COMFORT SEQUELS

THE PSYCHOLOGY OF MOVIE SEQUELS
FROM THE   80S AND 90S

D1519373

COMFORT SEQUELS

THE PSYCHOLOGY OF MOVIE SEQUELS FROM THE 80S AND 90S

Emily Marinelli

Cover design by Morgan Kerchner
Author Photo by Lauren Propps
Edited by David Bushman
Book designed by Scott Ryan
All interviews were conducted in a conversational style
and have been edited for grammar and clarity

Published in the USA by Fayetteville Mafia Press
Columbus, Ohio

Contact Information
Email: FayettevilleMafiaPress@gmail.com
Website: TuckerDSPress.com
Twitter: @FMPBooks
Instagram: @Fayettevillemafiapress

For Mom, Grandma, and Gramma ET:
my Steel Magnolias

And for my B, I miss you every day.

CONTENTS

—AUTHORS NOTE—

Comfort Sequels is about my favorite movie sequels from the eighties and nineties. It's full of fun movie facts, psychology, glitter, and my chats with celebrities. This book is about queer joy and also my lived experiences with trauma. So sweet readers, in this book I address difficult topics such as domestic violence, addiction, poverty, neglect, bullying, drug use, body image issues, and disordered eating.

These movie sequels are dear to my heart and have helped me through many hard times. But I recognize some of the stories and tropes simply do not hold up in today's world. Using a social justice lens, I call out problematic aspects and invite you to do the same as you revisit these often forgotten and mostly unloved films.

Many stories in this book are exactly as I remember them, with names and some identity markers changed to protect privacy. With others, I have taken creative liberties and thus produced a work of true creative nonfiction.

What remains unchanged are the people who have loved me, supported me, and elevated me through the years. Thank you and I love you.

Finally, if you think *Grease* is better than *Grease 2*, this book will change your mind and your life.

You're welcome.

—Introduction—

"Back To School Again"

"Sweetie, are you sure you wanna watch it again?" My single mom, working twelve hour days to make ends meet, cannot fathom my desire to view *Grease 2* yet again. As soon as she picks me up from school, I beg her to put it on. Sixth grade is not nearly as exciting as the return of the T-Birds and Pink Ladies. I wait patiently all day at Carver Middle School in Tulsa, Oklahoma, in the hope of returning in the evening to the school of my dreams; Rydell High.

"Yes, momma, I need to watch it one more time. I'm learning the 'Back to School Again' dance number, and I have to get all the moves right." The tiny living room that doubled as a dining room in the house we are renting couldn't contain my Pink Lady spirit. Four small dining chairs surround a Formica table adjacent to a brown dilapidated couch right out of *Roseanne*. The largest piece in the room is the entertainment center, a thrift store find, which takes up an entire wall. This is where I spend most of my time.

My mom, still dressed in Kmart high heels and a shoulder-padded navy suit with bejeweled buttons down the front, laughs and slides the tape into the gray-and-black Panasonic VHS player. My grubby fingers, sticky with my after-school snack of Easy Cheese and Ritz crackers, turn the dials on the TV to find the channel that will allow the movie to play.

The VHS FBI warning comes into focus; large, scary, blue letters hover above the Department of Justice seal. I show off by closing my eyes and reciting it word for word from memory. "Federal law provides severe civil and criminal penalties. . . . " "Great job, honey, that's impressive!" My mom praises my ability to remember the disclaimer and leaves to start dinner before going back to grading papers.

I set up the dining chairs in a line to denote different parts of the *Grease 2* opening-credit spectacular. Two chairs create the semblance of a pink Studebaker I can sit atop like Sharon (Maureen Teefy) during the Pink Ladies pledge. Chair number three is for my T-Bird motorcycle entrance segment. While not critical to the choreography, the fourth chair has no real purpose except that it allows me to jump from a height for dramatic effect in the middle of the room.

The most challenging part of the almost-seven-minute "Back to School Again" opening number is the various microdialogue character introductions. For these, I have to be creative. While holding a geography textbook, I poke my head through a gap window in the entertainment center, creating a makeshift school bus, just like Frenchy (Didi Conn). Tiny pom-poms from my Skipper doll (younger sister to Barbie) work great for my impressions of the twin cheerleaders, and I use my mom's Aqua Net to spray my hair just like Ms. Mason (Connie Stevens) does to her bouffant hairdo. The whole scene would not be complete unless I'm chewing gum in a too-cool-for-school way. The Winterfresh hangs on my mouth's edge, and as it drips down to my chin, I smack it back quickly while pretending not to notice or care how others perceive me.

"Back to School Again," explodes onto the screen with fantastical colors and synchronized dancing. The song tells the relatable story of a summer vacation ending too soon and the bummer of starting fall classes. The opening song lyrics begin "Spending my vacation in the summer sun/Gettin' lots of action havin' lots of fun/ Scorin' like a bandit 'til the bubble burst/Suddenly it got to be September first." September sneaks up out of nowhere, and Rydell students don't want to go back. "The Board of Education took away my parole." The lyrics are not completely appropriate for kids, but hey, I'm twelve after all and have heard much worse.

I do the Twist, the Swim, and the Pony with the students of Rydell while working hard to not accidentally swallow my gum on a Grapevine turn. My sticky and now sweaty fingers fumble with the VCR buttons to get the choreography just right. Pause . . . rewind. Pause . . . rewind. Pause . . . Fast Forward. I can feel my mom's gentle tolerance from the kitchen as she tells me, "Honey, let's start putting your things away and set the table for dinner." Huffing and puffing from the sixties dance moves repetition, I yell out, "But mom, I really need to get this ending down!"

Here it goes: I weave in and out between the chairs theatrically, run in place as the music holds . . . "Whoa, whoa, I gotta go back, back, back to school......................" and execute a shoulder somersault right as the song blasts "AGAIN!" Bam! Studebaker chairs one and two crash to the ground; the Winterfresh, in a perfect ball, propels from my mouth onto the TV screen just as my mom comes in holding our casserole dinners. Nailed it! Just in time for tuna.

Michelle Pfeiffer and the Pink Ladies of *Grease 2* do the dance steps on the screen for little Emily to emulate at home. (Photos courtesy of Paramount Pictures)

Lifelines

The next day, I would actually have to go back to middle school, and school wasn't a great place for me. I was a nerdy, shy, chubby kid, just beginning to question my sexuality. I wore bulky sweaters and too-tight jeans. I sprayed my fine, thin, curly brown hair with Malibu Musk spritz and didn't wear deodorant. I got good grades and actually cared about what my teachers thought of me. Probably I cared a little too much. Kids were assholes, called me names, made fun of me in the hallway and at recess. I would find quiet places to read library books and just wait until the 3:15 bell.

I wanted to disappear. With movies like *Grease 2*, I could disappear. I could get lost in the soundtrack. I could do my ladder moves along with Michelle Pfeiffer and sing out the letters to her song "C-O-O-L-R-I-D-E-R" (the letters are repeated many times in this song's coda, in case anyone forgets how to spell it). I could learn questionable biological information alongside Tab Hunter in "Reproduction" and explore sexual euphemisms and learn basic bowling skills in "Score Tonight" with Adrian Zmed and Lorna Luft. I could find safety in the music and lose myself with these misfit characters. This unforgettable sequel became a lifeline for me.

I watched movies over and over because of the comfort they provided, the familiarity, the predictability. The VHS rewind button was my companion. Unlike the chaos of my childhood, I knew what to expect with silly eighties and nineties films. They became surrogate parents to me. I could recite all the dialogue from *Ghostbusters* by memory. I could immerse myself in *Gremlins*, wondering what it would be like to befriend a Mogwai, or in *My Girl*, wondering what it would be like to live in a morgue and lose your best friend to a bee sting.

Like for so many children of working-class parents, TV and movies were my babysitter. We moved around a lot. My family was chaotic, with addiction, codependency, financial and housing instability, emotional and physical violence, and untreated mental health challenges. My parents ugly-divorced when I was three. My mother worked multiple jobs to take care of me. My father was absent. Many days I was left to my own entertainment.

Movies were both an escape and a connection. Like books, they helped me survive and connected me to another world. The movies I loved to watch on repeat—*Grease, My Girl, Karate Kid, NeverEnding Story, Mannequin*—touched my heart this way. They were teddy bears, next to me at night. *But hold on. There were sequels to these films? You mean there could possibly be more of these movies that were so joyful? So safe? So familiar?*

For the Love of Sequels

If you love the original, how could you ruin a good thing by making a sequel? Movie sequels of the eighties and nineties weren't sacrilegious to me, the way they are for some. For me, they were just *more* of a good thing. More comfort. More security. More safety. More family. More home. More ridiculousness. More laughter. More predictability. More of the universe we love—exploring something new while maintaining the familiar.

When a film touches me, makes me deep belly laugh, and has that feel-good spirit, I want more of it. I want the continuing story. I want the same story, even, just recycled and offered in a slightly new way. What felt so good about the original could come back twofold— the same, but also different.

Movie sequels from this period don't have a lot of heavy content or drama or intensity. They don't have overwhelming plot lines. They don't fray your nerves; they just make you feel good. My life was overwhelming enough.

Sequel scripts were lullabies, nursery rhymes, songs that put me to bed at night. I remember reciting lines repeatedly with my cousins and to myself. I made sense of the world through the sequels' dialogue. "Yeah, I know," a simple three-word phrase from *Grease 2*, enunciated in Maxwell Caulfield's sultry British accent, could've been a throwaway line, but my cousins and I folded it into our conversations daily.

Classic lines from *Mannequin Two: On the Move* are part of my family lore. In this film, the manager of the department store, Mr. James, walks around with his two assistants, espousing catchphrases that they then repeat back to him and frantically jot down on notepads: "Deplore neglect, demand respect" and "Make a showplace of the workplace." I loved them! They work great in the film and lend themselves to my impersonation of Mr. James walking around my house, my cousin behind me taking notes as my assistant, doing a call and response.

My eight-year-old-self watching *Mannequin Two* when it came out in the theater would never have conceived that at age forty I would have the honor of interviewing Stu Pankin, (who plays Mr. James). She would never have known he would say he actually improvised these hilarious "interstitial interjections," as he calls them. Unbelievable. The lines I recited to feel connected to and comforted by *Mannequin Two* as a child and teenager were actually created by this incredible actor! It was truly amazing to have such a beautiful and intimate conversation with him. You won't want to miss that chapter.

Sequels were something I could control. I could watch them over and over by pushing a button on the VCR. After renting *Batman Returns* so many times from Blockbuster, I begged my mom to just buy the VHS for me. And one of the great things about movie sequels from the eighties and nineties is that a lot of times they would go to video quickly and end up in the sale bin at the flea market. So the answer was "Yes!" Yes, we could get them, because you could get three VHS tapes for ten dollars. Add to cart! I really could have them and watch them again and again and again and again.

What movie sequels do you love?
What movie sequels bring you comfort?

Comfort Sequels

I wrote this book to tell stories about my life through the movie sequels of my childhood. *Comfort Sequels: The Psychology of Movie Sequels from the 80s and 90s* celebrates the ludicrous campiness of these films and the nostalgia that they conjure. Every chapter is a love letter to a specific movie sequel. Personal stories are infused connecting each film to a different part of my life.

As a licensed psychotherapist and psychology professor now, I also bring my own conceptual spin to each film, with a psychological interpretation of characters, story arcs, or major themes. Because I'm a film nerd, I also include fun and random behind-the-scenes facts about each movie. Oh, and some incredible interviews too!

The book covers the following eleven comfort sequels; *The Great Muppet Caper, My Girl 2, Batman Returns, Mannequin Two: On the Move, Grease 2, Dream a Little Dream 2, Ghostbusters II, Karate Kid Part II, Teenage Mutant Ninja Turtles II: The Secret of the Ooze, The NeverEnding Story II: The Next Chapter*, and *The Evening Star*.

Comfort Sequels includes celebrity interviews that are a dream come true for that Easy Cheese and Ritz crackers sticky-fingered twelve year old. I spoke with Muppet puppeteer Steve Whitmire (creator of Rizzo the Rat, *The Great Muppet Caper*), Christine Ebersole (*My Girl 2*), Stuart Pankin (*Mannequin Two: On the Move*), Peter Mosen and Bryan Johnson (*Ghostbusters II*), Chris McDonald (Goose from *Grease 2*), Leif Green (Davey from *Grease 2*), and yes, even the Cool Rider himself, Maxwell Caulfield (Michael from *Grease 2*). To find out what he thinks about the tattoo portrait I have of him on my calf, you have to check out that chapter for yourself.

You may have noticed that I have left out such major film franchises as Back to the Future, Star Wars, Die Hard, Beverly Hills Cop, and Jurassic Park. The reasons for this are simple: 1) there are already MANY books, articles, and docuseries about them and 2) while they are all classics, they are not my nostalgic favorites. I didn't watch them as often growing up.

Stuart Henderson in his book on *The Hollywood Sequel: History & Form, 1911-2010*, says " . . . the defining characteristic of the sequel is its acknowledgment of a chronological narrative relationship with a prior installment" (Pg 3), meaning it's a continuing story from the previous film. I want to acknowledge that if we are going by what Henderson says, some of the films in this book may not *technically* meet the definition of a true sequel. Instead, they could be considered "a series" or a "soft remake." But for me, I will expand the frame here, as all of the movies included in this book are MY comfort sequels (and maybe yours too).

How I view sequels is informed by my experience as a white, working class, cisgender presenting but genderqueer identified queer person who is able-bodied and college educated. I recognize that what is comforting for me is not comforting for everyone.

Revisiting these films decades later, some plots, dialogue, and characterizations simply do not hold up. Elements of these films are blatantly racist, homophobic, classist, and ableist and reinforce problematic tropes and stereotypes. With all of this in mind, I intentionally made space for critiques of what does not hold up in today's world, and offer my social justice-oriented psychological perspectives on the films.

"Back to School Again"

Comfort Sequels takes you "Back to School Again," but not in the way of being trapped excruciatingly at a school desk, desperately waiting for the bell to ring for your escape. Not at all. You can come and go as you please here. No need to read this book in order. Jump in and flip around.

There is no right way to enjoy *Comfort Sequels*. However, in order to maximize your experience, I would recommend the following:

1. Surround yourself with cozy items. Find squishy pillows in your house. Perhaps grab a stuffed animal or your cuddly pet (my snuggly rescue dog does the trick for me).
2. Make a delicious beverage. Are you reading in summertime? If so, make an iced tea or get a soda. If it is chilly outside, brew a hot chocolate or chamomile tea.
3. Get comfy! Put on some comfy clothes or pajamas. Wrap yourself in soft sheets or warm blankets. Go lie outside in the sun. Curl up by the fireplace.
4. Grab that after-school snack you had when you were younger. That's right, take a trip down the grocery store memory lane. It's okay if the snack is full of high fructose corn syrup and has no nutritional value. It's delicious and you know it!

I grab my Easy Cheese and Ritz crackers, Diet Dr Pepper, and Little Debbie Zebra Cakes, just like when I was twelve. My sweet rescue pup lays her head on the *Grease 2*-themed pillow next to me on the couch and settles in. I drape my Pink Lady jacket around my shoulders and slowly lower my shades, just like Michelle Pfeiffer.

I turn to the *Grease 2* chapter and start reading. I press play. The principal, confident and excited for the semester to start, tells her assistant principal that this will be a "great new school year." The "Back to School Again" instrumental intro interrupts the calmness of the scene. Rydell students flood the screen and trample over the two school administrators. The words pour over me. I smile and reach for my stick of Winterfresh gum. Pause, rewind, play.

The Great Muppet Caper

Greenhouse, Redhouse

Our little single-family house on Sandusky Street in Tulsa Oklahoma, is seafoam green on the outside with milky cream walls on the inside. We call it the Greenhouse, even though we don't have any actual plants, only fake, plastic ones from the fabric store. The Greenhouse sits in the middle of a working-class neighborhood with streets filled with potholes and looping strands of tar used to repair asphalt cracks. It's the only house my parents ever owned. On the verge of a divorce, it's the last place they will ever live together.

It's 1986, and I'm four years old. Despite the house being tiny, it feels huge to me. I run into the living room and jump up on the white hand-me-down couch. Next to it sits a waterworn oak side table. A globe lamp from a garage sale sits on top. Two threadbare dining room chairs flank the couch. Sunlight peeks through a wagon wheel window right next to the front door, and I hopscotch carefully back and forth through the shadow spokes on the light gray carpet speckled with stains.

Rustling sounds in the kitchen alert me that Mom is wiping down counters. Muffled voices in the den tell me Dad is watching TV. I know better than to disturb either one of them. They have been yelling all morning, and now that they are apart, things are finally calm and quiet.

I jump back and forth through the wagon wheel shadow spokes and think about Grandma and Grandpa. I wish I could be with them right now. Grandma and Grandpa (my mom's parents) are only a ten-minute drive from here. They live in what I call the Redhouse, because it's covered in red brick and has a front porch that Grandpa painted bright red. Grandma and I play on the big swing set they have in the backyard, which is also red, with white trim down the sides.

The Redhouse feels like home. It's a place I go every day while Mom and Dad are at work. Grandma always greets me with a huge hug; her arms engulf me, and she smells like fried Crisco oil, talcum powder, and Oil of Olay perfume. Against my neck I feel the bristles from her gray-and-white, tightly curled wig. Her cheeks are always cheery, and their warmth feels good against my skin. She kisses me and leaves little pink lipstick prints on my forehead. Pulling Kleenex from her bra, she licks a finger and dabs it on my skin before wiping away the marks. She smiles and tells me how beautiful I look.

Today is not a Redhouse day. It's a Greenhouse day. I run to the yellow phone hanging from the kitchen wall and ask Mom if I can call Grandma. "Sure, honey" she says, and dials for me because I can't reach that high. When Grandma answers, I tell her that I miss her a lot and ask if she can make my favorite breakfast: cheesy eggs and bacon.

"Baby Girl, of course I will. Next time you come over, I will do a whole big breakfast for you with all the fixin's."

"But Grandma, can I come over now?" I want her now.

"Well, sweetie, you're with your mom and dad today, but in just two days time, you will be over and I will set up the grocery store for you." I love the Fisher Price cash register and the little plastic fruit and vegetable pieces that Grandma comes in to buy from me. I charge her anywhere from one dollar to a hundred dollars depending on my mood, and she pays with her fake money without hesitation. Two days feels like a lifetime. I don't think I can wait that long, I miss her too much.

"But Grandma, I need you," I say, and the tears that are always just under the surface come pouring down my face; snot begins to form a bubble in my button nose. I take the long yellow coil phone cord around the corner. I don't want Mom to see me cry. I know that would only make her sadder.

"Sweetheart, listen to me. You are strong. You are gonna be okay. Here's what I want you to do." I'm pant-crying, but I can hear her and hang onto her every word. "I want you to go into your room and look at your *Sesame Street* characters on the wall. Each one of them is a part of me watching over you. I spent lots of time painting them to look exactly like Bert and Ernie and Cookie Monster. Those Muppets are angels protecting you."

I sniff and try to catch my breath. "But Grandma, I miss you." She pauses, considers what to say next to make me feel better.

"You know the Disney characters I painted for you?"

"Yes, Grandma," I say, and I flash to the life-size Snow White and all the dwarfs, Dumbo, and of course my favorite, Robin Hood. Grandma spent a year designing and painting those, and Grandpa cut them out in his woodshed and hung them on the back fence at the Redhouse. Strangers see them from the busy street and stop to ask if the Redhouse is a day care and if they can leave their kids there. They can't. It's my special place.

"Robin Hood protects you when you're here with me, and the Muppets protect you when you're at home with your mom and dad." Her words hug me.

"Ok, Grandma."

"I will see you in two days. In the meantime, go visit your Muppet friends on the wall and tell them hi for me. I love you, Baby Girl."

"Love you, Grandma."

I give the phone back to my mom and make my way down the hall, past my dad's Magnolia-pattern jardiniere and pedestal from his Roseville pottery collection. I hear stories about how much he loves it and how expensive it was. Sometimes when my parents fight, I imagine climbing up the side of the cabinet and pushing it to the floor so it breaks into a million pieces.

The Greenhouse doesn't feel safe like the Redhouse, except for my room. I spend most of my time here. Following Grandma's

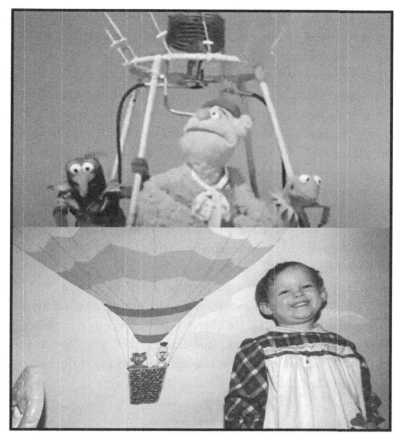

From screen to wall, my Grandma brought the Muppets to life in my childhood bedroom. (Photos courtesy of Universal Pictures, Em Marinelli)

instructions, I climb to the top of my Little Tikes playhouse. On my sky-covered painted bedroom walls are a smattering of hot-air balloons with *Sesame Street* characters popping out of the baskets. Each character has Grandma's touch, places where the paint is a little more blobby, places where I can still see the pencil marks underneath the paint from her wall sketch. I sometimes imagine ascending into the air with the Muppets as my flight guides.

I take a moment to pull up my itchy and sagging light pink tights. My red-and-green plaid dress has a little heart shape on the right shoulder, and I trace it with my stubby pointer finger. My brown hair, cut short in a pageboy, is almost nonexistent. Sandy-brown hair strands lace my forehead. The wisps are thin and show the stress of having survived an almost fatal bout with pneumonia last year, sending me to the hospital for three months.

Bert and Ernie smile over one basket and wave at me. I wave back at them. Suspended above, the unlikely pair of Grover and Oscar the Grouch share a basket too. Their balloon is smaller as it makes it way higher into the sky. The Muppets do what Grandma said. They protect me and tell me without words that I can go wherever I want to. I wave to them all and tell them hi. "Hi, everyone. Grandma says hi too."

I scoop up my soft, felt Kermit doll who lives in my playhouse. I talk to him the way Miss Piggy does. "Kermie, Grandma loves you so much, and she's sorry she can't be here today. We will see her soon. Now, what we are gonna do might be a little bit scary, but it's gonna be okay. I promise."

I hold him tight in my arms, look at Bert and Ernie, and slide down the length of the red-and-yellow slide, my tights sticking to the sides a little. When I'm safe on the ground, I look at his white eyes, each with a black line and oval pupil crossed through. "See, it wasn't that bad, was it, Kermie?" And just as quickly as I reach the bottom, I climb back up the ladder, ready to slide down again.

***

At this point in time, there are things my little, four-year-old self knows, but there are also things she doesn't.

What she doesn't know is that her mom is having a mental breakdown and will soon be hospitalized for bipolar psychosis and anorexia.

What she doesn't know is that her dad will serve her mom divorce papers while her mom is in the psych ward at St. Francis hospital.

What she doesn't know is that her parent's custody battle will continue behind legal doors.

What she will soon know is that there will be one week when her dad stays in the Greenhouse with her. Then he will leave and Mom will come to stay with her in the Greenhouse. Then Mom will leave and Dad will return. They will rotate back and forth. She will mostly stay in her room while her parents are a revolving door around her.

What she does know is that at some point she will start going to Grandma and Grandpa's Redhouse more and more. Grandma will make her favorite cheesy eggs and toast with extra melted butter. They will make her laugh, and she will get to watch movies on VHS as many times as she wants.

Some of these things she will learn later in her childhood. Some of these things she will not learn until she is an adult, in graduate school for psychology, where she will study to become a therapist.

For all of what she doesn't know, there is something she does—and it will sustain her for years to come: Grandma and the Muppets love her and are there for her no matter what. And she loves them back just the same, if not more.

The Great Muppet Caper Recap

I watch *The Great Muppet Caper* for the first time in the Greenhouse on one of my dad's designated weeks. I sit next to him on the scratchy couch in the den. He snacks on off-brand tortilla chips that sometimes poke into his gums and a big bowl of Pace picante sauce. I have Campbell's soup, and he doesn't notice that I take out the little square chicken pieces so I can just slurp up the little doughy stars.

Last week, Mom and I brought my *Sesame Street* table and chairs set into the den corner, and I look over at them now. The faces of Big Bird, Cookie Monster, Oscar, and Bert and Ernie on the back of the chairs make me smile. I talk to them like I talk to the hot-air balloon Muppets on my bedroom wall. I think about Grandma each time I do and feel her with me, even though she's not here.

As soon as *The Great Muppet Caper* starts, my dad yawns. The movie opens with the theft of jewels belonging to famous London fashion designer Lady Holiday (played by Dame Diana Rigg). They are stolen on the street in broad daylight. Kermit, Fozzie, and Gonzo, inept investigative journalists at the *Chronicle*, fail to get the thieves on film. Instead, they take lots of pictures of chickens directly across the street. Charming, but not helpful. Needless to say, they're about to be fired, so in a last-ditch effort to save their jobs, they fly to London to interview Lady Holiday, track down the jewels, and catch the thieves themselves.

Thrown into the bottom of the plane like cargo, the trio have limited resources for this UK adventure and end up staying at the Happiness Hotel (my all-time-favorite song from the film) for free. The hotel, where we meet the rest of the Muppet gang, is beyond run-down; "there are bugs and there are lice," but you'll "never beat the price." Nevertheless, it is their home away from home during the investigation, and their stay here involves love, disguises, and Electric Mayhem (infamous Muppet rock band).

I ask Dad if we can rewind and listen to "Happiness Hotel" again, and he doesn't care, says he's tired and is going to rest for a while anyway. He leaves and goes to his bedroom for a nap. He naps a lot these days, even more than before. I know how to operate the VCR by standing on the Big Bird plastic chair from my *Sesame Street* set. "Hang on, Kermit." I always have my Kermit doll next to me now. "I promise you can hear the song again soon." After watching "Happiness Hotel" three more times and learning the chorus, I try to remember where it is in the movie so that I can rewind the tape back to the song later and watch it again.

Back to the movie: the trio soon meet Miss Piggy, whom Kermit mistakes for Lady Holiday. Honest mistake. Miss Piggy is actually her secretary, and she doesn't correct him, leading him to believe she is in fact the famous, rich socialite designer. I look at Kermit during this part and laugh, knowing something he doesn't know. I know she's not the real Lady Holiday, but he doesn't. I'm not worried, I know it will work out and he will learn the truth somehow. On his date night out on the town with Miss Piggy, Kermit learns her true identity when the real Lady Holiday is robbed again. This time right in front of them. Gonzo captures this one on film, but sadly, the picture is destroyed before it can fully develop.

Kermit, Fozzie, Gonzo, and Miss Piggy learn the jewel thieves are beautiful fashion models led by Lady Holidays' brother Nicky (Charles Grodin). In an epic water ballet sequence, Nicky falls in love with Miss Piggy. With Kermit, he sings a love-battle duet showcasing their infatuation with her. I rewind this song a few times, laughing at Kermit singing "all the world ever wanted was you, a dream come true."

Nicky ends up framing Miss Piggy for the recent heist, landing her in jail. In a fury, Miss Piggy yells, "You can't even sing; your voice was dubbed!" Classic. But I don't worry; I know she is Miss Piggy and will never let iron bars stop her from being the fierce queen she is.

Learning of the next planned robbery, the trio of journalists, along with Miss Piggy and the entire Muppet gang, take matters into their own hands and stage the ultimate Muppet caper. Lady Holiday's famous baseball diamond, being held safely at the Mallory Gallery, is the target of the robbers, and the Muppet crew breaks in to stop them. A game of hot potato quickly turns into a full-blown baseball game, and the Muppets get the diamond from the thieves.

Nicky takes Kermit hostage, and in the way only Miss Piggy could, she saves the day. She bends her jail cell bars, escapes, drives a big rig, jumps on a motorcycle, and crash-lands through the stained glass window of the gallery just in time to crash into Nicky, release Kermit, punch out the robber models, and get the diamond back. I just love her.

All ends as it should in the world of the Muppets. The thieves are apprehended, the baseball diamond is returned, and, we assume, the journalists get to keep their jobs. The Happiness Hotel gang and all our protagonists are thrown like cargo into the hold of a plane bound for the US. Unfortunately, this plane doesn't land, so they are each thrown out into the air with parachutes. Like the beginning of the film, the end shows the Muppets floating in the sky, calm, making jokes as the credits run by them.

I consider rewinding the movie to the "Happiness Hotel" song because I have the "welcome home, welcome home" part stuck in my head. But I love the movie so much I decide to start it at the very beginning. "We are gonna start it over, Kermie," I say to Kermit, who sits eagerly in my lap. "I know how much you liked it." The hot-air balloon comes into focus over a bright blue sky. Like in my bedroom, I wave to Fozzie, Gonzo, and Kermit onscreen, tell them hi and that I love them.

Holding Environment

The Greenhouse is where we start our lives together as a nuclear family—

me, my mom, and my dad. A promise of a fairy tale life beginning together. The dream that is supposed to last happy-forever-after.

But it doesn't happen. The Greenhouse is full of chaos and confusion. Not just for me, but for all of us. Postdivorce, both of my parents will move elsewhere. My dad will move in with—and then marry—an abusive woman. My mom will move from rental to rental and then marry an abusive man.

The Redhouse becomes my safe place. Child psychotherapist D. W. Winnicott describes the surroundings of a child as they develop a "holding environment." As a psychotherapist now, I explain the holding environment to my classes and clients as imperfect but predictable, safe, containing.

What is needed during this developmental time is "good enough" parenting. "Good enough" parenting means that parents are not perfect; they make mistakes, but are attuned to the needs of the child and do the best they can to meet them while setting appropriate limits and boundaries. It is an environment free from physical, emotional, and sexual abuse, where they can literally be held through growing pains.

Mom takes care of me the best she can, but it's Grandma who is my consistent primary caregiver during this time. When I was just a baby, Mom used to drop me off at Grandma's every day before heading to Tulsa Community College to teach statistics and algebra. She would lovingly hand me over to Grandma before running out the door to get to class on time. And because Grandpa left to sell used car parts and fishing rods at the local pawn shop, most days it was just me and Grandma.

And we had so much fun.

Little, six-month-old me sniffs the air as bacon and homemade biscuits with extra butter linger in the Redhouse air. Grandma kisses me all over in her doughy arms. Grandma has food to cook, laundry to fold, and garments to hem to make extra money. She snuggles me into the "nest" she makes for me on the dining room table so she can have her hands free. It consists of a manger of fluffy pillows and my Kermit doll, tucked under my arm, his head cradling my neck.

In elementary school, when I get sick and sent home from school,

I always get to go to Grandma's. She pulls out a fitted magenta sheet fresh from the laundry basket to cover the couch, creasing the fabric between the cushions. My "sickbed" includes a TV tray with a "sick bell" I can ring if I need her and lots of liquids. The best one she calls "a sip of Coke": a Diet Coke over ice in a red, plastic-handled glass.

I lose myself in *Sesame Street*, *Mister Rogers' Neighborhood*, and an assortment of musicals Grandma has on VHS: *An American in Paris*, *State Fair*, *Flower Drum Song*, and our favorite, *Oklahoma* (for our state's namesake but also because we both have crushes on Gordon MacRae). I feel better in no time at all.

The holding environment is not just about a place of containment free of abuse. It is about rules and structure reinforced by caregivers. A "good enough" parent, Grandma sets boundaries with me at the Redhouse: playtime, TV, and bedtime limits. She makes sure I have a balance of fun and rules. She's an imperfect caregiver, like all caregivers, because perfection doesn't exist. But she's attuned to my emotional and physical needs almost always.

During this time, my mom gives me the best holding environment she can. Throughout my childhood, she's such a supportive parent, showing up for all my major life events, taking crying calls from me, loving me unequivocally. At the Greenhouse, she will have a mental health break from reality. And even when she's so sick, she makes the "good enough" parenting choice to take me to Grandma's. She makes sure I'm safe at the Redhouse until she comes home from the hospital and can take care of me again. No parenting is perfect, but it's about knowing limitations and asking for help when needed.

"Good Enough" Muppets

The Muppet movies are not technically sequels, as they don't tell a continued story. But the characters, like the ones floating on my bedroom wall, return in each film. Each Muppet story is a different one, but as in a traveling theater, the same creatures come back, playing new roles. They don't age; they are just themselves.

From the *The Muppet Show* (1976-1981) to *The Muppets* film (2011), the Muppets are a holding environment for me, as they are for so many other children and even adults. I know I can count on

Kermit, Miss Piggy, Gonzo, Fozzie, and my favorite, Rizzo the Rat. Even when the Muppets get upset, they aren't mean to each other. Even when they fight, they show unconditional love.

The Great Muppet Caper begins with the opening musical number, "Hey a Movie!" The song literally explains all of what the film has in store: "They'll be heroes bold; they'll be comedy." Kermit's stanza reinforces the containment when he sings "There'll be crooks and cops! There'll be villainy! But with us on call, we'll fix it all real easily." It's a heads-up there will be hard and stressful moments, but I can breathe and relax in their caper. A reminder it will all work out in the end.

As the film opens, Kermit and Fozzie and Gonzo float in a hot-air balloon on a beautiful sunny day. "Nice up here isn't it?" Kermit offers. Anxious Fozzie responds with a barrage of fearful questions, "What if we drift off to sea? What if we are never heard from again? What if there's a storm or we get struck by lightning?"

True to his weird nature, Gonzo answers Fozzie's fears with "That would be neat!" Fozzie is not sure it would be neat; his furry face looks down below and squeezes into a ball of fear. "Listen, nothing is going to happen. This is just the opening credits," Kermit's soft frog face reminds him. Likewise he reminds me that I'm safe. This is a kids movie; nothing bad is going to happen.

But Fozzie, still unsure, asks, "How long are these opening credits?" Kermit, as the "good enough" parent, replies, "Just another minute or so." And that is what the characters and I need to hear. Soon the film will start. This movie's got me.

Kermit's role is to help Gonzo and Fozzie tolerate both their distress and excitement over what's to come. With the uncertainty of what will happen as the caper unfolds and how they will get down from the sky, Kermit's is the soothing voice of calm and containment. He attunes to their needs and reassures them they are safe without irritation or annoyance.

Kermit later leads the group's team effort to plot Miss Piggy's jailbreak, while also leaving space for collaboration. He sets loving limits with Miss Piggy, who has deceived him. He is the perfect straight man to these Muppet misfits.

Holding boundaries, setting limits, making mistakes and owning them, Kermit is not at all perfect. Being "good enough" is about being human, or in this case, being frog. It is about leaving space for everyone to work together, have blunders, and be loved and accepted whoever, whatever, and however they are.

Redhouse, Greenhouse

Grandma's Muppet paintings that float from the big screen into my bedroom sky are safe, secure, and reliable. In the midst of all the changes and uncertainty of my childhood, they are known, familiar, warm, and funny. A reminder of the Redhouse, even when I'm not there.

They make me smile. I can count on them. I know them. They are consistent. They come back again and again. They are predictable and yet surprise me. They make me laugh, no matter my age. They are timeless.

But in real life things change. In 2006, I'm twenty-four years old. Grandma and Grandpa move to Florida and will stay there until they die. Grandma gets sick with Alzheimer's and slowly loses short-term and then long-term memory. Some words leave her first; then she loses speech altogether. Mom is her primary caregiver and is with her 24-7.

When I visit them, mom and I make bacon and cheesy eggs like Grandma used to make for me. We refill her "sip of Coke" in a red-handled cup. We do our best to create a holding environment for her as she transitions from being an elder back to being a child. Grandma holds baby dolls and regresses to an infant-like state. Mom and I lean in, unwavering, meeting her needs until the end, when she's in a different world entirely. Even after she's left this world, I still feel her energy and her love. It lives inside of me.

***

Today the Redhouse stands on the corner of Haskell and Harvard in Tulsa. The Disney characters still live on the backyard fence. The yellow on Snow White's dress and Robin Hood's emerald green hat are sun bleached, and the wood is cracked from age. But they remain, holding strong after almost forty years. I like to think whoever lives in the Redhouse now has kids or grandkids. I like to imagine them playing in the backyard with the characters watching over them, protecting them.

Last year I drove by the Greenhouse. I hadn't seen it since I lived there as a child. The aquatic green is now covered in beige bricks, the shutters black, the roof newly redone. There are new working-class Okie additions. The owners built a covered carport that shades a rusty pickup truck. American flags splatter the yard along with tire treads, muffler parts, and four different broken birdbaths with cherub statues in various states of disrepair. Potted plants, trash, and a swing cover the porch.

What remains unchanged is the wagon wheel window that looks out onto the busy street and reflects sunlight into the living room. I like to think that a little girl lives there and plays in the shadow of the spokes. I like to think she has refuge in my old bedroom and gets to have my *Sesame Street* characters on the wall above her. Maybe she needs a Muppet to watch over her, to set limits, and to love her. Maybe Bert and Ernie wave to her from their balloon. And maybe, just maybe, she waves back at them too.

The Muppet Way of Doing Things: An Interview with Steve Whitmire

Relatable. A bit of an outsider, looking in. More an *observer* than the star. But despite that, he has a lot of heart. And solid comedic timing. I mean, okay, he's a rat, for crying out loud! I know, it's pretty random. But of all the amazing Muppets, of which there are many, my favorite has always been and will always be Rizzo the Rat.

Did you know Rizzo was named after none other than Dustin Hoffman's character in *Midnight Cowboy*? I mean, how awesome is that? I learn this during my email conversation with Steve Whitmire, the creator of Rizzo the Rat himself.

Steve has been a part of the Muppet world right from the start, beginning with *The Muppet Show*, then moving on to *Sesame Street*, *Fraggle Rock*, *Labyrinth*, *The Dark Crystal*, and all the Muppet films. Each time Rizzo's shown up as a recurring character throughout the Muppet universe, it's been Steve making Rizzo do what Rizzo does.

In *The Great Muppet Caper*, Rizzo is a bellhop who lives in the Happiness Hotel with his other rat friends. They carry luggage upstairs because the elevator is stuck, and I love watching their little legs move so fast underneath the weight of the huge suitcases. Rizzo has a frenzied dance break in the middle of the "Happiness Hotel" musical number, and as a child, I would try to do it along with him, falling over every time.

In the song "Couldn't We Ride?," a love song between Kermit and Miss Piggy, the Muppet gang show up to ride bikes alongside them. It's such a beautiful, melodic number, but I can't help but laugh when Rizzo and his three rat friends show up in their own four-seat bike. Mom and I watching this scene over the years would be in awe of how, in 1981, the puppeteers created this tandem-bike sequence. I never would've thought that in *Comfort Sequels*, I would finally get to find out how they pulled this off.

In my interview with him, Steve took time to write thoughtful and honest answers about his work on the Muppets. He tells hilarious stories about creating Rizzo and filming *The Great Muppet Caper*. Steve shares what motivates and inspires his art and why *The Golden Girls* is one of his favorite comfort shows. Here's the wizardry of Steve Whitmire:

Emily Marinelli: How did you get involved with the Muppets?

Steve Whitmire: I became a Muppet fanatic in my early teenage years, during a time when there was no internet, and Jim [Henson, creator of the Muppets] was mostly doing appearances as an act on variety shows like *The Ed Sullivan Show*. When Sesame Street started, I was ten years old, too old for the curriculum but obsessed with the Muppet characters and the scenario of them all living on an urban street with the humans. Each episode was like visiting a theme park on television. I began trying to make my own puppets in the Muppet style with a moving mouth and focused eyes, and I wrote a letter to Jim Henson asking if he had written any books on puppet building. A few months later he wrote back, a huge thing for a ten-year-old. The fact that he actually took the time to write back to me motivated me even more. Looking back, it's funny to think that in a sense, he was collaborating with me even then, years before we would actually meet.

After nine years of learning on my own and eventually doing a local live show of my own, I attended a regional puppetry festival where I briefly met Caroll Spinney, the performer and originator of Big Bird and Oscar the Grouch. I was eighteen and wasn't looking for a job - I just wanted to meet someone who worked with the Muppets.

Caroll saw a short puppet performance I was asked to do at the festival. We exchanged addresses, but frankly, I never thought I'd hear from him again. But a few months later he contacted me to say that Jim (who was doing *The Muppet Show* in London) was looking for new puppeteers, and Caroll was planning to recommend me.

One of my most memorable life experiences was eventually hearing from Jim in a telephone call from London during which he offered me a job. I joined his team in the middle of Season 3 of *The Muppet Show* and worked on virtually every Muppet project for the next four decades.

Emily: For some, Muppet films are not considered to be sequels in a sense that they don't have a continuing storyline from film to film. Each Muppet film is unique and not dependent on the film that came before it. Each film changes in theme, style, tone, and genre. Why was the decision made to have this stand-alone film structure?

Steve: Well, I think it was probably not a decision that was pondered. Jim was always looking to the "next" thing creatively, and I think, whether it was a Muppet film or a complete departure like *The Dark Crystal*, that likely meant each project was a stand-alone story. In the case of *The Muppet Show*, Muppets (like us) were a repertory company of players who could be cast in any number of stories.

Emily: *The Great Muppet Caper* is my all-time-favorite Muppet film. Any favorite moments or memorable days making the film you want to share?

Steve: Oh, so many memories...when we arrived in the UK to begin shooting, we started with the scenes at the Mallory Gallery. They were overnight shoots so it made sense to do them prior to our bodies accessing the time change.

I became ill with some sort of flu—high fever, chills . . . felt terrible!

Still, it was all-hands-on-deck because I was needed on set, so my recollection is puppeteering Rowlf the Dog outside in the cold night air, lying on the damp ground feeling awful but being wrapped up in Rowlf like a warm blanket between takes!

Another night shoot was the Electric Mayhem bus driving around Piccadilly Circus. We were all having fun and laughing as we worked. We passed a pub in the wee hours as people were spilling out, and so, presuming they would all like it, all the Muppets waved and shouted to the patrons at the pub.

We could not see them, since we were hidden in the bus, but all I remember is hearing a guy yell, "Fuck off back to America!" We all got a big laugh out of a very unexpected jeer!

Emily: What do you think makes *The Great Muppet Caper* and the Muppets in general so comforting for audiences?

Steve: A consistent relationship between the audience and the characters that began with *Sesame Street* and was solidified during *The Muppet Show* years. It carried the Muppets forward for many years.

That relationship has largely diminished at this point as the characters are rebooted and reinvented, which is quite different from a sequel done by the originators. Jim's influence has sadly been rejected and replaced with formula-driven directions that claim to revive the Muppets but rely on the interpretation of objective, cliché traits of the characters that disregard their growth and depth. It goes to show that within the classic Muppets, depth of character can't be synthesized. It really must be passed along from individual to individual and between the right people.

Emily: You invented Rizzo the Rat, my personal favorite Muppet. What was the process like crafting him?

Steve: On *The Muppet Show*, Jim encouraged new puppeteers to grab a puppet of our choice and populate the background of the backstage scenes. He didn't give us specific instructions. He simply told us to do whatever we wanted in the background.

One day I was rummaging through a storage area filled with boxes of puppets, costumes, and props, and I came across an old rat puppet on a long stick that didn't do anything except bounce around. I think it was one of several such stick puppets built for a television special called *The Muppet Musicians of Bremen*.

So, the next time we shot the backstage on *The Muppet Show*, I had this ugly, tattered little rat stand next to Kermit at his desk throughout the full scene with other lead characters. All I did with the rat was have him stand there silently, listening and reacting subtly to what was being said in the scene. He was just a bystander eavesdropping on the conversation.

The moment the floor director said "Cut" at the end of the scene, Jim broke out of Kermit's character into laughter. As he laughed, he turned to me and said, "Where did you get that terrible puppet?" I told him, and he said, "We're going to make that rat a star."

At Jim's request, I went about rebuilding the puppet with help from one of the all-time-greatest puppet builders, Jane Gootnick. I redesigned the mechanism so that I would be able to get my hand inside the puppet rather than have him on an extended stick and sculpted his new head shape and little hands out of clay to be cast from latex rubber. It gave the new puppet a more distinctive look. Frank Oz suggested the name Rizzo based on Dustin Hoffman's character in *Midnight Cowboy*.

But a funny thing happened for *Caper*. New puppets were built for the film, and my redesigned Rizzo somehow didn't get used as the character. Instead, when shooting began and I showed up on set, the workshop had chosen to go back to the rats on sticks,, and yet another puppet was built to be Rizzo. It looked completely different, nothing like the puppet we had all arrived at during *The Muppet Show* era. I recall being really disappointed about that, but it was too late to change, so I had to use a puppet I wasn't crazy about.

I think at that stage Rizzo was such an incidental character that he got lost in the shuffle during the build in advance of the film. The thinking seemed to be that there was just a bunch of rats, with no real focus on Rizzo himself. It took me several years to really get comfortable with the character. In *The Great Muppet Caper*, he was still not fully formed for me, but I was happy that he was included here and there. It was actually *The Muppets Take Manhattan* when the character began to fully gel for me.

Emily: Rizzo and the rats in general are featured in the song "Happiness Hotel" in the film. What do you remember about filming that musical number?

Steve: For that song, I did the banjo player on the balcony (the one with the long yellow hair). It was the early rat on a stick that was used for the moment in the song where we see Rizzo dancing—that's about all it would do!

Emily: Each time I watch *Muppet Caper*, I'm in awe watching the famous bicycle scene "Couldn't We Ride?" What do you remember filming that song? How in the world did the Muppets, but especially the rats, ride the tandem bike?

Steve: Those were times when special effects were mostly practical, meaning what you saw on the screen is what was done during the shooting of the scene. There were various rigs to have the Muppets

How'd they get the Muppets to ride a bike in *The Great Muppet Caper?* Steve Whitmire knows. (Photo courtesy of Universal Pictures)

riding so many bikes together, puppeteers in overhead "cherry-picker"'cranes, some radio-controlled puppet heads, many of the bicycles attached together below the camera frame to build a huge rig that would stay upright.

Emily: What does being a puppeteer mean to you today?

Steve: Objectively for me, being a puppeteer has always meant being involved in every aspect of production, from the conception of a project through to the editing and promotion—it still is. It is an all-encompassing endeavor. From the standpoint of the actual performing, puppeteering at its core is acting, just as any actor would do. The obvious difference is that the performance is rendered through an otherwise inanimate object on one's hand rather than via one's own body and face (although puppeteers are notorious for their overexaggerated facial expressions as they emote through the puppet).

But, frankly, I don't think about the puppeteer part a lot. What carries real meaning for me is to have done all that I was able to do to see Jim's direct influence remain a part of the Muppets for as long as that was possible. That influence is still my subconscious, driving motivation. I am convinced that Jim was less interested in his so-called legacy than he was in seeing his methodologies become a lineage, a way of seeing and doing things to be passed down that included his willingness to literally forfeit a significant portion of his own creative vision so that those with whom he chose to surround himself could realize their own.

Still, there was an almost unspoken basis for his "Muppet way of doing things," a context within which a broad Muppet group dynamic acted as a filter through which our work came into being. I've heard it said that "Jim never told us what to do." I would rephrase that to say "Jim told us what to do by giving us a broad direction, but he never told us how to do it." We were free to create how we contributed to the vision within the context of our particular jobs to a very large degree.

There is a bit of a myth surrounding the environment Jim nurtured that a bunch of people came to work everyday, did whatever they

Steve Whitmire and Rizzo the Rat are together in this classic photo behind the scenes. (Photo courtesy of Universal Pictures)

wanted to do all day long, and at the end of the week Jim signed their paycheck. Jim didn't hire everybody. He was choosy about those who worked closest with him in an ongoing relationship. We all worked in support of the broad framework of his vision. It just so happened that doing so was a pleasure because of the man himself, and so his vision became the vision for us all.

Emily: What other movie series or sequels or TV shows do you find comforting?

Steve: LOVE *The Golden Girls*. That style of character-based humor never stops being funny. In contrast (and maybe not so comforting), I quite like action movies like the Bourne franchise of films or the James Bond movies. The old 1960s Adam West *Batman* series brings back so many childhood memories.

You might find it funny that I generally have no interest in watching animated or puppet films or television! I love doing it, but never watch it. I think that's because I don't think of what I do as puppetry per se. I think of it as storytelling with strong characters (who happen to be puppets).

Emily: What are you working on now?

Steve: Well, I've been doing a live stream on YouTube for several years called *CAVE - iN* with Weldon the I.T. Guy. For Weldon, I.T. stands for "internet troll," and that's what Weldon is, both as a species and a profession. He lives alone in his cave and spends his time hacking other peoples' lives.

The point of the show was to give myself the opportunity to do what I have always considered my favorite part of bringing these characters to life: spontaneously ad-libbing in an interactive way with the audience. *CAVE - iN* is a call-in show where viewers can talk to Weldon live about Weldon's favorite topic, their most miserable life experiences (he's a troll, after all). *CAVE - iN* literally has no budget. But with the help of my longtime friend and Muppet writer Jim Lewis, producer Liam Nelson, and puppeteer Melissa Whitmire (who is also my wife), doing *CAVE - iN* has given me the chance to conceive, write, produce, direct, perform, and edit both the show itself as well as midshow production pieces that I consider to be a continuation of the type of sketches we did way back on *The Muppet Show*.

But my driving goal is to do this work as long as I can, and with people who do it from a passionate place. If that can translate into something becoming financially successful, so be it, but I have always done this work because NOT doing it was not an option.

My Girl 2

It's 1987. I'm five years old. My parent's divorce finalizes, and despite a terrible legal battle, Mom gets custody of me. She rents a tiny white duplex on the wrong side of town. It's all she can afford on her teacher's salary in Tulsa. Inside she decorates with seashell lamps, beach-landscape framed art, and eighties soft-pastel decor. We watch PBS shows like *3-2-1 Contact*, and *The Little Princess* with Shirley Temple on VHS. She reads aloud to me from her *Jonathan Livingston Seagull* book at night before bed.

It's just the two of us, a single mom with a small kid, living in a scary neighborhood. Outside are drug deals, gunshots, and loud men working on cars and motorcycles. Inside are the sounds of the ocean from a conch shell Mom holds up to my ear. Music is around us all the time. We play *Sesame Street* and *Woody Woodpecker* vinyls and have dance parades around the little living room and kitchen.

I always ask her to sing "Candle on the Water" from *Pete's Dragon* while she's cooking dinner. "Okay, but you have to help me; you sing so much better than I do, sweetie." And I sing along with her, "I'll be your candle on the water, my love for you always burn," and it makes me remember the lighthouse from the movie and how Nora is waiting for her love to come back home from the sea.

To help me remember our address, Mom makes up a song, and we practice it together. The melody is simple, "1537 South 67th East

Ave, Tulsa, Oklahoma 74112." We won't live here for very long, and as I type this today, I still remember this duplex address only because of that song.

On a warm Tulsa summer day, she pulls me in a red Radio Flyer wagon up the street to Circle K. "Don't ever touch those, baby." She points to what look like orange and clear plastic strips on the sidewalk. I now know them to be syringes. Mom always worries someone will hurt us or try to kidnap me and reminds me about stranger danger. "Sweetie, make sure to stay close by me and don't ever get into a car with anyone who is not me, your dad, or Grandma and Grandpa."

We get Coke-flavored slushies and a can of Pringles to share. The rest of the wagon is loaded with toilet paper, a six-pack of Tab, Pudding Pops, and Kix cereal. I help her pull the wagon back home while eating a strawberry freeze pop that drips sticky pink dots on my white-and-purple sleeveless jumper.

At night we spoon in her bed. I'm scared of the dark, so she rubs my forehead and lightly scratches my back. She sings my own personalized lullaby: "Emily is my little girl, Emily is my little girl, Emily is my little girl, Emily's my little girl. I love her, I love my little girl, I love her, I love my little girl, I love her, I love my little girl, I love my little girl."

The repetitive melody washes over me, rocks me to sleep, reminds me I'm safe. During the night, when I wake up scared from a bad dream, Mom is there, soothing me, singing to me to calm my nerves.

My Girl 2 Recap

I see *My Girl* in the theater with Mom when it comes out in 1991. I'm nine years old. I'm instantly obsessed and go back to see it as much as I can even though I blubber each time Thomas J. dies. Up until then, it didn't really occur to me that kids could die. It's haunting, heartbreaking, and also exciting. I loved sardonic Vada, a writer, a loner with one best friend who had teacher crushes. She's me.

Then, in 1994, *My Girl 2* comes out. I'm twelve and convince Mom to let me walk one block up to the Tulsa Promenade Mall movie theater to see it by myself. I'm glad I'm alone, because it's so much more teen-crush romance than the first film. I identify with Vada's strength and want to make out with Austin O'Brien. It's a love letter to LA, and I'm already a fan of Hollywood, so it boosts my desire to visit and maybe even live there someday. *My Girl 2* far surpasses the first film and quickly becomes my comfort sequel.

In *My Girl 2*, thirteen-year-old Vada (Anna Chlumsky) pulls out an antique light blue-tinged tin box. Faded rabbits and foxes dance in a circle on the top. A passport, some theater programs, a brown paper bag with a handwritten date on it, and a baby book, mostly blank, live inside. Relics from the past. Small treasures from a life Vada never knew.

A hand-cut black-and-white headshot is pasted on the inside sleeve of the government-issued passport. A gorgeous woman centers the frame. Sandy hair curls down to her shoulders, parted on the side. She wears a flower power dress with polyester sharp high collars. Her lips part wide; her smile jumps into you. No question, even in this faded passport photo she is the life of the party.

Written in cursive along the left side of the picture is her name: Margaret Anne Muldovan. Later in life she will marry Harry Sultenfuss and become Maggie Sultenfuss.

She is Vada's mother.

Vada has never met her before.

In Vada's creative writing class, the students are tasked to write about "someone who has achieved something" and whom "you've never met." Students in her class, including Devon Gummersall (aka Brian Krakow from *My So-Called Life*) as a one-liner class clown, spew 1970s obvious choices such as Farrah Fawcett and Elvis Presley. Some giggle. Some yawn. No one seems to take the assignment seriously.

The teacher asks Vada what she has come up with. "My mother." I have goosebumps. Vada lands those two words in a nervous tilt.

"Your mother?" The English teacher considers, confused.

Vada nods, "I never met my mother."

Her words send whispers and head turns from her classmates, who are now thinking this assignment might not just be a joke after all.

Maggie died while giving birth to Vada. She grew up with her undertaker father, Harry (Dan Aykroyd), who lives in a funeral home in Pennsylvania with his now-pregnant wife and Vada's stepmom,

Shelly (Jamie Lee Curtis). Vada is surrounded by love but wants to fill in the answers to questions about her past, particularly as Shelly is about to give birth. *What is it like to have no memories of your mother?* I can't even begin to imagine what that must be like for Vada, and I cheer her on this journey.

In order to move forward, she has to go back. Vada has to visit Los Angeles, where Maggie grew up. After much back-and-forth with her overprotective and hypochondriac dad, who is terrified of her traveling alone, Vada flies to Hollywood to begin her investigation.

Vada does not have much to go on as she begins her adventure aside from the few keepsakes in the antique box and piecemeal anecdotes from her father. Remember, it's 1974, years before the internet. Years before cell phones and Google Maps. Hell, we don't even have these tech advances in 1994, when the movie comes out. Anyway, Vada's work is cut out for her. Finding out about her mother is no simple task.

In LA, Vada stays with her Uncle Phil (Richard Masur); his girlfriend, Rose (Christine Ebersole—more on her in the next chapter); and Rose's son, Nick (Austin O'Brien). Vada spends her days exploring the sights and sounds of the city with Nick as her tour guide and eventual love interest.

They become a chosen family for Vada. Uncle Phil and Rose are surrogate parents during her stay. They shower her with love and kindness. They reinforce boundaries, enforce consequences, and at the same time hold space for her independence and adventure. Vada needs this support as she uncovers secrets and clues to her mother's life and reconnects to her mother's herstory.

Through meeting characters in her mother's life story, she realizes that her mom was complex and imperfect. She finds out that as a teen Maggie got kicked out of school for smoking cigarettes. An activist, Maggie staged a walkout over gender injustices and the Vietnam War in college. The biggest missing piece she finds out is that Maggie was married before meeting Vada's dad, a secret she carried with her to the end.

Okay, so check this out: upon discovering Maggie's previous marriage, Vada actually guilt trips a cop into getting intel about

Maggie's first husband. Like WHAT? She gets his license plate number and most recent address and shows up at his door to talk to him. Can you believe it? Fearless and slightly dangerous choices all around for a thirteen-year-old. Amazing badassery. Get it, Vada.

Her borderline-stalking antics work, and she meets her mother's ex-husband, Jeffrey (J.D. Souther). Vada tells him everything. The class assignment that brought her here. The discovery of her mom as a rebel, a performer, a shit-starter. She shows Jeffrey the brown-paper lunch bag with a date on it that no one seems to be able to place.

Until now.

Jeffrey looks at the bag, smiles, and says "chestnuts." The bag was once filled with the chestnuts that Maggie and Jeffrey ate on a street corner after they had eloped. The date scratched on the bag is the day they got married.

"Do you have any pictures of my mom?" Vada asks, hoping to increase her collection of tin box artifacts. "I have something better," he says as he brings her into his living room and sets up his reel-to-reel.

I'm so excited to see what he is going to show her. Is this the first time she will see her mom? And the movie answers my question with Maggie's beautiful face lighting up the screen. In fits and starts, the film offers Maggie laughing, floating in a pool, chasing someone off-screen, being playful for the camera, and taking bows during a curtain call of *A Doll's House*. Vada is seeing her mother alive for the first time.

Wonder and awe widen Vada's big blue eyes as she watches her mother projected on the wall of this stranger's living room. Maggie unconsciously twists one curl of hair, just like her daughter does when she is excited or nervous. The likeness is uncanny. Jeffrey, like Vada, is overcome by emotion as he watches this woman he loved who left the world too soon.

The reel flips to a picnic table that comes into focus with friends, drinks, food, and laughter. Maggie, center of the party, begins to sing. You can hear a pin drop as the Chaplin lyrics pour from her mouth: *Smile though your heart is aching/Smile even though it's breaking/When there are clouds in the sky, you'll get by.*

Suddenly there is no reel-to-reel; the world around Vada disappears.

In its place a mother sings directly to her daughter. "Smile" is a lullaby to Vada. The lullaby she never got to have in real life.

In this moment, my heart aches for Vada. I feel so lucky that I get to have my mom in my life who sings lullabies to me. Especially the "Emily Is My Little Girl" lullaby. Tears spill from my eyes, matching Vada's sadness, anger, and grief multitudes that are limited by language.

In finally seeing her mother alive and learning more than what can be told in the little box of keepsakes, Vada can begin to grieve. With many questions finally answered, she can start making sense of her mother's story, and thus her own.

The Algebra Fairy

All through K-12 school, I'm terrible in math. Later, in women's studies classes in college, I will learn that many girls struggle in math, in large part because they aren't systemically supported in STEM the same way boys are. I'm sure that was a part of it for me, but also, math just sucked. I hated it. Still do. Thankfully, now there are apps and TurboTax, so my need to understand multiplication and long division is not as dire as it once was.

But in the mid nineties, when I'm in middle school, math matters greatly. I'm failing pre algebra, a class that sounds college chic but in reality is boring af. Mom, a longtime math professor, is quietly disappointed in my deficiency but is a cheerleader with the utmost patience.

"Sweetie, let's review how to solve for x,"

I shake my head no.

"Mom, it's impossible. Why do I need to know this? How does this help me in life?"

The numbers blur together on the page, and I know I'm in trouble when even the word problems are an unsolvable labyrinth. I dramatically throw my brown grocery bag-covered textbook on the floor next to my bed. It makes a loud thump on the beige carpet and lands in between Nirvana's *In Utero* CD case and my *All Over Me* and *Grease 2* VHS covers. I'm incorrigible.

My disdain for math doesn't get better; it gets worse. Even thinking about going to class makes my heart race, my glands sweat, and my stomach turn. I throw up before class. I try to work through it and sometimes I can, but anxiety and panic take over. One night I stay up until 2:00 a.m. trying to get through a long equation that is due first period the next morning.

Eventually I give up and write a note on Lisa Frank spiral torn paper. I leave it outside my door.

Momma, I just can't do this. Can you help me? I'm so sorry I tried so hard and I'm so tired and I can't stop crying. Thank you. I love you.

I draw a big heart next to my plea, hoping that will drive the point home. I leave my textbook open to the correct page and circle the problem with my No. 2 pencil. Closing the door to my bedroom, I press play on *My Girl 2*, and Vada's story cradles me to sleep.

My alarm is an asshole, going off at 7:00 a.m., and I groan-stumble out of bed. It takes me a foggy minute to remember the homework due in Ms. Stewart's class, and the monster gripping my gut returns. I open my door to find a trifold note on top of my textbook.

Algebra homework is now complete. Step by step guide is included. Love, the Algebra Fairy.

Over the years, I ask the Algebra Fairy for help only when I'm really in trouble. I learn enough algebra to pass my classes, but that's as far as my math career goes. But sliding notes under my bedroom door becomes an ongoing, adorable way Mom communicates.

Gone for a walk, Eggs and bacon on the stove are for you. Love, Algebra Fairy.

Here's a little gift the Easter Bunny wanted me to share with you. Hoppity hop hop hop! Xo Algebra Fairy. And next to the Easter egg-covered is a white bunny stuffed animal, a Cadbury Egg and a five-pack of yellow marshmallow Peeps in the shape of baby chicks.

I cuddle up with my Algebra Fairy. (Photo courtesy of Em Marinelli)

Algebra Fairy is going to Albertsons. Do you want chicken for dinner? Yes _ No_ or Write in your own answer_.

I mark "Yes," think twice, and scratch it out. I opt to write in my own answer: *Fettucine Alfredo, please!*

I keep the notes in a box under my bed. I paint it sky blue with Puffy paint and place a few fox and bunny stickers in a circle around the top, just like Vada's. I admire Mom's beautiful penmanship, her tight cursive from a time when it was taught in schools as part of the English curriculum.

Later, when I move to California for college, I bring the box with me. I save the Hallmark cards Mom sends me in care packages for holidays and for "just because" reasons. I keep it under my bed to feel close to her and touch it with my toes when I can't sleep.

Mood Rings As Mementos

Did you ever own a mood ring? I did, thanks to the Claire's store in the mall. I'm thirteen, the same age as Vada, and I wear it proudly to middle school. It connects me to *My Girl 2*; I love looking at it during class. It transports me to seventies glam and to Vada's world.

I wait for the dull-black coloration in the ring to brighten into a joyful or excited red. I worry a brown hue will show the world I'm nervous or anxious (likely about math or asshole kids at school), and I hold my ring up to the sun to manipulate the tinge.

Usually the ring stays black, even when I huff my hot breath over the silver. Sometimes a deep ocean blue emerges, and I wonder why. *Am I feeling calm? Am I in love? Maybe I'm just sleepy after a cafeteria lunch of pizza and wacky cake?* In case you're wondering, wacky cake is just cheap chocolate cake with frosting that is labeled wacky for reasons I still can't comprehend. And yes, it's delicious.

Mood rings are made with crystal material that respond to heat. The ring tracks emotional responses that make our bodies hot or cold. Physiology aside, it's the symbolism that makes mood rings cool. Like tarot decks, astrology, or any other way we look for signs from the universe, mood rings reflect that which can't totally be explained by science.

A Magic 8 ball on our finger, mood rings show us what we deeply desire, reflect what we feel inside, tell us whether or not we should proceed or stop and pivot immediately. They give us access to our emotions, and for preteens like myself and Vada, having our inside world reflected clearly on the outside is extremely validating. The meaning we make is subjective and based on intuition. This is what magic is all about.

And Vada needs some magic in her life. She suffers in middle school, trying to fit in and find herself. She is understandably upset when she's kicked out of her room to make space for the new baby nursery. All of this, plus her normal teen hormones and stressors. Shit is hard.

In middle school I'm Vada trying to fit in with the popular kids. The message from other kids and the larger world is clear—in order to be lovable, you must be thin. I starve myself, chain smoke Marlboro

Lights, and exercise for hours every day to fit this ask. I retreat to reading *Sweet Valley High*, Danielle Steel, and other fantastical romance stories to escape my reality.

I smoke pot, start to realize I'm not totally straight (maybe bi?), and fall in love with actually straight girls who never reciprocate my adoration but instead flirt in an unrequited endless loop. On weekends I go to the movies alone or watch rented indie queer films in my room. I tape episodes of *Ellen* on syndication and label them with made-up names. I write episode descriptions on notebook paper and slide them into Maxwell VHS covers.

Vada is lost, like me. Deep down, she believes that since Maggie died during childbirth, her death is Vada's fault. Believing she killed her mother is too big of a responsibility for any teen to have. Vada carries this weight in her psyche. It follows her in shadows; it peeks into her sense of self-worth.

In the first film, Thomas J. (Macaulay Culkin), her best friend, tries to retrieve her mood ring, which fell near a beehive. He is stung by many bees and dies of an allergic reaction. I cry and cry when Vada sees him in his open casket. "His face hurts," she wails. "Where are his glasses? He can't see without his glasses." Her torment is mood ring-palpable. The hole in her heart is massive.

No one should have to endure a loss like this. Especially someone so young. Her message from the universe is clear: when she lets people into her life and world, they perish. Once again, because of Vada, someone she loved and cared for has passed.

Her mood ring is a reminder of Thomas J. The ring made it through the bee stings and signifies a part of him that survived, a part of him she can actually hold on to. The ring is his love for her, which has also survived. The mood ring acts as a constant object for Vada. Friends and mothers leave; mood rings stay.

Wearing the ring every day is a ritualistic connection to what has been lost. There is strength in seeing her internal grief displayed externally on her finger. All the more reason it is extremely upsetting when Nick (Austin O'Brien), in *My Girl 2*, tries on her mood ring and pretends to drop it in the La Brea Tar Pits. He does this after Vada tells him the story of losing Thomas J. *Why the fuck would Nick think it was okay to pretend to accidentally drop her ring in the tar pits?*

Obviously, his so-called playfulness is a defense against his discomfort at learning of the loss of her best friend. But still, it is kind of unforgivable. He is unknowingly forcing her to confront the actual loss once again. I hold on tighter to my mood ring when I see him do this, as if Vada and I are one and I can't risk losing my ring for dumb boy antics.

Okay, yes, he's a preteen boy—clueless, cute, and crushable. He's immature and prone to joking and being mean. But at the same time, he's reasonable and has principles. He's soft and attuned. He validates Vada's emotions when she is distraught at various roadblocks in the search for her mother. When Maggie's friend has a meltdown at the secondhand store, Nick physically holds her to comfort and support her.

While these are not things to write home about, they are fairly advanced for a white boy of thirteen and show us that he has the potential for at least some emotional maturity and depth. Nick grows on us, and my little teenage heart fell for his sharp humor and intimate

Austin O'Brien and Anna Chlumsky on the journey to find her mother.
(Photo courtesy of Columbia Pictures)

gestures of adoration toward Vada. Over the course of the sequel, the audience (along with Vada) begins to imagine life moving on in the form of this new exciting love interest.

Nick and Vada's cheesy dialogue is the stuff that every tween in the mid nineties loves to hear and certainly makes this movie the perfect amount of hokey. At the film's end, Nick is waiting on the tarmac for Vada as she is about to board the plane to fly home. Wind blows through his sandy brown bowl-cut hair, soft piano and violin music flows, and the dialogue ascends:

Vada: "Listen, I'm sorry you had to sacrifice your entire vacation."
Nick: "Some sacrifices are worth it."
Vada: "You mean it wasn't that terrible?"
Nick: "I wouldn't say it was terrible. It was kind of an . . . "
Vada: "An adventure?"
Nick: "Part adventure . . . part miracle"

The kiss is nervous middle school tender, curious, exciting, and sweet. I wanted a tarmac first kiss like that so badly! I seek out the air draft pockets when boarding a plane and hope a cute boy or girl (who would also be on a mandated family trip) would grab me and kiss me.

Fashion from the early seventies, bell bottoms, clogs, and peasant shirts, made a resurgence in the early nineties, so I was right on time and looked the part. Even in my stylized getup, an airport stolen first kiss never happened for me, but I still listened to my *My Girl 2* soundtrack on my Walkman, dreaming of my runway send-off.

Slowly Vada softens to Nick, and maybe she falls in love again. Nick will never be Thomas J., but being able to experience the joy, pain, annoyance, and excitement that new love brings is mood ring magic. The inside jokes they cocreate, the adventures they embark on, open up parts of Vada that have been lost.

For me, my mood ring becomes a lifeline to *My Girl* and *My Girl 2*. At school, when I'm bullied for being overweight or when I have panic attacks in math or P.E., I can look down at my mood ring and think about Vada and Nick. I turn it around and around my finger and feel a little less anxious. I fiddle with it, and I'm pleasantly distracted.

I wear it when I have my first real kiss, at age thirteen, just like Vada. I'm not at an airport tarmac after all, but at Broadway summer camp. The whole summer I'm crushed out on this boy, Jake, who is Austin O'Brien meets baby Kurt Cobain. Dreamy.

I flirt with him when I'm picked to sing "So Long Dearie" from *Hello Dolly* as part of the end-of-camp summer showcase. I boldly approach him; greasy blond and auburn hair strands fall into his eyes. I sing, "I'm gonna learn to dance and drink and smoke a cigarette," and I brush my purple boa against his acne-splotched face.

For some reason, at home I obsessively watch the song "Love with All the Trimmings" from *On a Clear Day You Can See Forever* and think about Jake. I become Barbra Streisand and immerse myself in the movie by drinking Mom's White Zinfandel from a goblet and clinking my nails against the glass. I imagine I'm singing to Jake, like Barbra as Melinda sings to Robert, her gorgeously tanned love interest and soon-to-be husband.

On the last day of camp, Jake and I wait to be picked up in the corridor of Eisenhower Elementary school. Everyone else is already gone. It's just us. Our backpacks are on the tiled floor next to us; his stickered skateboard is propped up against the wall. I see Mom pulling up in her white Mazda, and I hide behind the door frame so she won't see me. Our dialogue is Nick-and-Vada worthy.

Emily: "My ride's here." I look down and become suddenly shy.
Jake: "Damn, I wish we had more time." Shifting weight in his Airwalks, he nervously pulls on either side of his No Fear T-Shirt.
Emily: "Me too. I'm gonna miss you."
Jake: "Here's my number; call me sometime." And he hands me his scribbled digits on the back of a Broadway camp showcase program. I'm impressed that he's prewritten it in anticipation of this moment.
Emily: "Okay, I will." I twiddle my mood ring as sweat begins to collect under my armpits, and I can only hope my Secret deodorant will hold.
Jake: "Meeting you has been . . . " and he trails off.

Emily: "It's been really cool." Really cool? I think. Fuck, why did I say that?
Jake: "I was gonna say rad."

He gives me a piercing look, and I know what's about to happen. Gently caressing my right cheek in his hand, he draws my face up to his. Right away I know this isn't his first kiss, and I'm happy to follow his lead, moving my tongue where he directs his. I'm warm all over. The sun hits the mood ring on my pudgy ring finger, and it turns from saddle brown to violet and finally lands on a bright, emanating royal blue.

"Just Smile"

Vada grew up in a mortuary, with death around every corner. Vada's dad, Harry, tries to normalize death. He speaks about it matter-of-factly. It is his day job, after all. It's just the family business.

But just because death surrounds Vada doesn't mean she has healthy outlets for processing and integrating it. Vada's heart is fractured. She suffers the soul-pain of losing both a parent and her best friend from the first film.

Vada projects the fear of loss and abandonment onto her stepmom, Shelly, who is close to giving birth to Vada's half sibling. She fears Shelly will also die during delivery, the way her mother did. If she couldn't save her mom, or her best friend, at least she can save her stepmom and her baby.

If Vada can witness a corrective childbirth experience through Shelly, she can begin to heal her own grief and loss. The birth of Vada's new sibling is a reminder that so many things in life can change. Life moves on, and yet some things remain: love, connection, family.

And music!

The Sultenfuss Funeral Parlor is a family home filled with music. *My Girl 2* opens with the family joyfully belting "Our House" as they prepare a funeral showing. Later in the film a very pregnant Shelly gently sings "Baby Love" to her soon-to-be-born child, with Harry on tuba in accompaniment.

At the film's end, Vada arrives back in Pennsylvania to find her new baby brother is born and Shelly is safe and healthy. Shelly had experienced complications during pregnancy, so to say everyone is relieved is an understatement. The cycle of death and birth comes fully around, as Vada takes her new brother into her arms, rocks him gently, looks directly into his eyes, and sings:

"If you smile through your fear and sorrows
Smile and maybe tomorrow
You see the sun come shining through for you, if you just Smile."

Just like her mother sang to her in the film reel, Vada is passing on this generational message through song. By bringing "Smile," as a song ritual into this musical family, Vada brings in her mother's spirit too. The "Smile" lullaby now becomes a little secret, not just between her and her mom, but now also between her and her new brother.

"Emily Is My Little Girl"

There will never be a relationship like the one I have with my Mom. We are soul connected in ways I have never been with anyone else. Today, as I type this chapter, she's seventy-two, just retired from fifty years of teaching, and lives in Pensacola, Florida, her dream of being so close to her deep love, the ocean, finally realized.

My whole life she told me how she was so afraid of slipping into Alzheimer's, like her mother (my grandmother) and her brother (my uncle). Despite her prevention efforts, in the past year she has started to lose her short-term memory. Remembering the day of the week is checking the wall calendar dozens of times. Remembering how to drive outside of a five mile radius is damn near impossible. Remembering what she did yesterday is out of reach.

What hasn't changed is the way she sings to me.

I stay with her on and off throughout the year now. We parade around her nautical drenched apartment and sing like we used to. Before making a shopping run to Ross Dress for Less, she does the "Follow the yellow brick road" dance from *The Wizard of Oz* to the tune of "Shop til you drop," a made-up classic from childhood.

I walk into her compact kitchen, tight with copious sets of lighthouse mugs and plates that spill out from the cupboards onto the counter. She hums "Candle on the Water" while making Jiffy cornbread with creamed corn, black-eyed peas from a can, and roast beef slow cooked in a Crock-Pot and topped with McCormick pot roast seasoning from a packet. It's a meal she's cooked a million times and is second nature to her now.

At night I snug under the seashell comforter in the guest room, and gripped by lifelong insomnia, I ask her to sing to me. Her manicured nails lightly scratch my back and mix with the lull of her song. It's as if thirty years haven't passed. I'm little again and afraid of the dark, and she's there to comfort and soothe me. Despite forgetting what she had for breakfast, she remembers every word to my very own "Emily Is My Little Girl" lullaby, and I quickly fall asleep.

***

Grief is not so much about healing as it is about integrating loss. Processing grief may never come to an end. Losing someone we love always stays with us but gets resituated into our lives over time.

There may never come a day where Vada wakes up and has no feelings at all about her mother's death. It is more likely that she will feel less and less responsibility, guilt, and shame over time. The pain will change, lessen, move, settle.

As my mom's disease progresses, I may never wake up and just miraculously feel okay or better. Some days are terrible and I want to scream; some days are easier and quieter; some days I have more patience and acceptance. I look at my new mood ring, given to me by my queer chosen family on my fortieth birthday, and ask it for guidance, to reflect whatever is my internal truth in any given moment.

All these years later, Mom still writes little notes and slides them under the door. Her cursive is a little looser than in years before; the notes are a little strained but hold the levity and love they always did.

Emily there is pot roast in the crockpot help yourself, Love, Algebra Fairy

Here's a little gift Santa left for me to give you. Love, Algebra Fairy.
The note sits on top of a little Golden Book about Dolly Parton,

whom she knows I adore. I mean, who doesn't love Dolly?

Going to Publix, do you need anything? Love, Algebra Fairy. With a box to check "Yes" or "No."

I consider for a second and then make a third box: "No, thank you Algebra Fairy, but I love you very much"

The box I made like Vada's won't hold all the cards, original poems, and notes she's sent me over the years. The Algebra Fairy notes alone could fill their own box. Now they fill tubs and part of a filing cabinet. I still keep the original box close and reread them when I can't sleep. While Vada holds on to parts of her mom to try to understand her, I now hold parts of mine to try to remember how she once was, and I am curious about what our future will be.

What will come next for Vada? While the third *My Girl* film never got off the ground (it was in the works for many years), I like to imagine an exciting life for her. Maybe she keeps cultivating her craft as a writer. Maybe she continues her fearless journalism. Maybe she follows in her mother's footsteps. Or maybe she makes a new path entirely.

Vada's journey to learn about her mom helps her put pieces together of her own herstory. She takes risks, she falls in love, she finds her own womanhood, she finds a new sense of family. Maggie's lullaby both starts and stops with the word "smile." It creates a sense of closure and also calls for a new beginning. The "smile" that travels many places and beckons Vada to do the same. That calls her into a never-ending world of adventure and wonder.

After the Ball:
An Interview With
Christine Ebersole

In *My Girl 2*, Christine Ebersole plays Rose Zsigmond; the girlfriend to Vada's Uncle Phil. Rose runs the family auto body shop and is a firecracker, a no-nonsense manager with a huge, loving heart. A solid mother to Nick, Rose soon becomes an important maternal figure for Vada too.

Ebersole's credits run off the page. Star of TV, film, and the stage for almost fifty years, Christine is simply a legend. Her film highlights include *Tootsie, Amadeus, Ghost Dad, The Wolf of Wall Street*, and *Licorice Pizza*. Her TV shows include *Ally McBeal, Murphy Brown, Will & Grace, Unbreakable Kimmy Schmidt, Pose, The Kominsky Method*, and *Bob Hearts Abishola*.

On Broadway, she portrayed Elizabeth Arden in *War Paint* (with Patti Lupone) and Elvira in *Blithe Spirit* and won the 2001 Tony for Best Actress in a Musical as Dorothy Brock in the revival of *42nd Street*. I know her best, aside from *My Girl 2*, from her Tony Award-winning performance as Little and Big Edie Bouvier Beale in the 2007 musical *Grey Gardens*.

I was nervous-excited waiting for her call. I didn't need to be.

Christine is a gentle diva powerhouse, and it was magical to talk with her. Like Rose, Christine is warm, to the point, and hilarious. She is empathic; her responses are thoughtful, and it is clear she loves her family and her craft. I could feel her maternal warmth, and on this short call, I felt like the Vada to her Rose.

She ends our talk with little terms of endearment that come out quickly before we hang up. Her words got stuck on my tongue like wacky cake. I wanted to take them in and taste them again and again. Swish them around and get them stuck in the roof of my mouth. Swallow the sweetness in little bits, and still save some for later. Here's the enchantment of Christine Ebersole:

Emily Marinelli: What do you remember about getting involved with *My Girl 2*?

Christine Ebersole: Well, I got offered the movie, and we were right in the throes of adopting a child, our firstborn. The director, Howard Zieff, was unbelievably accommodating, because I was so nervous about taking a movie while he was a tiny baby. But Howard was like, "We will get you a nanny and put up a room for you, and we will just do everything we can." He was so kind and so accommodating.

Elijah was born, and he came on the set with me! So it's a very special time for me, and I remember that movie so fondly because our family was just starting. Everybody on the set was so happy to have a baby, I mean he was just forty-eight hours old! So I have those special memories. Everybody I worked with, everybody on the set, was just so kind and welcoming and just made it all possible.

Emily: Wow, that is amazing. It is such an important time to be so close and to bond with your baby when they are that little. Thank you for sharing that. I love your character Rose in the film. She is unapologetic and loving. She's an incredible mom. She's a strong businesswoman. How did you prepare to play her?

Christine: I think the key is the writing. If the writing makes sense and is strong, the characters just sort of naturally come out. My personality is certainly lended to it, but it's really in the writing that really dictates how it's played. So I'm grateful that it was well constructed.

Emily: Rose has some hilarious one-liners: "I don't suppose your father gave you permission to pierce your ears?" To which Vada replies, "Not exactly." "Well, just don't shave your legs. Your father will never let you visit us again if I send you back hairless and full of holes."

Christine: It's about being honest. Speaking honestly, truthfully. How you are in life, you are in art. This character is very straightforward, no frills, she's just a straight-ahead kind of a gal. So it's just approached from that manner. She wasn't fussy.

Emily: And you create this dimension of softness with her. A maternal softness. Now hearing about your baby on the set as well and thinking about your mothering to Nick, I'm seeing these beautiful parallels around motherhood. I see you and Phil as parental roles for Vada too.

Character actor Richard Masur and Broadway legend Christine Ebersole in *My Girl 2*. (Photo courtesy of Columbia Pictures)

Christine: It was really great working with Richard Masur and all those people I got to work those scenes with. Everything was just easy, just because of the people involved. It wasn't fraught. It was a beautiful story, and it was about caring and loving and looking out. Themes that certainly resonate with me. It was all right there for the taking.

Emily: Your character holds an important role for Vada as she grieves her mom and Thomas J. How do you see these themes of grief and healing play out in the film?

Christine: Healing is a broad term. I think it's more; *how do you integrate the experience into your life?* You know, if you have a cut on your hand and the cut heals, then the cut goes away. But I think grief is a little different in the sense that grief never goes away. But you figure out how to integrate the experience into your life so you can move forward with it. And I really don't know, because my mother lived to be a hundred, so I don't know that experience. But I know some of my friends who lost their father when they were eleven, and it's something you never forget. You're never healed from it, but it's a matter of how you integrate that loss into the fabric of your life and move forward with it and hope it doesn't prevent you from moving forward. And [Vada's] quest for that was an act in itself of moving forward, of trying to discover things about her mother so she could weave them into the fabric of her life.

Emily: Any other memorable moments while filming?

Christine: Anna Chlumsky was a darling, very sweet girl. I mean everybody, it just had that kind of vibe, you know, that kind of nurturing vibe on the set. Everybody was in it together. We all obviously loved the story and were privileged and thrilled to be a part of it.

Emily: You can feel on the screen the cohesion and family energy between all of you.

Christine: Yeah! Yeah, it's really true! I have nothing but the fondest memories of that and especially because of what was happening on a personal level and just how generous the production was to accommodate the event that was happening in my life.

Emily: This book is about the comfort that movie sequels/series bring, the sense of security they provide. What do you think makes *My Girl 2* so comforting for audiences?

Christine: Finding stability that was offered to Vada in this uncertain world she was inhabiting. Offering stability from two people who loved one another and who were committed to one another. The definition of family is commitment and dedication and willingness to face any kind of struggle or battles ahead. It's the fortress of that strength that you thrive from any challenges that come your way. So I think it's what Richard Masur's character and mine represented, that stability for her. So there's something comforting about that, I feel.

Emily: What other movie series or sequels do you find comforting? What is your version of comfort sequels?

Christine: It's odd because I've been doing this for almost fifty years, and yet I don't watch TV or movies [laughs], in full disclosure. So I really wouldn't be the person to ask about that. For sequels, I could say *Godfather 2*, but I'm not sure that's comforting [we both laugh].

Emily: I mean, it's a great movie, but it's an intense one.

Christine: It's not the warm and fuzzy feeling you get from *My Girl 2*. *My Girl 2* is a sequel, but it stands on its own. We look for comfort in different ways, and I don't derive a lot of comfort from watching TV and movies. It's mostly listening to music, talking with friends, and reading the Bible. That's a constant source of comfort. Certainly music, I love listening to music, and the kind of music I listen to depends on the time of day and what's going on.

Emily: I had the once-in-a-lifetime, transformational experience to see you in the Broadway musical *Grey Gardens* in 2007. You embodied Little Edie, her passion, her fragility, her artistry, and her confusion.

Christine: It was a life-changing experience for me as well. You don't know how these things happen; the opportunity was just presented. And I was able to embody those women [Little and Big Edie] through identification of their struggle. So what I tried to do was bring humanity to these women. And could identify with the struggle, which is why I was able to do it on the level that I was.

And I don't really understand it. I really don't. It's being present with what's happening. It's a hard thing to describe. How do you portray something and have a portal of that experience that can be a window for others that are watching or viewing it to have an emotional experience themselves? And that's where the sharing comes in. It's not presentational in that sense, it's representational. It was a juggernaut that will never ever be replicated. So I'm grateful that I was a part of that, and I really had such respect and admiration and compassion for these women.

Emily: Anything you are working on now you would like to share?

Christine: I have an album coming out. Interestingly the album cover is literally within the same time frame of *My Girl 2*, because right after *My Girl 2*, I was offered a job at the Paper Mill Playhouse in New Jersey of a Broadway-bound musical called *Paper Moon*, which is based on the movie with Ryan O'Neal and Tatum O'Neal. I was playing the part of Trixie Delight, which was played by Madeline Kahn in the film.

It was like minutes after we finished filming *My Girl 2*, we got on a plane. Elijah was like three weeks old, and when I did *My Girl 2*, he was two days old. So we got on a plane and we came to New York. The cover of the album is a photograph of me backstage at the Paper Mill Playhouse, and I have a wig cap on and I'm in my dressing room with my husband, Bill. It's taken looking in this dressing room mirror with lights around it. Bill is holding Elijah, and I'm standing behind Bill

Christine Ebersole's CD cover was taken during *My Girl 2*.
(Photo courtesy of Provident Music Group)

in this incredible statement of love and the beginning of family, and Elijah is in Bill's arms yawning. It's just the sweetest thing you've ever seen. That was literally three weeks after filming *My Girl 2*. I wrapped up the film and went to New York. So the picture could've been from *My Girl 2*.

And that's the cover of the album, *After the Ball*, because the narrative is about when the children grow up and become independent and we grow older and how you move forward. That was the inspiration for that, was when we were all empty nesters, when they had all left home and were in college. That's why it's called *After the Ball*. What do you do after the ball, after the party?

That was when we were all together, the happy chaos that surrounds that, when kids are growing up. Then suddenly they're gone and you're older, and then what? It's the most heartfelt work that I've done in terms of music because it was inspired by that. It's like a crossroads.

Emily: A lot of parents will appreciate and relate to these questions, and I love the *My Girl 2* tie-in. It's all there. It is such an honor to talk to you and an unbelievable opportunity.

Christine: All the best on the book. I can't wait to read it. Will you send me an autographed copy?

Emily: Of course I will. Thank you so much for your time. I wish you well.

Christine: Thank you for helping me remember those wonderful experiences. Thanks, dear. Lots of love. Take care.

Batman Returns

"I am Catwoman; hear me roar!"

"Shabby" is probably the best way to characterize my first attempt at becoming Catwoman. "Thrifty" or "creative" could also describe it.

My Walmart all-in-one-bag Catwoman costume basically consists of a trash bag with two arm holes, and white-tape stitch lines zigzagging across the front. The leggings are more of the same; rain pants that flap in the wind. Stick-on whiskers slide off my cheeks with each streak of sweat. Fuchsia Lee Press-On Nails serve as my cat claws.

I am ten.

Snookums, my English bulldog, ate the plastic cat tail that came with the costume. So a tabby-colored tiger tail from another hand-me-down dance-recital costume has to fill in. I have it pinned to the rain pants, and not only does it not match, it also ends up creating a big hole right between my butt cheeks. When it finally tears off completely, I decide to use it as a whip.

It's a one-size-fits-all kids costume, but I'm a little thicker, so the pants snug into me and begin melting in places when hit by the sun. The headpiece is too hot to wear in Oklahoma in July, so I use leftover Halloween face paint to fashion a dark eye mask with two holes. As if that were any more fashion forward. I'm serving up old-Hollywood bandit realness in the backyard of our duplex rental.

I trip over a cemetery of My Little Ponies ground into the red dirt underneath our oak tree and face-plant into a sinkhole that Snookums made. I taste face paint and bologna-sandwich leftovers in my mouth and feel inner-thigh chafing—already well underway—as the pants cling with humidity to my stubby legs.

But I'm determined. I stand up, covered in earth, pick off sticky burrs from my ensemble, and survey the damage. All is intact, just a little cut on my bandit forehead where I landed. I kick a Bud Light can out of the way and head to my trampoline. I have Catwoman work to do.

I press play on my Goodwill thrift store Sharp pastel-pink boom box. Janet Jackson's cassette single "Black Cat" begins to blare and vibrate, and my heart begins to race. While not related to *Batman Returns*, it is the pop/rock anthem I need to fully become the character.

I mount the tall trampoline one leg at a time, the springs boing-ing, my pants ripping even more as I come to a standing position on the jumping mat. My mom looks out the kitchen window and smiles, waving a yellow rubber-gloved hand at me. She shakes her head of sandy blond hair and mouths "Be careful, sweetie!"

"1,2,3,4!" Janet calls in the epic electric guitar to start. I'm already out of breath.

"Michelle, this one's for you," I say out loud, as if Michelle Pfeiffer will cosmically hear me and telepathically know I'm about to execute a trampoline routine in her honor.

I begin the precision sequence I have spent hours practicing:
Eight regular bounces with pointed toes,
Seat drop,
Knee drop,
Cat drop.
Allow for buoyancy.
Pause for effect on all fours just in time for the "Black Cat" chorus:
"Black cat, nine lives
Short days, long nights"
Meow like a cat.
Scratch my pink nails in the air.
Fall my way back to standing position.

Wipe a cat whisker off my face.

Smear face paint streaks on the trash bag.

Sing along with Janet:

"Livin' on the edge
Not afraid to die"

Scream out loud, "I am Catwoman; hear me roar!"

Cat whip the pretend enemy next to me with the recycled tail.

Trip over pants leg.

Almost fall through the springs.

Try not to die.

Come back to center.

Brace myself to jump high again for the next eight count.

Repeat the whole sequence.

I would like to think that Eartha Kitt would've found humor in my backyard Catwoman attempt. Julie Newmar would've rolled her eyes but loved me all the same. But it was Michelle Pfeiffer as Catwoman in the 1992 sequel *Batman Returns* whom I wanted to be. Or maybe it was Michelle whom I wanted. Or both.

Batman Returns Recap

It's 1992. Mom and I are at the matinee show at the dollar movies, and I'm a little scared as the screen goes completely black. Snowflakes fall over the WB logo as Danny Elfman's score leads us into the backstory of the Cobblepot family; a rich man (played by Paul Reubens), his wife, and their deformed baby.

They keep the baby in a covered cage so he can't see out and we can't see in. His little penguin flippers pop out and violently grab the house cat for a tasty meal. This little baby, who happens to be a penguin/human, is being abused by his parents. I suddenly find it hard to swallow my popcorn as my stomach tightens. I feel sad for him and don't have the words to put to this injustice.

The Cobblepots are disgusted with their son and don't know what to do with him. He is not totally human. He is not totally penguin. He is a hybrid, seabird and human. A freak. So, on Christmas Day, with seemingly no other choice to make, they throw him into the icy river, which is also the sewer system of Gotham.

The camera follows the baby carriage into the underground world of an abandoned arctic theme park, Arctic World. Penguin baby actually survives. Live penguins greet him and take him in as one of their own. The opening credits roll.

Fast-forward to Christmas Day in Gotham thirty three years later. Disgusting corporate mogul Max Shreck (Christopher Walken) is going to build a new power plant in Gotham as a scheme to make more money off the city. Selina Kyle (aka Michelle Pfeiffer, aka MY Catwoman) is his assistant. She enters the high-rise office shy, fumbling, unsure of herself. She attempts to ask an insightful question to a group of businessmen who have convened to discuss said power plant.

Max patronizingly and misogynistically retorts, "I'm afraid we haven't properly housebroken Ms. Kyle. In the plus column, though, she makes a hell of a cup of coffee." The men around the table grumble-laugh. Selina doesn't ask her question. She berates herself after they leave. I'm so sad for her; she's like the baby penguin, trapped in a cage, unloved.

Soon after, she innocently discovers the truth of the power plant scheme and decides to tell Max. Bad idea, Selina. Max actually pushes her out the window of the high-rise office building. As if he wasn't already the worst human, now he's also a murderer. But as terrible as it is for Selina to die, this moment is also the beginning of her rebirth. Laying on the ground in the dusty snow, whiskery hair falling in her face, blood trickling from her head and mouth, Selina has lost her life.

Thankfully, she has eight more.

Cue the cats. Strays emerge from trash cans, pop out from behind buildings, jump down from rooftops. They knead all over her. They nibble her. They beg her to join them. To come home. To turn into Catwoman.

Cue me in the movie theater on the edge of my seat. How could she have survived such a fall? How are the cats rescuing her? I imagine crawling my way to save Selina from her demise too. She needs me. I immediately whisper to Mom asking if we can get a cat when we get home. She just smiles and offers me some more Junior Mints; her nonanswer is of course a no. We have our hands full with Snookums.

Cat-scratch-feverishly, Selina transforms her single-cat-lady apartment filled with childish pink vintage knickknacks into a sultry cat den. She breaks the neon pink sign in her room, transforming the message from a sweet "Hello There" to "Hell Here." I will write "Hell Here" in neon pink Crayola Marker as soon as I get home and tape it to my bedroom wall. It won't last long, as Mom will realize it isn't the best parenting move to let me keep it up there.

Selina grabs a black vinyl rain jacket and somehow reshapes it into a full-bodied, perfectly fitted rubber catsuit, complete with stiletto boots. She emerges on the screen, a newly mutated feline/human. How did she do that? Amazing. She's beautiful and so sexy I can barely stand it.

I watch as Selina and Bruce Wayne fall in love by day but fight each other by night as their alter egos. I notice pangs of annoyance and jealousy as Bruce gets to dance and flirt with Selina, who is now fully Catwoman, no question.

The men in the story are way less interesting but plot important. Max is now in cahoots with Penguin and has him run for mayor so he can take control of the city. Penguin plans to kill all the newborn babies in the city (in retaliation for his own demise and parental disregard as a child).

Penguins' other shady activities in the film include kidnapping the Ice Princess, kidnapping a baby, and eventually even kidnapping Max. Lots of kidnapping. All for different and I'm sure important reasons. He even stages a penguin torpedo takeover. He is a busy guy.

Catwoman teams up with Penguin against Batman and all the good he represents. Of course Batman prevails. He is able to rewire the bombs set by Penguin and blow up Penguin's lair in Arctic World, thereby rescuing all the children of Gotham and saving the day.

This is fine, but all I really want is more Catwoman. All I can do is wait for her to come back on screen. When she does, there's a tingling between my legs and I shove my Diet Coke fountain drink there to cool it down.

And then, she's back.

And the unthinkable happens.

Catwoman kills Max and HERSELF at the same time. Wait,

WHAT? MY Michelle, MY Catwoman, has perished? It's too much for me. I know she was never set up to succeed. But did she have to die?

I'm despondent. My mom looks over, seeing how upset I am, and gently squeezes my hand. I know what I saw, but I have a feeling she is not totally gone. I can feel Catwoman still purring somewhere close by.

Penguin's is the next death to come. Black blood and gore eke out from his mouth. A sad creature in a world that never understood him. As he takes his last breath, his body falls onto the ice.

We circle back to when we found him at the beginning of the film, discarded by the Cobblepots, taken in by the penguins. He is one of them; they are his true family. The penguins beautifully and ritualistically escort his body back into the water with them. We watch his slow submergence, the penguins surrounding him in the water. An aquatic funeral cradle. This part gets me crying. Even though he's a bad guy, he's been hurt too and deserves better.

The film ends with Batman. Of course it does; he is the franchise namesake. On his way home from all the mess of the day, he stops his car in a dark alleyway (Gotham sure is full of them). He picks up a black cat thinking maybe he found Selina. He thought he saw her in a shadow. But no one is there. He looks around, gets back in his car, and heads home. He sure needs rest after all that went down.

But then, a bat signal rises high in the sky, over the buildings of Gotham, summoning Batman again. As the film comes to end, there she is. Catwoman appears and looks up to the signal. We see only her back, but we know it's her. The life comes back into me, and I can breathe again.

Nine lives. "That's right; she had one life left, Mom," I whisper to Mom, who laughs and says, "That's right, sweetie," squeezing my hand. What will Catwoman do next? Where will she go? What women will she help? When will I see her again? She shimmies her shoulders, shaking off the past, opening us to possibilities of the future. The end credits take us out. That's all we get.

For now.

True/False/Shadow Selves

Batman Returns is about the beauty and sadness of freaks. Penguin and Catwoman are reminders of how mainstream society can't accept what is different. They represent what is beautiful and also what is sad about being a freak in a conformist world.

In 1992, I could relate.

Growing up, I spend every weekend and some school nights with my friend Jenny. I feel an electric jolt come through me when we are together. It hits me when I least expect it. Like when we stay up late laughing and talking and snacking on Bagel Bites on her waterbed.

I press play on her tape deck and then slide under the covers to meet her. I perform a full lip sync to New Kids on the Block's "Time Is on Our Side" and watch the waterbed's ripple effect from my boy band dance moves. I pretend to offer her a bouquet on the part where I lip-synch, "If I sent you flowers, would you walk away or would it be enough to make you stay?"and her dimples pop out, making me giddy with excitement and desire.

Before her mom announces fresh pancakes and Cool Whip in the morning, I wake up. Jenny's still asleep. I stay completely still so the waterbed doesn't jostle. I want to have more time to just look at her while she's asleep. Pieces of her long, thick cinnamon hair are matted and stick to the sides of her sweaty face. One arm drapes over her Hugga Bunch doll, which kind of looks like a peach alien with pink eyes and a matching, glittery-pink diaper. The other arm reaches out toward my pillow, fingers slightly curled. I imagine what it would be like to intertwine our fingers and just sleep that way.

We spend the daylight hours playing outside. I still can't get over that there's a whole play shed that's just hers in the backyard. We set the small wooden table and chairs for dinner and grab tins before heading to the garden. Steely-gray and earth-brown sludge slides through her long fingers when we make mud pies. I decorate my pie with scattered rocks and an oak tree leaf. Hers is much more sophisticated, topped with a spray of Queen Anne's lace and a yellow marble.

When I watch *Batman Returns*, all I think about (besides Catwoman) is Jenny. I know she would love this movie. The next time she comes over to my house, I tell her all about the movie and how amazing Catwoman is. I want to show her my Catwoman trampoline routine, but in the end I'm too shy. Instead I play Janet Jackson's "Black Cat" while we jump up and down on the trampoline and talk about Girl Scouts.

Soon she's going on a camping trip. I've never been camping and feel jealous that she knows how to camp and gets to be in the wilderness with other girls in her troop. Since I can't relate, I launch into "We're the girls from Beverly Hills," and she meets my *Troop Beverly Hills* movie call and responds, "Beverly Hills, what a thrill." I decide then and there to join Girl Scouts because I want to be closer to her.

I'm supposed to have crushes on boys. But what I think about is kissing Jenny. I wonder what it would feel like. I imagine standing facing each other in her play shed, window and door closed. I imagine cradling her often sunburned cheek with my small hand. I imagine pulling her face toward me, looking down at her full lips. I imagine her dimples moving from smile to serious as I touch my little mouth to hers.

I know how wrong it is to like girls. The world teaches me that, and so do the kids at school. I hear derogatory names being thrown out for anyone perceived to be gay. Kids get beat up for being different all the time.

It's bad enough already being fat; I don't need my queerness added into the mix. In elementary school, I'm made fun of daily for being overweight. I wear layer upon layer of clothing to hide my body; bulky sweaters and huge puffy jackets cover my frame. I sit in the back of the classroom so kids will hopefully forget about me. I stay quiet and subservient in classes. I curl up with *The Babysitters Club* during recess instead of talking to anyone. I eat lunch outside, alone behind the cafeteria. I put on my masks in order to survive. In fifth grade I even write a poem called "My Masks" and submit it for an English assignment.

Child psychotherapist D. W. Winnicott describes the idea of the "true self" as an authentic way of being and relating. We are our "true selves" when we are present and showing up from a place of authenticity and realness. This is in opposition to his idea of the "false self," in which we put on a mask, act how others might want us to, or

The false selves of Catwoman and Batman dance at a costume party.
(Photo courtesy of Warner Bros.)

hide our true identities.

At school I'm Selina, doing as I'm told, making good grades, falling in line. I'm a "false self," just trying to survive. When I'm home, behind closed doors, in Catwoman drag, in full trampoline performance, my "true self" can emerge.

When Selina and Bruce attend the masquerade ball, they're the only people who don't wear masks. I like to think this is because they are their "false selves" when forced to be in the world as humans rather than disguised in their superhero identities.

I like to think they are their "true selves"when they actually have a mask on (as Catwoman and Batman). The real world has hurt them too much; they're unable to simply be themselves. Only in their masked state, disguised as animals, can they be authentic. Only in their animal state can they be their "true selves." When humans aren't enough, when humans should do better, animals take over.

But maybe there is something else going on too. Their secret Batman and Catwoman selves were born of unprocessed trauma; as such, their secret, animal selves remain relegated to the shadows, not quite fully integrated into the psyche. In this way, these powerful what

Jung would call Shadow parts, remain split off from the psyche as a whole. Their Shadow sides come out to protect and to fight, to do what Bruce and Selina can't do in real life. Bruce wasn't able to save his parents from being killed; Selina wasn't able to fight back in a man's toxic world. But these alter egos emerge from the shadows in order to do the tough work that must be done. They may not be totally "true" in the Winnicott way, but they are the truest parts of their essence in a post-traumatic existence.

Catwoman as Feminist Vigilante

Independent and sassy, undeniably curious, smart, mysterious, and magical, cats have a mind of their own. There is something feral about even the most house-trained cat. Sometimes they can be supersweet and cuddly. Other times they can be total assholes, not listening, knocking over important house items, scratching furniture, biting and clawing. They do what they want and scoff at the consequences. Ultimately they just want to be loved. This is all of what Catwoman encompasses and more.

In her first feminist vigilante act as a she-ro, she saves a woman from sexual assault by kicking a perpetrator's ass. Right away we know who she is and what she's about.

Pfeiffer's Catwoman is an emboldened, wild creature, a badass bitch, taking what she wants. She avenges patriarchy with her fighting powers and extremely tight-fitting catsuit. She is not the scared, shy, oppressed Selina Kyle in a man's world. Everything perishes in Catwoman's wake: buildings burn, things blow up, she leaves behind chaos and destruction.

Catwoman transforms from a fragile, hurt, traumatized woman to a dominant, mischievous, renegade feline superhero. Yet her sadness and confusion still endure. A sadness over not being seen in pain for so long. A sadness that Batman and Penguin both identify with and yet can't fully understand.

Catwoman asks us to look at systems that oppress women, and she shows us the psychological damage they can create. She shows us the power of resisting and not conforming to traditional female societal roles.

Becoming a cat unleashes her independent, not-taking-any-shit self. Becoming a cat allows her to give expression to a dangerous, powerful side of herself that she otherwise wouldn't—and couldn't. Becoming a cat gives her permission to live out the full expression of her shadow side.

Selina needed to die in order for Catwoman to be born. The archetypal docile servant, Selina—a 1950s secretary to sexist, evil Mad Men tycoons—is no longer what women want or need in today's world. And really, did the world ever need that?

Catwoman is ridding the world of corporate monsters, men who would otherwise continue to damage the world. Male executives who will always win because of their money and power. In a world made for such men, 1992's Catwoman offers a kind of blueprint for an on-the-ground response, a way to deal with a world that seeks to disempower her.

Whereas Selina could never find love, her Catwoman shadow alter ego drips with eroticism, and it spills over into the new Selina, post-Catwoman evolution. The new Selina and Bruce try to find each other in their "false selves," but their shadow, animal personae get in the way. She's Catwoman. She's got no time for romance with a man. She's got Catwoman work to do.

At the end of the film, Catwoman tries to kill Max (remember, he murdered her first by throwing Selina out the window), and Batman attempts to stop her. "Let's just take him to jail," he pleads. But Catwoman knows the way out of patriarchy is to take care of it herself. She knows Max would never be convicted in court; he's too rich and powerful. There are no systems that actually hold him accountable. He must die. He killed her; now she must kill him.

Batman begs her to go home with him. He appeals to her animal persona which has an opportunity to meet his. "We are the same—split right down the center." Then Batman takes off his mask, a HUGE no-no in the Batman franchise world.

It doesn't work. She is gone. Selina might actually love or lust after Bruce, but after becoming Catwoman, she is something else now. She's not the scared little secretary Selina. She's not and will never be a housewife to a rich man in a castle on the hill.

Instead of allowing men/the law to govern what should come next for Max, she writes the story. Electrocuting herself and Max at the same time, she controls the narrative. Both die.

I am not necessarily agreeing with her choice to murder Max (although it's satisfying to see after a film full of his douchebaggery). But I am suggesting her character represents a site of resistance, born of trauma, that could be repurposed for societal transformation. Her actions show that sometimes women have to take matters into their own hands for things to change.

Penguin As the "Elephant Man"

Like with Catwoman and Batman, Penguin's shadow side emerges when he is his animal persona. In the comics and in TV's 1960s *Batman* lore, Penguin is less of a mythical penguin/human character than he is in *Batman Returns*. In some Batman fandom, he is portrayed as a bad guy gangster who waddles and kind of looks penguin-y, like Burgess Meredith on the Batman TV series in the sixties. Otherwise, his birdlike quality doesn't go any further than his demeanor.

He was made into the Danny DeVito freak he needed to become in *Batman Returns* in order to tell this particular Batman story. In this story, his parents are humans, playing God by deciding who lives and dies; namely their son. There is a biblical quality about the act of putting baby Penguin in a basket and sending him down the river. Penguin's desire to kill all the first-born children of Gotham also echoes the Messiah-like rise of his power to the carnival freaks.

Penguin's story is about the dangers that arise when men have too much power, when greed and corruption take over and lead to violence. *But why do Batman and Catwoman get to live when Penguin doesn't? What about Penguin makes him more inclined to bite someone's nose off when he is criticized about his looks? Why is his story more gruesome than Batman's loss of his parents as a child, or Catwoman's attempted murder?*

I don't have any easy answers. There are a myriad of factors that go into how someone responds to their traumatic life circumstances. Penguin has what is known as "complex trauma" (traumatic events that happen more than once, over a period of time), as do Batman and Catwoman. So why (aside from the obvious reality that he needed to

The Penguin as a modern day Elephant Man in Tim Burton's *Batman Returns*.
(Photo courtesy of Warner Bros.)

be the major villain of the story) is he more predisposed toward harm than the others? I don't know. What I do know is that this Penguin never stood a chance.

David Lynch's 1980 film *The Elephant Man* depicts Joseph Merrick's experience living with deformities in late 1800s England. Famously, the Elephant Man (portrayed by John Hurt) says, "I am not an animal; I am not an animal; I am a human being." As Penguin searches for and eventually finds his parents' identities, and learns they have passed, he has a similar cinematic moment. From the cemetery, reporters yell "Penguin," to which he responds, "A penguin is a bird that cannot fly. I am a man. I have a name. Oswald Cobblepot." He claims his identity with solemn righteousness.

But Oswald will never belong among humans, even when he tries to obtain prestige by running for mayor. When he is rejected by the community and made a fool publicly by Batman, he retracts his Elephant Man-like pronouncement: "My name is not Oswald; it's Penguin. I am not a human being; I am an animal, cold-blooded."

Cold-blooded. His attempt at humanness is over. This freak can reign only among carnies and within his penguin species. The only place he finds reverence is in the sewer, underground, among the garbage, hidden away. Penguins can't fly, so too this Penguin never stood a chance to soar away from his misery and trauma. Like most penguins who need cold aquatic climates, this Penguin can't survive outside of his ice castle.

Penguin doesn't measure up to the expectations of what his rich capitalistic ableist parents wanted their firstborn son to be. He just wants to be included and to belong. He just wants love. While we don't know what happened to Penguin in utero, we do know that as a baby he was fed and protected by his penguin family. Penguin never received this love and care from humans.

I completely understand Penguin's rage. It is a natural response to the circumstances that life has presented to him. What he chose to do with that rage is unacceptable. Could he have made different choices and not resorted to violence and murder as a result of his lot in life? Absolutely. But the hostility itself comes from a very understandable place.

• *What would it be like if we just loved and celebrated freaks like Penguin?*
• *What would it be like if Penguin had a place in this world to be loved and accepted just as he is?*

The original trauma of his parents rejecting him, orphaning him into the world, compounded by trauma after trauma as he is rejected by people every day, creates the split-off Penguin shadow self that we meet in *Batman Returns*. The rejection and repulsion narrative gets reinforced again and again.

As a young kid watching *Batman Returns*, I of course did not understand Penguin's plight with the fullness and psychological astuteness I do now. But I could connect with what it was like to be misunderstood, bullied, and a freak of sorts. I was a loner, and like Penguin, I made up a world around me that made sense, where I fit in, where I was in charge. Of course I didn't cause mass destruction or try to kill newborn babies.

The Beauty of Freaks

When all of our parts are integrated, Jung calls it (capital S) Self.

I wonder what an integrated Self would look like for Batman, Catwoman, and Penguin. How would their "true selves" be presented to the world? What would happen to their superhero personae? In the terrible world of Gotham, is self-integration even possible?

Penguin and Catwoman are hated, judged, and abandoned by the world. They represent that which does not fit in with the corporate greed of Gotham. I see them as byproducts of capitalism and patriarchy, systems that discard women and penguin-ey/nontraditional men.

Catwoman was born from a lifetime of misogyny and being treated like a second-class citizen. Penguin was discarded from birth and learned he can't survive as a man in a society that will never accept him.

It's clear that both don't always make the greatest life choices. They act out destructively to survive. But I see their actions as understandable rage responses to living in a world that has hurt them so deeply.

I love the beauty and redemption in their stories' arcs. Locations of resistance and alternative narratives, they are not all monster. Penguin reclaims agency and embraces his animal self. Catwoman becomes the feminist vigilante that Selina never could.

These freaks I loved as a child I still love today. They show me that it's powerful to be different and not belong. They show me that freaks can be beautiful. They rise up and fight for justice. They can and should be loved not in spite of that, but because of that.

As a kid, I was aware of my otherness. I was aware of my Catwoman obsession and crush. I was aware of how awful it feels to be bullied, and was accustomed to being alone. But I wasn't aware, until now, that during this time I was transforming my trauma as a child into play immersion in *Batman Returns*.

Catwoman and Penguin freaks, like my little self, are looking to belong, to be seen and to be loved. On the trampoline, I look for connection, containment, a way to channel my own experiences in the world and make sense of them. I become my own "true self"—a queer, animal persona version of Catwoman—because it has to come out somewhere.

In the end, I never tell Jenny how I feel. We never kiss. We never date. We never dress in tight cat bodysuits and defend women who are about to be assaulted in alleyways. Years pull us in different directions. Our story is an unrequited fantasy.

Recently I reconnected with her, and it's a friendly and loving exchange. In our talk, it's clear that ours is the kind of friendship where we don't have to stay in catchup for too long. We go to deeper and more real places: mental health, marriage, relationships, grieving and loss, meaning of life.

Right away she gets my name and pronouns right, and my queerness and my gender queerness are just fully accepted by her. It's incredible. What I thought was so freakish for so long, and still do sometimes, was just a nonissue. She congratulates me on being a therapist and writer. She fully loves and accepts all of me.

I still have "false selves." Everyone does. I've been socialized female, so of course I still have Selina inside of me. It still takes effort to put my Catwoman shadow side out in the world and continue to integrate her into my full true self. But when I do, I'm more confident and empowered. I can love more fully, I can live more freely, and I can use my feminist she-ro powers for good.

Mannequin Two: On the Move: An Interview With Stuart Pankin

As a young queer kid growing up in Oklahoma, most of my gay pop culture reference points were white, often wealthy, cisgender men. I had access to standard Blockbuster VHS fare like *Love! Valour! Compassion!*, *In & Out*, *The Birdcage*, *Jeffrey*, and the like.

I loved those movies, of course, but I needed other fabulous queer icons as over-the-top as I was. I needed huge eighties, neon, geometric-shaped sunglasses. I needed vibrant, flowy blouses and handkerchiefs tied to wrists. I needed unapologetic Black male feminine energy. I needed Hollywood Montrose's flamboyant, stereotypical flavor of gay. The fact that his name in the film is Hollywood Montrose is a gay miracle in and of itself.

I originally published the article you are about to read, "Stuart Pankin on *Mannequin Two: On the Move*, 30 Years Later," in 2021 on the pop culture website *25YL*, now *Film Obsessive*. What's missing from my earlier article is my deep adoration and respect for the magical fairy queerness of the late, great, Hollywood Montrose (Meshach Taylor of *Designing Women* fame). So before you read about the wonderment of *Mannequin Two*, I want to take a moment to appreciate his genius.

Hollywood is a fierce queer superhero. In the original *Mannequin*, he single-handedly fights off the bad guys using just a water hose while exclaiming, "There are two things I love to do: fight and kiss boys!" Yes, he is wearing his signature shades while he says this, and yes he occasionally squeals with delight during the hosing process. He is queering film combat. So good.

In *Mannequin Two*, he disguises himself as Army Sergeant Butch Montrose. Dressed head to toe in an olive green uniform, he successfully accomplishes his plan to break Jason out of prison. Impressive. But not nearly as spectacular as his orchestration of the entire Hauptmann-Koenig dance ensemble presentation to help Jessie (Jason's true love) escape the clutches of Count Spretzle.

Time and time again, it is not Jason but Hollywood who saves the day. As a Black queer man, he is of course relegated to being a sidekick to Jason, the white cisgender straight protagonist in this 1991 comfort sequel. But these major moments in both films demonstrate that Meshach is carving out a new kind of gay hero archetype that beautifully fucks with gender norms. *Mannequin* and *Mannequin Two* literally would not be the same without him.

Yes, there are problematic aspects to having a presumably straight man play a queer character in general. Yes, the writing lifts Hollywood's sexual innuendos a bit too far at times. Yes, his melodramatic, heartbroken window dresser persona is sometimes overdrawn.

And yet, I TOTALLY know men who are just like him: nursing a breakup, concerned about their looks, struck by impossible gay body image standards, and facing the intersections of homophobia and racism. Men who are as fashionably amazing, as quick-witted and savvy, and as complex and nuanced as Taylor's portrayal. Men who, like Hollywood, drive pink Cadillacs but when the going gets tough will not hesitate to hose a bitch who gets in their way.

Thank you, Meshach, for giving me a queer icon I will never forget. For giving me *The Wizard of Oz* nods. For giving me "cheekbones" and Diana Ross realness. For reminding my queer little self that "nothing's gonna stop me now." I miss your brilliance. You are loved.

"Stuart Pankin on Mannequin Two—30 Years Later"

In a dank, sticky-floored, small movie theater, with once-cushioned chairs now falling apart, a wide-eyed eight-year-old girl sits with a huge fake-butter popcorn tub dripping in her lap. Her crimped hair held by a purple scrunchy. She sports a *Jem and the Holograms* bejeweled tee with yet another scrunchy holding up the side of the extralarge shirt. An important reminder: you can never have too many scrunchies.

She sits in the front row next to her cousins, who are just as excited as she is, and her mother and aunt, who are clearly annoyed at being along for the ride. It is the thick of a Florida summer, and with no AC, this theater has seen better days. The cartoon Coke and popcorn duo dance on the screen, previews play out (*Jurassic Park*, *My Girl*), and then the movie starts: *Mannequin Two: On the Move.*

Instead of a backdrop of Edfu, Egypt, with a sexy Kim Cattrall, such as in the 1987, original *Mannequin*, we are transported to the Germanic Kingdom of Hauptmann-Koenig. It is the age-old fairytale of a prince finding his true love in the form of a peasant girl, who is then turned into a mannequin by an evil sorcerer (looking strikingly similar to Bernie of *Weekend at Bernie's* fame) in a spell that lasts 1000 years. Typical.

The peasant girl Jessie (Kristy Swanson) is awakened by her true

In the club, William Ragsdale and Kristy Swanson fall in medieval-love to Gene Miller's unforgettable tune "I Can't Believe My Eyes."
(Photo courtesy of Gladden Entertainment)

love, Jason (William Ragsdale), one thousand years later, in 1991 Philadelphia, and my eight-year-old self is as spellbound as the enchanted peasant girl. In the opening credits, Jason seems so cool to me as he runs late to his first day of work at the department store, brushing his teeth with a Diet Coke as he speeds along in his jeep. I tap my jelly sandals in time to the song "Wake Up" and will attempt to brush my teeth just like Jason as soon as I get home.

As the movie unfolds, we see the world through Jessie's eyes as she comes into twentieth-century consciousness. We see the timelessness of a love story through the generations. We see a misunderstood mannequin struggling to be free from men who want to own and possess her. We see sword fencing, we see a fabled hot-air balloon showdown, we see a medieval and modern slow dance sequence at a club, we see chivalry that is "not dead." We see an ever-so-slightly-recycled plot of *Mannequin* with new and exciting twists and hilarious characters.

My cousins and I can barely contain ourselves. We love this movie. I look over at my mom and aunt, who I imagine will be asleep by now, but who instead have tears streaming down their faces from laughing so hard. Despite their best efforts to remain indifferent, they love it too. When the movie ends, we can't stop talking about it. We go back the next day to see it again. And the next day. We went back every day our parents would take us and would act out scenes at home in between. *Mannequin Two* is an instant family classic. A film we will watch on repeat for years to come. A film our family still quotes and references to this day.

The real crown jewel of the film is the manager of the department store Prince and Company, Mr. James, played by the incomparable Stuart Pankin, whose one-liners and comedic timing steal the film. For the thirty-year anniversary of *Mannequin Two* this year, I had the delight of interviewing Stuart, who is the sweetest and kindest man and every bit the opposite of his tightly wound character in the movie.

Well-known for his voice role as Earl Sinclair (the dad) in *Dinosaurs*, Stu is an incredible actor with hundreds of stage, film, and TV credits to his name. Films and shows like *Not Necessarily the News*, *Arachnophobia*, *Fatal Attraction*, *The Artist*, *The Dirt Bike Kid*, and *Curb Your Enthusiasm* are just a few of many in his filmography. I joked that I, of course, was interviewing him about *Mannequin Two*, a film that completely flopped at the box office and that Rotten Tomatoes gave a 13 percent rating. Poking fun at Rotten Tomatoes then became a running joke in our talk together.

Stu has a way that makes you feel at ease, has a warm presence, is humble, and speaks in earnest. He made me deep belly laugh multiple times, and in our short conversation together, I felt we were kindred spirits. In our talk, he tells stories of filming *Mannequin Two*, revisits familiar places in Philadelphia where he grew up, and shares memories of working on set with Meshach Taylor, William Ragsdale, Kristy Swanson, Cynthia Harris, and Terry Kiser. He tells a hilarious story about filming the ending scene to Starship's "Nothing's Gonna Stop Us Now." We reflect on the importance of nostalgia as it relates to pop culture and the role it has played in our lives. We discuss how we ascribe meaning to film based on where we are and who we are with, and how *Mannequin Two* holds up thirty years later.

Emily Marinelli: You're from Philadelphia, where *Mannequin Two* was filmed. Did you grow up there?

Stuart Pankin: Oh yeah, I lived there until I was eleven, then we went to Massachusetts for about two and a half years. Then we moved back until I went to college, then we moved to New York. So I was in Philadelphia a long time. All those formative years.

Emily: A major site of filming in the movie is Wanamaker's department store (aka Prince and Company), which is a historic landmark. What do you remember about Wanamaker's?

Stuart: As a kid we used to go downtown to Wanamaker's. There was a statue with an eagle, and that was a phrase in Philadelphia when people wanted to get together: "Meet me at the eagle," and that meant go to Wanamaker's, shop around, have lunch, whatever. Yeah, Wanamaker's was a classic department store in my time. It was great to film there. We filmed there all the time.

Emily: Did you ever see the gigantic pipe organ in Wanamaker's? I read that it was the world's largest pipe organ.

Stuart: I did see it. When you are on the first floor, the atrium goes up past two or three floors. I think the organ was tucked in the back. It was a beautiful store.

Emily: Was the whole movie filmed in Philadelphia?

Stuart: It was all Philadelphia. Mostly Wanamaker's, a person's house, on the street (Terry and his goons filmed on the streets of Philadelphia), and Schuylkill River, where I used to row as a kid. My mom was still alive then, so we got to see her. My son came, and we stayed near the Independence Square area, which is a great, beautiful place with a lot of history. There was a set for Meshach [Hollywood Montrose] when he had the big, splashy spectacular at the end. We actually went to a club with a stage and filmed it there. That was a big few days of filming. It was a really nice experience to be back in Philadelphia and film it in my hometown.

Emily: I'm curious if you saw *Mannequin* before signing on to the second one?

Stuart: If I did, I don't remember a lot about it. I remember James Spader was in it, and he was really good. I think my friend Steve Vinovich had a part in it too. But I don't remember a lot about it. I'm sure I saw it, but I'm not sure if I consciously saw it before we went to film the second one, 'cause they were very different. But yes, I remember it. How did *Mannequin* do? What did Rotten Tomatoes think about it? [Laughs.]

Emily: {Laughs.] I don't know; I'd have to look it up, I think it did a lot better. But for me, *Mannequin Two* is and will always be No. 1! It is just the best.

Stuart: Good! I was looking at a few clips today before talking to you, and it ain't bad, you know? It's kinda funny, and the people in it—Billy Ragsdale, Kristy Swanson, and Meshach Taylor and Terry Kiser—these are really skillful, wonderful people. I remember the director giving us leeway to write scenes. He literally said, "We need a scene!" The scene when I went to Cynthia Harris (who was a friend of ours), who played Billy Ragsdale's mother. She was great—she actually babysat for our son when we were filming in Philadelphia. But the director actually came to us and said, "We need a scene." When I go there and give her a fake name, he said, "We need to punch that out; could you guys write that scene?" and we did. He was very accommodating for us actors. Cynthia is a terrific lady. We have been Christmas-card friends for years.

Emily: That scene you are describing is hilarious. It makes me laugh out loud every time because you are filming a video for a dating service with Cynthia Harris. You realize at some point that her son [William Ragsdale] is your employee at the department store. You then take the VHS and start pulling out the tape and then hitting it against the wall. I was gonna ask you what you remember about that.

Stuart: I thought it was really funny, I remember improvising when I was hitting the tape (it was somebody's house), and I was banging the VHS tape against the wall. I think I chipped it, so I reached into my pocket and said, "Here is ten dollars, and I will pay for it." It was that kind of set, where we had the liberties and the freedom to feel comfortable about improvising or even, during the scripted acting scenes, just having a nice time.

Emily: You mention the late, great Meshach Taylor. You have a lot of scenes with him. Anything you remember and would be willing to share about working with him?

Stuart: Well, I just remember him being extremely funny and a nice guy. We used to eat together occasionally. He was a pro, because he had done the first one. I just remember him being a nice guy, funny. That character that he played—I saw the scene of him recently where he pretended to be the army guy trying to be butch—it was wonderful, very funny. He was terrific, died much too soon. When I saw the clips and I saw us working together, I remembered how much fun it was to be with him and to work with him.

Emily: There is a scene where Terry Kiser is coming out of his little Hauptmann-Koenig plane and the goons are there, and you're there with Hollywood and you're both just turning your heads to view Terry's wart hair that's protruding from his face. You say, "What a pleasure it is to have you hair . . . wart . . . here. What a pleasure it is to have you here!" Because no one can deal with his wart hair. In my family we still quote "What a pleasure it is to have you hair."

Stuart: What I remember is that we filmed it at some sort of small airport. He got out of the plane and we did the scene, and again I saw it recently and was happy with it. Sometimes an actor sees himself—a lot of actors say they don't watch themselves; I watch myself all the time (I'm too self-involved not to) [laughs]. It was very funny, Meshach and I, we coordinated the head thing and all that. It was great. And Terry was great too.

Meshach Taylor and Stuart Pankin side tilting at Terry Kiser's wart hair.
(Photo courtesy of Gladden Entertainment)

Emily: You have all of my favorite lines in the movie, including the managerial catchphrases that you say with your staff: "Deplore neglect, demand respect," "Make a showplace of the workplace," etc.

Stuart: Not to brag, but I wrote all those! I mean, I put those in.

Emily: WHAT?! You did?

Stuart: Yes, I decided that might be a nice little running gag, which paid off at the end when they shoot me and I say, "I need help," "Stop it." [And the staff repeats the phrases instead of actually getting him help]. It paid off on that. [Director Stewart Raffill] gave me leeway to do that, and I wrote all those interstitial interjections.

Emily: You mention the big scene at the end with the dance number, and there is fencing and shenanigans. You get punched in the face by Terry Kiser and then shot in the foot. Anything you remember about filming that part?

Stuart: As far as on the set, it was great, I mean getting punched by Terry and getting shot and having all those repeated things with the minions. It was a big production as I recall, a big stage. I don't remember where it was, but it was a big venue. Billy came down on a wire onto the stage and there was fencing and shooting——it was a huge, complicated production. There were hundreds of extras. I just remember looking around thinking, Wow, this could be good! Unfortunately, Rotten Tomatoes didn't think so, but I think so!

Emily (laughing): They don't know anything!

Stuart (laughing): They know nothing! They're ROTTEN!

Emily: Any other days or memorable moments you remember during filming you might want to share?

Stuart: Yeah, I remember when I was finished, when I was wrapped,

I went to the airport, and it was a very busy travel day; they couldn't get me on the plane. I called the production office, and they got me on another plane from Philadelphia, which stopped in Washington and then went on to Los Angeles. Okay, great, I'm done with the movie and everything. The East Coast was rainy. We took off in Philly, landed in Washington, I'm sitting in the first row because they give you good seats. The door opens, and a flight attendant comes in and says, "Mr. Pankin?" And I go, "Yeah?" And she says "Could you come with me? You're wanted back in Philadelphia for some work on your movie." I went, "What are you talking about?"

So I got off the plane, I think I flew back that night to Philadelphia to do a scene. It turned out to be the end scene, where they were driving away in the car at the very end of the movie. I remember the room I was staying in. It wasn't even on the top floor. It was leaking, rain was pouring into this hotel (I won't say what hotel). I changed rooms because I couldn't sleep in that room. I put a wastebasket with towels to catch the drips so I could get some sleep. I show up the next day on the set. If you remember (you probably do), when we all get in the car with a bunch of people in the car and the car drives away, do you remember that scene?

Emily: Yes of course.

Stuart: They could have used a watermelon with a wig! Nobody saw my face. Nobody saw my back. Nobody saw nothin'! [Laughs.] And they called me back to do that. Look at that scene again. You can't see me; it doesn't matter who I was. Seriously, they could've used a mop with a bucket on its head! So that I remember very well.

As far as other things, it was just a very pleasant shoot. I remember buying some things at Wanamaker's for my wife because they give you a discount that was a nice perk. And just hanging around Philadelphia, being with my family, was nice. It was a pleasant experience because they were nice people and Stewart Rafill was a nice guy. Of course he never cast me again, but I'll talk to Rotten Tomatoes about him [laughing].

Emily: I wanted to ask you a funny question. When I talk to people about *Mannequin Two: On the Move*, I'm always curious why they think it is subtitled On the Move. Why do YOU think it is called On the Move?

Stuart: I have no idea. Maybe it has to do with her being shipped from Hauptmann-Koenig to Philadelphia? Well, "on the move"—she was on the move in the movie. She was all over the place! South Street and dancing in bubble baths. But as far as why it was called On the Move, I don't know. I mean they never consulted me about the title [laughs].

Emily: There is a fan base for this film. I feel like it is an underground fan base, but I'm curious: have fans talked to you about this movie? What do they ask you about?

Stuart: You know, I hate to disappoint you. Not a lot of people talk to me about *Mannequin Two* because not that many people saw it, unfortunately. I don't even think my son and his wife have seen it. No, not a lot of people mention it. You know, *Dinosaurs*, which I'm involved with, has just been released on Disney+, and I'm getting a lot of autograph requests on that because it is now much more out in the open than it was. And there are other things people remember me from, but not a lot of people know me from *Mannequin Two* or mention that to me, for better or for worse, I'd be thrilled to be remembered for it! I'm happy with the work I did, and I'm happy with the movie, so I'm not gonna say, "Oh no, no, no, no, I wasn't in *Mannequin Two*." I would say, "Sure I was, thank you very much." But they don't; they just don't.

Emily: This year, *Mannequin Two* is having its thirtieth anniversary. Describe what it is about the film that has made it so memorable and long-lasting. And things from the movie that hold up now and those that don't.

Stuart: Oh, that's a tough question. What holds up? The performances hold up. I mean, Meshach's performance was memorable in both the movies; that's why they brought him back, because he did that so well. That certainly holds up—among the fan base, I'm assuming. Sort of an iconic character that people point to. Billy and Kristy did a terrific job. I love Billy Ragsdale. I think he is a terrific actor, I've seen him in other things, and I just think he's really good. So is Kristy; she has had a wonderful career. Cynthia Harris has had a great career, I think mostly on stage; she has done a lot of stage work. People remember the performances. People, when they see movies, latch on to certain things. Some people remember the goons; some people remember and latch on to Terry because he was famous for . . . what's the one where he died?

Emily: *Weekend at Bernie's.*

Stuart: *Weekend At Bernie's*, yes, so they might look at him and remember that. People might remember me for something, I don't know. [*Mannequin Two*] didn't do great at the box office, but there are people like yourself where it resonates. There are movies—like I did a movie called *Scavenger Hunt*, which a friend of mine watches every month, and it didn't necessarily do great in the box office, but people latch on to certain movies for whatever reason.

[*Mannequin Two*] was a kind of broad comedy, and there are a lot of silly broad comedies today. It might be too silly for some people, for some "sophisticated" people [laughs]. I've seen movies in theaters where people scream at the jokes that I wouldn't clean off the bottom of my shoe. But that isn't *Mannequin* at all. I think it's pretty good. People react to movies and plays and television in certain ways; certain things touch them. And that's why it lives in you and lives in what you say is the fan base.

What doesn't hold up is what I said, like the broad comedy. People might not like the broad comedy. I've been doing comedy all my life, some of it broad, some of it not, and I think anything that is done well will be remembered positively to people who react positively to this kind of stuff. If you don't like fights in an air balloon, you're not gonna like the movie. But if you admire the skill and technical achievements, you're gonna like it, so it's such an individual thing: why someone likes something, why someone doesn't like something, what's gonna last forever, what's gonna be forgotten. Everyone's guess is as good as anybody else's.

Emily: As a younger person I saw *Mannequin Two* over and over again. It was like a blanket, a comfort. And it still resonates for me and brings back all those feelings of security and safety.

Stuart: You know, that's interesting. A lot of times we see movies and we associate them with happy times. Like every movie I've seen with my father and when I was young. Every one. I don't care if it's good or bad. I love it. Because I was with my father, and I love my father. When my parents and I used to go out to the movies together, I loved those movies. So you probably, maybe associate *Mannequin* with some time in your life that was great, and that's great!

Emily: I really like what you just said about making the connection based on who is around us at a certain time in our life.

Stuart: It's like you eat a food and you love it, and then you realize, *Oh I loved it when I was a kid with my grandmother and my mother.* You know, there were these associations that really make what's going around at the time count and memorable. Like what I said about these movies with my father: I remember many of them—they're not great movies, but I love them. Like *The Buccaneer* with Yul Brynner, and we saw *Planet of the Apes*. In Massachusetts we went to see *Teacher's Pet* with Clark Gable and Doris Day. And I'm sure there were others, because my dad and I used to hang a lot, but those three I remember.

Emily: Thanks so much, Stu I just really love your energy, and you have so much humility and humor. It was so fun to talk to you!

Stuart: Well, that's really kind, and I appreciate it, and it was a pleasure talking to you. I'm just very happy you reached out to me and happy to talk about *Mannequin Two* because I don't get a chance to talk about [it] that much. And it was a nice time in my life filming the movie in Philadelphia with my family and with all those good actors, so thanks for bringing that up.

It's thirty years later, and much of *Mannequin Two: On the Move* still holds up today. Impeccable comedic performances from Meshach and Stu, and the improvising and flexibility that Stu spoke about, are classic and make the film work. The amazing absurdity of the plot (why would a department store in Philadelphia care about hosting a display of an enchanted peasant girl from a tiny European country?) is awesome, niche, kitschy, and cult-status perfection. Not to mention the ridiculous early-nineties soundtrack featuring such classic nonhits as Gene Miller's "Wake Up," Gene Miller's "I Can't Believe My Eyes," Gene Miller's "Do It for Love," and Shoes's "Feel the Way That I Do." And of course a reprise of the actual hit song, Starship's "Nothing's Gonna Stop Us Now," from the first film.

Aspects of *Mannequin Two* that don't quite hold up today: gay male stereotypes reflected in Hollywood's character and the damsel in distress archetype that follows Jessie as the peasant girl/mannequin. Yet despite these early-nineties over-the-top characterizations, Taylor brings authenticity, fierceness, and tenderness to Hollywood, and Swanson's depiction of Jessie shows her strong determinism to fight against all odds for her true love and for her freedom. Lest we forget that Hollywood is the mastermind behind breaking Jason out of jail and saving his life numerous times, and Jessie reverses the necklace spell onto Count Spretzle (Terry Kiser) thereby making him into a mannequin, the ultimate revenge.

As Stu and I discussed, the broad comedy moments are not for all audiences of today (hot-air balloon fights, getting shot in the foot, getting punched in the nose, falling out of a moving van into a lake). At times the script is questionable at best (it went through so many rewrites and writers that it sometimes loses its way). Regardless of the shortcomings of some outdated content, the magic in this fairy-tale storyline stands the test of time and spans the decades (or centuries, if you will).

After all these years, I still remember sitting in the theater with my mom, aunt, and cousins on that sweltering Florida afternoon. I still remember the shirt I was wearing, the previews I saw, and how we all laughed until we cried. I'm thirty-eight now, and rewatching this film is just as exciting and hilarious as it was seeing it for the first time. *Mannequin Two* still makes my heart smile. It brings me back to that time of my childhood, and in each rewatch, I'm taken to the fantastical land of possibility, of true love winning over evil, to a simpler and more predictable time when we took family trips together and ate copiously buttered popcorn and family-sized Junior Mints just because we could.

My conversation with Stu turned into an opportunity for both of us to reflect on our childhoods and memories of seeing films with our families. As Stu remarked, "We see movies and we associate them with happy times." Nostalgia and meaning making are self-defined; so whether you are watching silly films like *Mannequin Two* or *Teacher's Pet* or something more serious, it doesn't matter. What makes a movie enjoyable is of course subjective, but for us, it had to do with whom we were with and what parts of the story resonated for us, not how well the movie did at the box office (or what Rotten Tomatoes had to say about it!). The plot, the acting, how a film is revered, is less important than the sentiment. What is most important is the connection you had to the characters, the way you felt watching it, and the people who were with you, when you saw it. That's what holds up the most.

Grease 2

It's the heat of a Georgia summer in the early nineties. Mom and I are visiting Uncle Gary's house. Even though I'm twelve, my middle-aged-women's Kmart attire is just my average, everyday wear, nothing special. I'm sporting red-and-orange culottes with a matching short-sleeved, gold-jeweled button-down shirt. The shoulder pads in this ensemble accentuate my curvy frame, giving me a top-heavy, triangular look. My brown, wavy hair is pulled back into a low ponytail. Electric bangs spray into a high fountain, held together with White Rain Extra Hold Hair Spritz. On my feet, generic black Payless flats.

The outfit brings some stares from my family, but that doesn't matter to me. All I want to do is eat copious Otter Pops and watch TV while the other kids (my cousins and their neighborhood friends) play adventure games outside. My fingers, sticky from the popsicles, cling to the boxy remote control, giving me the power to create the kind of afternoon I want. Safe in the AC, away from the humid hell outside, I surf channels, switching from *Growing Pains* to *ALF* to *Perfect Strangers*. I consider settling for *Saved by the Bell*, but it is an episode I've seen before, so I keep flipping. Then I happen upon what would become the most important moment in my world of cinematic comfort sequels.

A beautiful blond-haired, blue-eyed man, who is clearly supposed to be a teenager in high school, is singing. Okay, sweet, a musical, I'm in. I lift one shoulder pad and then the other in time to his ballad. He wears an oversized sea-blue sweater. His lyrics are sad, about how he lives inside a charade. He walks listlessly in a cafeteria, his tray holding a meatloaf brick with a soupy side of mashed potatoes. I'm enthralled.

Maxwell Caulfield singing "Charade" the scene that changed my life forever. (Photo courtesy of Paramount Pictures)

Cut to him solemnly drawing hearts encircled by even more hearts on lined notebook paper as he hits the high notes: "Charades, conceal me." I flash to my own notebook, the one I carry around in sixth grade. A Lisa Frank Trapper Keeper with pages of doodles, line after line of hearts, names of celebrities. I do this at lunch when other kids are smoking weed in the parking lot, making out at their lockers, laughing at inside jokes. I'm lonely like him, an outcast, a nerd. Even worse, I don't quite fit in with the actual nerds, so I'm really on my own.

The song dips with ". . . but can't you feel the real me." I wonder, What is the real me? As I sit here, watching whatever campy, dramatic, relatable movie this is, I feel more real than at school. Surviving stares, laughs, fat jokes, loneliness, I am him, lost in his own world, in a song no one else can hear. Also, he's cute. I stay on the channel transfixed, purple Otter Pop drips blending into my housewife romper.

And then I see it's a continued montage! Amazing. Teens laugh and carry on as blue-sweater guy walks down the school hallway.

He slams multiple lockers in frustration over said charade. Okay, loving these dramatics. He hooks his fingers into his too-tight jeans. What about this is not to love? I will soon discover this sultry British-accented faux teen is Michael Carrington, aka the Cool Rider.

As the film continues, I'm unable to leave the living room, not even on commercial breaks, in fear I would miss it starting up again. "Dinner!" Uncle Gary calls from the dining room. "Sorry, I'm busy; I'll eat later. Save me a pork chop," I yell back. My mom comes into check on me, her tan shoulders a little darker from being outside, her brown hair sun kissed gold. She understands my need to stay and see what is going to happen next. Gently touching my right shoulder pad, she says, "I'll make you a plate, honey; just make sure you eat soon, okay?" "I will. Thanks, mom, I love you."

What is this campy musical? What is this film that has Pink Ladies and T-Birds? What is Michelle Pfeiffer (aka my favorite Catwoman) doing in this film? *Remember, this is a time with no internet to quickly Google "What film has Michelle Pfeiffer singing at a talent show dressed as a Christmas tree?"* I don't know what to do. I need this film with me forever. Somehow.

I dare to leave during a commercial to assuage my growing impatience. "Uncle Gary, where is your TV Guide?" I storm into the dining room, interrupting the family gathering as everyone is holding hands and giving thanks for the pork chops. "Amen," he says, ending the prayer early, not angry with me at all. He smiles gently through his salt-and-pepper beard. "Over there, sweetie," he says, pointing me toward his recliner, where a Diet Coke and TV Guide live at all times.

I frantically search through the pages, crumpling and tearing some corners in my haste, searching for the title of this film. And there it is. Simple. It's *Grease 2*. Of course it is. How did I not know they made a sequel?! Turns out hardly anyone did, until it became a cult classic.

Dinner takes years. I sit in the corner, my legs bouncing incessantly, watching my mother's every bite until Mom can take me to the local movie rental store to try and find it. This is an Atlanta suburb, and they just don't carry it. We are told we can drive to Blockbuster, that they would probably have it in stock, but that's thirty minutes away.

We call. They do. I plead for Mom to drive the distance, hoping it will still be behind the VHS cover by the time we get there. Thankfully, it is.

Cue me taking over the VCR at my uncle's house. Cue me "be kind, rewind"-ing *Grease 2* to watch again right after it ends. Cue everyone else saying goodnight and going to bed and leaving me in the living room, cold pork chop in hand, watching *Grease 2* at a low volume so as not to disturb. I consider stashing the VHS in my suitcase on the drive back home to Tulsa. Would Blockbuster really miss it? Come on. But I don't want to risk not being able to see it in the future in case I get in trouble.

With each rewatch, my love for Michael (played by Maxwell Caulfield), that sweet, blue-sweatered British nerd, grows. My adoration of Stephanie (Michelle Pfeiffer) deepens, and my infatuation with *Grease 2* crystallizes. It continues to this day. As I type this sentence, I'm literally lying on a *Grease 2* pink-themed throw pillow in my living room. The obsession is real.

Grease 2 Recap

By this point, you might have some idea of what *Grease 2* means to me. In the introduction, I take you through my attempt to learn the choreo to "Back to School Again," the opening number. It involves four kitchen chairs, Skipper doll pom-poms, Aqua Net hairspray, and a stick of Winterfresh gum.

Grease 2 is easily my favorite sequel of all time. I can still recite every word of the script and sing every lyric by heart. The film came out the year I was born and is the stuff of legend in my family.

During my rewatch marathon at Uncle Gary's house, I find that *Grease 2* is a love story like no other. Okay, the Greasers are back, the Pink Ladies are back, even director Pat Birch from *Grease* is back for campy, kitschy cinema fun. But central to the narrative of this comfort sequel is a gender reversal story arc that the first film doesn't deliver (more on this later).

Set in 1961, two years after the original film, the story takes us back to Rydell High School. We meet Michael Carrington, a nerd from the UK, who is the cousin of Sandy, Olivia Newton-John, not featured in this film. Michael spends his high school days pining for the love of Stephanie Zinone (Michelle Pfeiffer), head of the Pink Ladies, a cool kid totally out of his league. The only thing she cares about is motorcycles and dreams of leaving her small town for a life of adventure.

In order to prove his worthiness to her, he not only very quickly learns how to ride a motorcycle, but basically becomes a professional daredevil stuntman overnight: scaling cop cars, doing wheelies, and jumping over the entire length of a large pool. If this won't win her love, I don't know what could. The only issue is that she doesn't know it's Michael who's performing all these incredible feats.

Michael does this all while keeping his identity a mystery (à la the "Charade" song montage that lured me into this film in the first place). He never reveals (until the end of the film, that is) that he is one and the same; by day he is Michael, the nerd helping her with her Shakespeare essay, and by night he's the Cool Rider, swerving in and out of the shadows.

The Cool Rider/Mystery Man is of course a major threat to the Greasers, led by Johnny Nogerelli (Adrian Zmed) and his trusty sidekick Goose (Chris McDonald). A masculinity face-off weaves throughout the film. A motorcycle chase, the presumed death of Michael, and a talent show tie between the T-Birds and Pink Ladies take us to the luau. Michael's pool stunt proves not only that he is alive, but also that he is worthy of being part of the gang and, most importantly, of Stephanie's love.

As Johnny gives Michael a T-Bird jacket, Stephanie and Michael embrace in a finale song that knocks "We Go Together" from *Grease* completely out of the ballpark. In a song title so dramatically different from its predecessor, "We'll Be Together" from *Grease 2* is in fact an iconic rival anthem. It has a slow build, a key change, and freeze-framed actors jumping up from a trampoline as the end credits roll. Phenomenal. Yo, *Grease*, what do you have to say about that? It just doesn't compare.

So true love prevails, and the film reminds viewers that we can in fact have it all, that "I can be me, and you can be you, and we're never-ending." That you can be a nerd and cool kid at the same time. That love has no identity borders and definitely not enough ketchup on burgers. As a culotte-wearing, introverted, obsessive queer nerd, these were the messages I needed to hear. It was just okay to be me. To not hide behind a charade.

"I kiss who I want, when I want"

The female narratives in this comfort sequel are what stand out from the first film. The gender story reversed in *Grease 2* has Stephanie (Michelle Pfeiffer) as the hip Pink Lady who rejects her position as the leader because she doesn't want to be forced to date the leader of the T-Birds (Johnny). Her independence is the most important thing. Get it, Steph.

In the bowling alley, Johnny asks for a kiss, and she refuses. She is unwilling to accept that she is "someone's chick." "I kiss who I want, when I want. In fact, I could kiss the next guy who walks through that door if I want." (By the way, I'm writing this dialogue from memory because, well, it's *Grease 2*.)

In a defiant move, she actually does. Without having said more than a hello to Michael before now, she lip locks him as soon as he comes through the glass doors. Talk about timing. Afterward, she looks past the dumbfounded T-Birds to the girls, gum smacks, says "Let's go!" and leaves, bringing the Pink Ladies with her. Damn, she's good. I wish I could have her confidence and unapologetic authenticity.

She queers and disrupts standards of femininity all the time. When Stephanie is not afraid to eat a burger in a very unladylike way and get ketchup all over her face, I make a habit of doing the same. That's right: girls can eat when they want, how they want. Right, Steph? She even has an after-school job as a gas station/auto shop attendant. How cool is that?

When not at school, she is perpetually in pants and rolled-up sleeves and gum smacking like there's no tomorrow. Without thinking, Steph comes to school still in her everyday-wear pants; only after getting a few wide-eyed glares does she quickly add a skirt on top, rolling up the bottoms of her leggings to hide them (because she would've been expelled otherwise).

In middle school, I graduate from my culotte Kmart frump and dress boyish too. I like low-riding jeans and flannels that I tie around my waist. Sporty Spice is an inspiration, and I find long track pants with rainbows down the side and a tank top just like hers. At thrift stores, I find men's collar work shirts with "Service Merchandise" and "Oklahoma Natural Gas Company" on the pocket, imagining I'm Steph working at the gas station and telling customers to "honk that horn where the sun don't shine" when they become unruly.

Grease 2 reflects the tension between the emerging Second Wave feminism of the early sixties and the receding fifties pressure to be the perfect housewife, meeting your husband's every need. The sixties bring us Jackie O, blossoming women's liberation movements, and counterculture protests, and *Grease 2* sits right at this precipice.

It's the tension between Stephanie proclaiming "Maybe I'm tired of being someone's chick," and Paulette (Lorna Luft) responding, "You're tired of being someone's chick? Are you feeling alright?" Or Stephanie kissing "who she wants, when she wants" next to the codependent, sexist sentiment of "Girl for All Seasons." (BTW, I still love that song, regardless.)

Later in the film, after the talent show practice, Michael incessantly tries to ask her on a date, and she says no. Multiple times. In understandable frustration, she finally says, "Listen, when are you gonna get the picture?" Cue the music for the showstopping "Cool Rider" anthem. Up until this point, you may have thought that "Cool Rider" was all about Maxwell Caulfield. Nope. This is Stephanie's song.

This is where she tells us what she wants in a guy: "a whole lot more than the boy next door." Actually, she wants "hell on wheels." She's telling us she doesn't want to settle down and have little T-Bird children; she wants a life of adventure and travel. A life with her Cool Rider on the road outside of her little town and fixed trajectory of a bored, happy-homemaker housewife. The fact that Michelle does her own stunts while riding the bike with her Michael/Mystery Man makes this whole thing even more sick.

The T-Birds are not in charge in this film. Their performance of the song "Prowlin'" is done beautifully, with fabulous choreo, and ties them for first place in the talent show. It can be read as rapey

Michelle Pfeiffer is responsible for teaching kids everywhere how to spell "Cool Rider." (Photo courtesy of Paramount Pictures)

and sexist, reinforcing patriarchal ideas of men preying on women and women's bodies (going "prowlin'"). But I soften to them because in true comedic T-Bird doofus fashion, the song delivers their clever plan: to meet sexy women at grocery stores. Really, you guys?

So this is pretty harmless and clueless really, and it works only because we know they are not actually those guys. We have seen them retreat in the face of danger (the rival Balmudo gang), their masculinity never an actual threat. If anything, the Pink Ladies walk all over them, and they are just boys trying to figure out how to fit in, like the rest of us.

Cool Kids Table

It's 1994. I'm twelve years old and in sixth grade at Carver Middle School in Tulsa, Oklahoma. The cool kids' table at lunchtime is, well, cool. No one sitting there is trying to be cool. They just are. No effort. Preppy J. Crew and Abercrombie-wearing soccer players, they are rich kids who live in Midtown and whose parents can afford to take them skiing on holidays. They all know each other from childhood and continue their friendships with no regard for anyone else.

I try so hard to make my way to sit at their table. I starve myself to lose weight and overexert myself by dancing every day after school for hours at Peggy Lanik Dance Studio. I find sale items in the Delia's catalog to match their designer outfits. I know it's impossible to reach their status, but dammit, I try.

One day I stand close to their table, hold my paper-bag lunch of bologna and cheese on Wonder bread, and talk to a classmate. She is one of the cool kids, but is nice to me. Just as I'm thinking maybe I can be invited into their group, an eighth-grade douchebag named Tommy glances my way. He smells my desperation as I look longingly at this group of pretty white kids. "Why don't you take a picture; it'll last longer," he yells at me, and the popular kids laugh in chorus to his *Wayne's World* reference. I want to die.

I'm used to it by now. Earlier that school year, a kid yelled "1-800-94-Jenny" at me as I sat down to eat my lunch. I'm doomed. Kids kept singing it to me when I walked down the halls. After this incident with Tommy, I stop eating lunch completely at school. I pray to lose weight so they will leave me alone. Or accept me. Why can't I be Stephanie? Not caring to fit in. Making her own rules.

Then, in seventh grade, I find my girls. Robin, Kat, and Mel, my version of a girl gang. Pink Ladies without T-Birds. Kat and Mel had known each other for years, and they teach me how to crochet and make feminist punk zines. I love them from day one, and they accept me into their coven. Robin is a grungy, cute stoner who smells like stale tobacco. We become kindred spirits by passing secret triangle notes in biology class. I bring her into what becomes our foursome. I soon find out Robin likes to drop acid and watch her dad's taped concerts of Rush and Heart on VHS. I go to her house and eat Ruffles, drink Pepsi, and play Donkey Kong.

The four of us hang out every weekend and make out with neighborhood boys, only when we want to. We kiss "who we want, when we want." We go to the mall and deliberately move clothing to the wrong sections in 5-7-9. We couldn't be any more on the nose when, as a gang of misfit girls, we wear "Misfit" long, baggy men's shirts with our black skirts, Doc Martens, and tights.

In faux goth attire, we ride the rides at Bell's Amusement Park and freak out the little kids. Our favorite is the Himalayan ride; we scream and scream and go faster and faster and try not to throw up. Robin and I take hits from her pipe before going through the Phantasmagoria haunted house, and despite its rickety appearance, we get scared. We stumble off the motorized cart and quench our munchies by splitting a funnel cake.

We thrift-store shop and chain-smoke Camel Lights in coffeehouses. When I get my learner's permit, I drive around town, and we rotate whose music we listen to on my Mazda tape deck. They end up getting sick of my showtunes (including my *Grease 2* soundtrack on cassette), but I make them listen anyway. By the end of the school year, these bitches are singing along to Michelle just like I hoped they would. I cast a queer spell, and it worked.

***

Like me and my Girl Gang, Steph and her Pink Ladies reflect one of the dualities of high school: we want to both fit in and also find our true self outside of cliques. Our little group of misfit toys created a world outside of the one that was presented to us. We wanted to have a place at the cool kids table but also to walk right past them. We reconciled this by making our own table, and when someone wanted to sit with us, we let them. An open invitation for outcasts. *Grease 2* is about making our own lunch tables and not conforming to what society asks of femininity. It asks us to consider whether wearing a skirt to fit a societal norm is what we really want to do.

In the original *Grease*, John Travolta and Olivia Newton-John find each other in coolness and nerdiness, meeting in the middle. John letters in track to be nerdy, and Olivia dons black spandex and red heels and tells him he better "shape up" in a killer song at a carnival. The nerd becomes cool; the cool becomes nerd. They fly away in a car together. Aww. The message is you have to completely change who you are to be loved. Eww.

Stephanie in the sequel is having none of that. She doesn't meet Michael in his nerdom. She knows what she wants, and gets it. While Michael does tutor her in an effort to get closer to her, she doesn't all of the sudden become an expert in Shakespeare or seem to give any more of a shit about her high school classes. She doesn't join the chess club or write an unforgettable essay spawned from her tutelage by Michael.

I love that she doesn't do any of that. She is who she is. She inspires me. Michael had to become the Cool Rider for her. Even though I love his Cool Rider-ness, I don't like the idea that anyone has to change who they are to find and receive love. That's not the greatest message of the film. I certainly should not have had to put myself through what I did to try and conform to high school pressures. No one should have to change who they are to be loved and accepted.

But Stephanie stays unwaveringly her. What really works in *Grease 2* is Stephanie as a strong female character and what she represents. In no way is Stephanie the dumb blonde girl archetype to Michael's British brain and brawn. She is a supersmart, sassy, no-shit-taking, free spirited, brilliant character. What makes the film so relatable and comforting is her strength and determination. For me, as a young girl and emerging queer kid, this representation mattered as it did for so many other young LGBTQ+ kids. Also in the *Batman Returns* chapter, it's clear how truly obsessed and crushed out I was with Michelle as Catwoman.

Grease 2 is predictable and safe and yet diverges from the formulaic path. It is unapologetically over-the-top (see the "Love Will Turn Back the Hands of Time" dream sequence) and has the ability to self mock and not take itself too seriously.

Viewers know we are in a fictional landscape that is outrageous, fantastical, and transcendent. For these reasons, the fandom has grown astronomically over the years. The film still plays in theaters, with sing-alongs where you can dress up and immerse yourself in Rydell High glam. Finally the world has caught up to where I was with the need to immerse myself in 1961's T-Bird and Pink Lady world. The film taught me that being an outcast is okay; being yourself is what's important. It taught me there's no one right way to be feminine or masculine and that gender is expansive. There is nothing more queer, more empowering, more inspirational, more fun, and more soothing than this sweet little comfort sequel.

Where Does the Pollen Go? An Interview with Chris McDonald

I never knew I had a crush on Goose until I met him over Zoom to ask him questions for this book. I couldn't tell if I was just excited or starstruck, but the sexual confusion was real.

When he appears on camera, his electric-blue eyes stun me. I'm at a loss for words. "Wow, we are wearing the same matching colors. And our glasses match too!" he offers enthusiastically. His red windbreaker with black-and-white trim echoes my red sweater covering a navy blue blouse, peppered with white seagulls. Both our glasses are thick, black, vintage chic. His shaggy eyebrows almost burst through the lenses; my thin brows hide underneath mine. "You're right!" I say, "So synchronistic of us." I'm trying to be cool, but words fail. And yet, right away I feel a twinship, a mirroring, a connection with him. I wonder if he feels it too. His energy is soft. It helps me remember to breathe.

His strong jawline opens into a smile. "So you are writing a book? That's so great!" He has an authentic presence that grounds me. His smile comes from somewhere else. Somewhere deep inside of him. A place from where his art must emerge. Yep, it's sexy.

"Thank you! Yes, I'm writing about sequels and what makes them comforting. *Grease 2* is my all-time favorite sequel!" I stumble out. I'm making sense, putting the right words together, but I'm nervous as hell, and my cadence is breathy staccato.

I'm interviewing a celebrity I never could have imagined I would get to speak to, but on top of that, Chris McDonald is a total dreamboat IRL! I had no idea I would get caught in his spell. I drift away into his handsomeness and lose track of my purpose and intention—to ask him nerdy questions about my favorite cult-classic film.

I take a deep breath to come into my focus and anchor back to why I'm here. As he begins to share his love for the film, my jitteriness begins to loosen. He is casual, funny, charming, brilliant, charismatic. I'm disarmed by his ease. He has a gentle, tender spirit.

I have one of those out-of-body experiences. I look down at myself from above. The above-me says, *Em, you are forty years old, sitting in an RV in Michigan, talking on Zoom to Chris McDonald, a.k.a. Goose, from Grease 2. Who the fuck are you? You are living the dream, girl.* I come back to my body and see his handsome face, patient and kind.

Chris McDonald's work is astounding, his filmography and TV list a mile long. He was Geena Davis's husband, Darryl Dickinson, in *Thelma & Louise*, Ward Cleaver in *Leave It to Beaver*, and Tappy Tibbons in *Requiem for a Dream*. You might remember him as the villainous Shooter McGavin in *Happy Gilmore* or most recently for his Emmy-nominated killer performance as CEO Marty Ghilain on HBO's *Hacks*.

I of course know him best from *Grease 2*, which happens to have been his first major film. In case you need a refresher, his character, Goose, is the super tall, intellectually dense, perfectly animated sidekick to the main T-Bird, Johnny. Parroting Johnny's every move, he steals scenes with just the right amount of broad comedy, but not too much. Everything he does is captivating. Your eyes move toward him even when the story doesn't.

In "Reproduction," a musical number that takes place in a high school sex education class with Tab Hunter as the teacher, Goose commands the camera. With his low bass, doo-wop flourishes, gyrating hip pops, and iconic sperm dance, the number ends with him hanging from a ceiling pipe. He sings "Where does the pollen go?" as he lands back at his school desk precisely at the last note of the song.

In our talk, he tells me all about filming that scene, revealing that he improvised his infamous semen moves. Our conversation takes twists and turns as he shares hilarious stories while filming, the prankster schemes he hatched on set, the rapport he had with the other T-Birds, and his pure joy of being in this movie musical.

We both get a little emotional as I share what his performance has meant to me and how the film was a constant source of comfort in my childhood. Like me, his genuine love of *Grease 2* shines through in our chat, a fact that makes me love him more (if that was even possible). Here's the talented dreamboat Chris McDonald:

Emily Marinelli: How did you get involved with *Grease 2*?

Chris McDonald: Well, when I came to town in like 1979, the biggest thing was *Grease* and a little thing called *Saturday Night Fever*, so John Travolta was in the zeitgeist of the world. When this opportunity for *Grease 2* came along, I was brought in, and I was trying to get Johnny Nogerelli's part. But you couldn't wash the Irish off my face. So I got really close to getting that part, and they said no. And I was devastated. I went back, and I sat in my little bungalow apartment just kind of staring at the walls, and then the phone rang and it was Pat Birch saying, "Come back tomorrow; we are gonna do some mixing and matching. We love you; you're just not that Johnny Nogerelli type." And I said, "I get it." So I went back; I had nothing to lose. I had a complete blast mixing and matching the T-Birds and Pink Ladies. And Alan Carr was there and Robert Stigwood, and Bill Oakes, the other producer, was there. There were tons of kids, and we were dancing and flirting. So that night I got it. And I was like *what a turnaround from complete devastation*. So it was the best of times after the worst of times.

Emily: I'm so glad you got Goose; he's the perfect part for you. He's hilarious, he's goofy, he's got these great lines, and the way he says "albu-mans" and "Roy Orbi-son's" is hysterical. You can tell he's a goofball, but he also has a lot of heart and is hilarious and sweet. How did you prepare to become a T-Bird?

Chris: That was a lot of fun, because I just saw the dynamic of what was happening, Johnny is the alpha dog, and then it was me and Peter and Leif. And I thought, I'm gonna try it like hero worship, like you would in high school. So Johnny is the man, and I would do anything for him.

We danced every day, and I was in great shape. I was dancing like crazy. Pat Birch, our director, God love her, she just put us through our paces, and that whole opening sequence, "Back to School Again," was a complete blast. But if you look closely, I'm the only one who's out of sync during the "da da da" [he sings the part where they do the twist]. I'm the one standing up, and I just go backwards, and I thought, *What the hell?* And they kept that in, and I was like *Oh my God*, because we did it like ten times. It was the one time I was going the opposite way, which was pretty funny.

Emily: It's kind of perfect for the character.

Chris: Yes, just a beat behind. But what was really cool was our rehearsal period. I had been riding motorcycles since I was like eight. So I was doing some really bad things. We were at this empty high school that they were gonna tear down in Norwalk, California, and I was driving up and down the stairs, through the hallways. It was so easy for me to drive a motorcycle, and the other guys were trying to follow me, and I was like "No, don't do that." They couldn't come down, and they fell. I had so much fun, because those hours were just free time for me to ride around on motorcycles.

Emily: You were riding inside the building, like up and down the stairs?!

Chris: Yes, inside the building. My father saw the movie and was like "That would never happen on my watch." He was the principal of my own high school, so that was crazy. So I was breaking all the rules and getting into the bad T-Bird in me.

I had such great times doing all this crazy stuff we were allowed to do. We had a lot of night shooting; that was really the only thing that wasn't at the school. Different places around, and I had to drive the motorcycle around. There was some great camaraderie.

There was this one big jump that the stunt guy Gary Davis did; he took that bike and put it into the water of the big pool in one take. And it was exciting, because if he overshoots it he could really get hurt, and if he undershoots it, he could really hurt people, and there's a lot of people around. So that whole thing was really exciting and took forever to set up. But he pulled it off, and it was fantastic, and all the people who were standing around the pool, the stunt guys, they were part of the Greaser gang that are our rivals. Then Gary Davis as Michael Carrington does this great jump and just lands it; it was just really exciting. That was a great number. That's when all of us are together, and everybody had their moment, and it was just one of those things. And it was no complaining. It was cold. We shot it, and it was probably in the fifties, and we had our Greaser jackets and we were fine, but some of those poor girls were freezing.

Emily: I love Goose hauling Davey around in that sidecar.

McDonald driving the bike with the side car in the musical number "Prowlin'." (Photo courtesy of Paramount Pictures)

Chris: That sidecar was tricky. I think that's probably why they put me on it instead of my own bike. Peter had never ridden before, and Adrian was pretty good on a bike. Leif didn't have to ride, but they gave the best rider the sidecar. It's so hard; you can't corner with the damn thing, I mean it's a classic; they are Honda 305s with this big appendage on it, so cornering was a bitch. I hated it. But it was a lot of fun. You never had to put a kickstand down. It had four tires.

Emily: Rydell High allegedly was supposed to be in 1961's California. So why do you think everyone in *Grease 2* has New York accents?

Chris: We were playacting, trying to be tough. We were trying to be like one of those "Hey, how you doin',Vinnie?" and "Hey, get over here!" So we all kind of adopted this "Hey, Johnny, what're doin'?" like you're a tough guy from New York movies. And that's what kids do. I mean, I did it in high school too, imitating other people. Really funny.

Emily: Were you in musicals before signing on to the film?

Chris: No. Funnily enough, my father also directed all the plays in my high school, and my sisters and brothers got all the leads in all these classic musicals. I was in the pit. I was a very good trumpet player. I was never onstage, but I was there every night when they did the shows. So it was a little payback for the family when the old Chris from the pit is up onstage singing and dancing. It was kind of funny, but to answer your question, no, not until that time, but I certainly had it in my genes, that's for sure.

Emily: You sure do. There's so much singing and dancing in the movie. How was that for you?

Chris: A complete blast. Really athletic. You had to be a good athlete to do the things [Pat Birch] was doing. I absolutely loved dancing. I was sweating, I was dancing, and there were all these beautiful girls, and I was like I love my life.

It was so fun to do that and then do goofy things like "Let's bowl, let's bowl, let's rock and roll," and I threw the ball down and it was in the other lane that I made the strike. So it wasn't even on the straight strike; it was like this one. Crazy stuff like that I was trying.

I think it really helped to define who Goose was: basically a guy who, as much as he worships Johnny, he has a lot of life in him. He's got a lot of spirit. It was really fun; all the dancing was great. There were some seriously excellent dancers too; the guys were spinning like this, and oh my God, wonderful, talented people. Pat choreographed [*Grease*], and then she directed [*Grease 2*]. So she knew the period. She knew the dancing; she made it her own. Louis St. Louis did a beautiful soundtrack. It was a treat doing that much dancing, and I just looked forward to it every day.

Emily: What were some of your favorite musical numbers in the movie?

Chris: The opening number and the ending number are both great bookends for the movie. It's fantastic, and so many dancers involved in unison, doing their thing, teachers arriving and all that stuff, that was great. But "Reproduction," right up there!

Chris McDonald improvised some of the choreography in the "Reproduction" dance number. (Photo courtesy of Paramount Pictures)

Emily: The sperm dance is my favorite part of the whole song. You're just a swimming sperm; it's so amazing.

Chris: I got to say, "Where does the pollen go?" I was ad-libbing that stuff like I'm a sperm [laughing]. Just swimming, trying to find the egg. That was filmed at the high school. We rehearsed at the soundstage in Paramount, which was a real thrill, I mean to be working inside one of these massive soundstages, but yeah, all that stuff was shot on location in Norwalk. "Prowlin'" was probably my favorite song, where we do all that riding and singing "Walk, talk like a T-Bird." I love it.

Emily: You guys are so good with the microphones and pulling back your jackets. Your work in this movie is amazing. And Goose really stands on his own. I mean, I know he's Johnny's sidekick, but you made him something. We look at you when we're watching it.

Chris: Really? Wow, you made my day; you made my year. Thank you, that's very sweet.

Emily: You're hilarious, and the energy that you take up on the screen, it doesn't overwhelm. It's just right.

Chris: Oh, that's great, wow! Put that in your book!

Emily: I will! It's really true, and I'm so glad I get to say it to you. It's been true for me since I was very little. So thank you.

Chris: Wow, thank you. I'm honored. That's a very, very sweet thing to say. Thank you.

Emily: This book is about the comfort that movie sequels bring, the sense of security they provide, the familiarity and predictability. What do you think makes *Grease 2* so comforting for audiences?

Chris: Well, I think from the woman's point of view, it's more current.

The first one is in its own time capsule, but this one is the woman making the choice. She's turning down the coolest guy in school because she wants something else. And we follow her, embodied by Michelle Pfeiffer in all her glory. She was absolutely beautiful, just tough and fun.

Women especially love *Grease 2*, because of its empowerment to girls. That's all due to the great writing of Pat Birch and telling it like it is through a woman director's eyes, which is terrific.

Emily: What other movies or music or TV shows do you find comforting? Your go-to pop culture comforts.

Chris: Stuff I grew up watching when I was your age watching *Grease 2*. Probably I was ten years old and I was watching *My Three Sons*, and then I got the honor of playing Ward Cleaver in *Leave It to Beaver*, the remake, and that was one I watched all the time. I thought this was kismet, because I loved that show. Beaver is always getting in trouble, and I'm the middle of seven children and I was always getting beat on by my brothers like that. So I really identified with the Beav and all of his problems, and that's comfort for me.

Musicwise, comfort to me, I grew up in the mid seventies, and so I was all about funk, James Brown, and Stevie Wonder, and I have a playlist, and when I want to get back into comfort/memory lane, I'll put that on. I went to this small school in upstate New York, Hobart and William Smith, and joined a fraternity because I was broke and my family didn't have money to send me to Ivy League schools. I was a jock, so they gave me a scholarship. I worked as a dishwasher at the Kappa Alpha fraternity, and that's when I played that playlist, and to this day, that's my comfort food. I'm cleaning up for twenty-five guys; that's how I got free room and board. So that was my job, and I just had that music playing, and they called me the "Funky Chicken in the Kitchen." To this day, I still go back to that soundtrack.

Emily: Did you have an idea when you were making *Grease 2* that it would have such a cult following?

Chris: That's an interesting question. I don't think anyone knows how well it's gonna do. But once *Grease 2* hit television, it went [makes rocket sound]. But you never know; they were doing things back then before what everyone does on the internet now. They were sending us out in groups. The T-Birds would take the West Coast and do all these tour packages talking to local stations; the Pink Ladies would do the East Coast, and then we'd flip, and that was really fun. We were just getting the hype up on a publicity tour.

We were the Tasmanian devils coming through town in a blur, hitting up two towns, and then the next day we'd hit another two towns, and then we'd get on a plane, and it was just so much fun. It was a pivotal moment in my career, and to be around the many people that I mentioned, a lot of them I stay very friendly with, and this is now forty years, which is crazy. It was a life-changing thing, and I felt, and I still feel, tremendous gratitude for being chosen, because everyone wanted to be in this movie. To this day people still say, "I loved it so much more than the first one. It's got everything in it." And I love hearing that.

Emily: It IS way better than the first one, and there's something about the movie that brings community together. It's like "Oh, you know *Grease 2*? Great, now we are family." That's the spirit you don't always get with all films. There's something really special about it [getting emotional].

Chris: That's very cool. Even though it's not considered the hit that the first one was, I mean it's John Travolta, what're you gonna do, hot as a pistol. But that's showbiz. It's always just up and down, up and down. *Grease 2* was a big up, and I kept that up for a really long time. Even to this day [getting emotional]. Even what you said just got me right in the heart and felt great. So thank you for that.

Emily: Thank you so much. It was amazing to talk to you.

Chris: You're most welcome.

Who's That Guy?
An Interview with
Leif Green

I reach out to T-Bird Davey Jaworski (Leif Green) over Facebook, not imagining he would reply. Why would he? I'm some random *Grease 2* fan. So when he agrees to meet with me, I'm tickled as pink as a Pink Lady.

As soon as he appears over Zoom, I see the same sweet, round, cherry cheeks; dark, pronounced eyebrows; and Tom Bosley nose that I remember so well. His once-russet brown hair is now peppery gray, but it's just as thick and curly as it was in 1982. A ceramic rooster, some candy dishes, several porcelain birds, and other colorful, mid-century modern kitsch surround him in the kitchen.

It's the perfect backdrop to what becomes an hour-and-a-half talk. We totally Kiki and could keep talking all afternoon. Don't worry: I have cut down the transcription for this book, but damn was it hard.

Davey might not be the most memorable T-Bird, but since the beginning of my *Grease 2* obsession, he was everything to me. To the straight eye, the queer guy might not be so obvious, but to my little gay self, I felt his otherness, and without knowing exactly why at the time, I felt our sameness.

Over the years, with each rewatch, my adult self sees how he steals scenes with his humor and sensitive masculinity. The shortest of all the T-Birds, Davey is the one who doesn't have his own motorcycle, but instead rides in Goose's sidecar.

In the "Who's That Guy?" musical number, he joins the Pink Ladies in singing about the mysterious sexy man at the bowling alley (spoiler: it's the Cool Rider). I can't help but wonder, Just who IS this fabulous guy? His high-pitched hyena laugh sprinkles throughout the film, and he executes a high split jump during "Score Tonight" that is incredible. I mean, he is just adorable.

We talk all things *Grease 2*, including his thoughts on the queer aesthetics of the film, and he shares a behind-the-scenes drag moment that I will never forget. The pièce de résistance is when he shows me the most jaw-dropping gay parlor trick I've ever seen. Seriously, I gasp.

He talks about his love for sewing doll clothes and how he had just started dabbling in flower arranging. I mean, he's truly a gay after my own heart. Here's the glittery goodness of Leif Green:

Emily Marinelli: I have three favorite parts of *Grease 2*, and they are all random. The first is Michael saying "Yeah I know" on the track field, the second is Chris saying "Where does the pollen go?" in "Reproduction" and third is your laugh. Tell me about that laugh.

Leif Green: I did the laugh, and then they took it and inserted it into different places. When we did the bomb shelter scene, that's just how I laughed, that's just how it came out. Maybe it was because I was crouched down in that weird position or something. A lot of our film is looped, because we filmed outdoors and it wasn't the clearest sound in the world. So we went back in postproduction and looped lots of stuff.

I remember I had to listen to that laugh and then recreate it. But at one point in "Reproduction," they just throw in my laugh. The mics were always on, and the cameras were always on. They almost always rolled a B camera during the musical numbers, sometimes a B and a C camera in case somebody else caught other things that were as interesting as what the A camera caught.

Emily: I'm SO glad they brought your laugh in again and again, because it's so good. It lifts up scenes. It's so funny.

Leif: When we saw the first rough cut, I was so sad. In the scenes where each of the T-Birds meet in private with Michael Carrington and pay him to do their homework, the pay off line is "I've got a rep to protect." When the kids are all leaving from the classroom of "Reproduction," Davey says, "Now, not a word of this to anybody," and Michael says, "Because you have a rep to protect," and fills it in, and that's the joke in the script. Obviously they had a funnier joke with Chris with the girl coming in and telling the principal that she's missed her last three periods. And that's the joke they chose to use. And I totally got it, even back then, but I was like *Wait, I wanted my little scene!*

Emily: Of course, because you see him writing your assignment and signing your name. And I always imagined that's how your character wrote. But I would've liked to have seen you say that to Micheal. It would've been so cute.

Leif: Yeah, and it kind of sets up for when he's the mystery biker for Davey too, because he sees him as a mysterious kind of superhero.

Emily: How did you get cast as Davey?

Leif: It made the most sense for me to be the part of Davey, because of the way I presented myself. I had gone in for a couple of dance calls, but then it got pretty serious with the Davey part. They had me sing a ballad and an up-tempo number I had done for a casting director in what would be considered off-Broadway in LA. It was the West Coast premiere of the show *Runaways*, and I got close, but they thought I was too wholesome, so I didn't get cast. But this kind of proves the theory that you should go audition for everything, because they remembered me from *Runaways* and brought me in for *Grease 2*.

So I auditioned for the casting directors, and they brought me in to sing for Louis St. Louis, the musical director for *Grease 2*. Afterwards, he told me he called Pat that day and told her they had found Davey and they didn't need to worry about that. But I didn't know that at the time. I had quite a few hoops to jump through. I was nervous because Matt Lattanzi [Brad] was also up for Davey, and he was Olivia Newton-John's boyfriend at the time. But he got Brad instead, and I was very happy, because I thought, *Oh, I'm not gonna break that tie.*

The very last audition we had, Maxwell and Michelle had already been cast, because they were behind the table with the people who were making decisions. They had three of each of the Pink Ladies and the T-Birds, and they just kept mixing and matching us. Then they contacted us not long after that and told us we had the parts.

Emily: How did you develop Davey's character?

Leif: Davey was easy for me because he was the only one who didn't feel threatened by Michael's character, the Cool Rider. He was actually enthralled, hero worshiped, crushed out.

Emily: RIGHT! I love it. And there you are in "Who's That Guy?" singing "He wears a pair of goggles like a man from outer space." It's clear you are enraptured with him in this mystery.

Leif: In my mind, Davey was not a very good T-Bird, and he knew that. But he got there, and he's gonna hold onto that spot. I thought there was more going on for him than the other three, because he said, "My dad wants me to go junior college after graduation," whereas I thought the other three parents didn't care about them. But Davey had parents who said, "You are going to do something." I felt that Davey had a little bit better of a home life. Being a gay man myself, I always thought Davey was gay and that he wasn't about to say anything, because it's 1961 and he's in high school, but he started to realize what was going on with the mysterious biker.

Emily: Hearing your queer read on this is so exciting to me because as a young queer person myself, I was watching this movie, and any movie really, looking for representation. I wanted to thank you for being a part of something that meant so much to me as a fan but also as a baby queer.

Leif: Michelle Pfeiffer's interpretation of Stephanie really spoke to a lot of queer women I've talked to. Like, "I'm free every day; it says so in the constitution." That was definitely queer coding as well.

I was completely out while we were filming the movie. There wasn't anybody who didn't know I was gay. I pursued a career a little bit longer, then didn't, but I wonder sometimes how I would've managed that. When *Fame* became a TV show, I screen tested for the gay character in that, so I told myself if I got that part I would say I was gay to the world, but I didn't get the part, so it didn't matter. It would've been interesting, because it was a little early for people coming out as gay and being professional actors.

Emily: Did you have any idea *Grease 2* was going to be a cult classic or a queer cult classic?

Leif: No. I remember thinking at that first rough cut, I was pretty convinced it wasn't gonna do well. I was too young to sit there and name what the problems were. And I wasn't a big fan of *Grease*, so I didn't know it very well.

They sent us on a promotional tour. They divided us up, and it was Chris and me and Peter, the three lesser T-Birds. We went up the West Coast, through Canada, and then met in New York for the big premiere. That's where we met up with everybody else at the end. About a third of the way through the promotional tour, the movie came out, and the local reviewers were like "Did you realize the movie was gonna be so bad?" And it was funny, because no one at Paramount had given us any feedback at all on how to behave at these press things that I recall.

And they certainly didn't say, "Now if people think the movie stinks and say that to you, here's what you should say." So I think we just flubbed it and said, "We think it's great." Then, about ten years or so went by, and cable TV needed to fill twenty-four hours, so *Grease 2* would play a lot. That's where these people who saw it over and over again, those are the big *Grease 2* fans. They would be forty, fifty years old.

Emily: That's me! That's where I first saw it on TV. I was born the year it came out. But I watched it on TV over and over. And then of course I rented it at the video store.

Leif: Right, then there's rentals and home ownership. And that's the time when young people would recognize me. Usually once every three months I would get recognized. And I was out to lunch with some friends, and it just so happened I got recognized twice that day. And no matter what I said, I couldn't convince my friend this didn't happen to me every hour every day. She's like "You're just being modest, because two people at two different random stores recognized you."

I thought it would just go completely into oblivion, because it was poorly received from critics and the public. And then, into the twenty-fifth year, when Facebook and social media came out, people started contacting me. Then they reproduced the album. Did you know about that?

Emily: No!

Leif: Oh yeah, I don't know where it is, but I gave liner notes. It's a recreation of the album with pics and new liner notes. It's recent. I have a lot of *Grease 2* memorabilia, and I readily gave it away to people. I wish I had been a little bit more judicious, because people who are real fans, who really care about the movie, I've met along the way, I have virtually nothing left to give. But I had cool stuff, and it would've been nice to give it to them. But I didn't know people were gonna love it so much.

Emily: What's your favorite musical number in *Grease 2*?

Leif: I really like "Reproduction." It's so confined. I know a lot of people like "Back to School Again" because it's not confined; it's so expansive. And I like that too, but we were challenged to make "Reproduction" because we couldn't go any further than outside of our desks. And it was something like I had never seen before.

It was really exciting, because most of us were making our first movie. Some of us had done some TV shows, commercials, maybe a Broadway show here or there. There were eight female and eight male dancers who were there every day. If you've watched it as many times as I'm sure you have, you will recognize them. They were as much a part of the movie as the T-Birds and Pink Ladies.

It was quite a fun atmosphere, not only to be doing a musical—those were few and far between when you are auditioning for things—and for it to be a musical set in a different time period, where costuming was a real thing, and props and all the cars. They basically rented thirty cars and used them as set dressing and anytime they needed them.

I remember when we filmed "Back to School Again" they had to shoot towards the school only, because if you turn the cameras around, it was all eighties strip malls. Someone got the bright idea of getting period school buses and just lining them so we could now go the other way. That was really smart. So it really did look like 1961. And that was really cool to me because I love history and time travel.

Emily: In "Score Tonight," you have that incredible jump split in the air in the bowling alley.

Leif: That was caught by the B camera. That was just me goofing around, and somebody caught it. We would rehearse the number and do it over and over, and I'm sure the B camera guy wanted to capture that. He follows it perfectly.

What's interesting to me is Charlie McGowan, who is one of the dancers, is also one of the Preptones. In the bowling alley scene, he grabs the ball and does a quintuple pirouette [five rotations]. And then he leans down and does a split jump like I did, but from the ground. I'm jumping off of the score area, so I've got lots of height from there. He's just doing it all from the ground. They left it in there, but it's in two different pieces. But man, he was a good dancer. He's in the movie version of *A Chorus Line* too.

Emily: Yes, I recognized him as the "I Can Do That" tap guy. I always wanted to know if that was him. That's amazing. So what was it like riding sidecar to Goose in the motorcycle and in general working with Chris McDonald in the film?

Leif: I already knew how to ride a motorcycle because I grew up in West Virginia and my brother was really into motorcycles. I think we all knew to some degree. I don't think anyone was that nervous to get on a bike. They played around with me driving a moped-type thing, which was funny, but nothing was funnier than the sidecar. I don't know if it was real that the motorcycle couldn't go in reverse or if I just made that up, but that's what we did.

In the scene where I'm supposed to fall into it, we had filmed that a few times, and at one point I fell off of it and really hurt my coccyx bone. I thought they would use that one, but because I was hurt that's why they probably didn't.

Chris and I had this whole thing that Davey was the keeper of the key, because Goose would lose it. So Davey always had the key and put it in and Goose would start it. It's funny, though, because on some level Davey is the most prestigious because he's being driven around.

Emily: Absolutely!

Leif: In *Grease 2*, the T-Birds aren't very cool. They always play for comedy. It's hysterical when they bring in the other gang, because it's all the stuntmen who were hired to do the movie. Not only are they rougher and tougher and would easily beat up the T- Birds at any point and at any time, but they're double the size of them. There are four T-Birds and there's like fifteen of Balmudo's gang. [Laughing.] It's like *Why would this gang of twenty eight year-old guys be interested in fighting these four high school wimps?*

Davey goes face-to-face with Balmudo in a way that he never intended to and could get beat to smithereens. And imagine the adrenaline that kid would've been feeling. I thought I was a goner, and then someone comes and saves me completely.

Emily: Right, the Cool Rider is Michelle's mystery hero, but he's also yours too.

Leif: One of the queerest moments on set happened backstage. Maxwell and I were sitting around talking. It was slow; we had nothing to do. In the school auditorium theater, which they use in the movie, every day they would show the dailies from the work from the day before. Actors were strictly forbidden to go to the dailies. So that's why we were waiting around, because all the cameramen, the big shots, all the above-line people, the director, all the producers were watching the dailies.

Maxwell and I were kidding around, asking why Davey would ever be a T-Bird; he's so faggy and sissy. And Maxwell said, "Well, you kind of look like Stockard Channing, so maybe Davey is somehow related to Rizzo and he got in only because of his family connection." So we just started laughing about that. And that turned into I should dress up as Rizzo.

Emily: Naturally.

Leif: It's pretty easy to dress in drag when you have an entire Paramount studio on location with clothes for the extras. They put me in a girdle and the longline brassiere that had the cone boobs. They had Rizzo's actual Pink Lady jacket I got to wear. Then the makeup folks did my makeup and put me in a wig to match hers, and they gave me sunglasses. They parade me around, and people are like "Look, it's Stockard Channing!"

We get to the side of the theater where they are watching the dailies. When you go in the side door, you're at stage level. So we crack open the door and can see imagery on the screen. Now, I don't know where I got the nerve, but I walked in front of all the big deals that were watching. I lower my glasses like Rizzo does in the very first scene, and I say, "This movie is shit; the first one's much better."

The *Grease/Grease 2* crossover no one expected: Leif as Stockard.
(Photo courtesy of Leif Green)

Everyone laughed so hard. We all got to go in, and that was the one time we were allowed to watch dailies. That was a big treat. This must've been early on, because we watched "Back to School Again," and that was the first thing we shot.

Emily: You were so bold! If you have a picture of you in drag as Stockard Channing I def wanna see that.

[Leif shows me a series of pictures from his files; the first one is of him as Davey.]

Leif: There's Michelle and I [blowing bubbles].

Emily: So cute. There's a lot of gum chewing in the film.

Leif: There it is [shows photo of him as Channing]. I do kind of look like her.

Emily: OMG, that is genius! You even got a clutch! You're in full

Rizzo drag, I'm obsessed. You do look like her. Thank you for sharing that with me. It's perfect. So tell me about Davey and Dolores's relationship.

Leif: There seems to be a little animosity between Davey and Dolores, but it was very clear that she wanted to become a Pink Lady, and to do so, she had to date a T-Bird. So she wanted Davey, who was unattached, to attach to her. And there were scenes between us all through the movie that were cut.

Same with Rhonda and Goose. When Rhonda has the tape on her nose, there was a scene filmed where Goose opened the door and slapped her on the nose, and that whole thing about her being in doubt of her nose was a storyline that didn't continue. So there are some loose ends in it that probably didn't bother the average viewer because the Michael and Stephanie story was intact, and that's the story that mattered.

Emily: I'm dying to see those scenes that were cut and wonder where they are.

Leif: When they are in the bowling alley and Dolores says "This bra is killing me" to Paulette and Paulette says "You wish," that isn't the end of the scene. Dolores slides over the seats more and comes to me. She's wearing a push-up bra to make her boobs bigger to impress Davey. So later, at the luau, she stuffs her bra, and Davey is convinced. So when she whispers to Michael that she's found herself another man, we all knew what that meant.

Emily: Right, that makes more sense having the context of seeing you two throughout the film and having that build up. We never get to see Dolores and Davey together. Where do you imagine their relationship would go from there?

Leif: [Laughs.] Not very far, 'cause I always imagined that Davey made his way to New York and was part of the Stonewall Riots.

Emily: THAT is the most magical answer you could've possibly given. That is fantastic.

Leif: If you look at Pam, who plays Dolores, she went on to play very gender-fluid characters, more than once mistaken as a boy. She had a long run on *Facts of Life* where she's discovered stealing or doing something bad, and everyone thinks she's a boy. She did a movie where she turns into a boy or wishes she was a boy. Lots of gender fluidity for her and for me as a gay T-Bird.

So yeah, Davey became a young gay activist, and probably Dolores realized she was a lesbian and moved with him.

Emily: That's right. They both came out. They both moved to New York, and they both became amazing activists.

Leif: Yes. In the final scene, when everyone is together, Pam is actually in the ninth grade in real life. She was the only real minor in the movie. So she could only work a certain amount of hours; then she had to go. A little person was hired to fill in some scenes to play her. So at some points I'm with this fifty-year-old little person in a brown wig, and other times I'm with Pam, who is fourteen, and I'm twenty one.

The scene when all of the couples kiss and are finally happy together, it was weird. I was totally gay. Pam was fourteen; I was twenty one. And I was kissing this stand-in little-person actor. The whole thing was very funny.

Also, toward the end of filming, Pam was in a car accident and broke her leg. That's why she doesn't jump at the end with me

Emily: You mean at the end credits when you jump in the air by yourself?

Leif: Right, it was a gymnast vault, and there was a big blue thing for us to land on. So if we are jumping into our future, Davey is jumping alone. He doesn't have a girl with him.

Emily: I love that. This book is all about what was comforting growing up. *Grease 2* was and is that for me. What do you think makes *Grease 2* so comforting for audiences?

Leif: I always thought *Grease 2* was a more PG version of *Grease*, because of Rizzo getting pregnant. It's a big plot point, and they don't sidestep it. Nothing like that comes close in *Grease 2*. It's a little bit more purified, so maybe that's what makes it more comforting. Anyone can really watch it. Now I watched something where a guy said every song in *Grease 2* is about sex. It's so perverted that way, and I guess that's not true in *Grease*.

Grease is more about *How do I keep my reputation and my identity?* People say she lowers her standards to be with Danny, but Danny did try to get a letter, but he also sheds the letterman's sweater and throws it down.

With *Grease 2*, there's so much going on, and the minute they switch it, with Stephanie, who's being pursued by the boy instead of the boy being pursued by the girl, all those dynamics and power struggles are really different. That's probably why *Grease 2* appeals to gender nonconformists now, because it's kind of a little bit all over the map.

Emily: What other movies or sequels or TV shows do you find comforting?

Leif: When you reached out to me for this interview, that's one of the reasons I answered so quickly, because that's me! I watch things over and over. My all-time favorite movie is *Meet Me in St. Louis* with Judy Garland. If you sat me down and I had to write down the dialogue for the whole movie, I'd probably get an A. I wouldn't get every word right, but I'd be darn close. It's my white noise.

I also love the *The Dick Van Dyke Show*, and it's actually on right now behind me. I like to have white noise on. *Driving Miss Daisy* is another one. That one has to do with the soundtrack as much as the characters and the story. The truth of the matter is I can do work, sit at the computer and work on an Excel doc or something, and it's just

Leif Green flying off into the future alone!
(Photo courtesy of Paramount Pictures)

there. I don't have to watch it. It's just there, like a friend.

Emily: Yes, it's comforting like a bedtime story or a lullaby you've heard a million times. I don't ever need to watch *Grease 2*. Like you with *Meet Me in St. Louis*, I could write down every word. But I want to, because when I see it, it brings out something in me I can't otherwise access.

Leif: It would be a fun thesis for somebody to explore why we watch and read the same things over and over. Some of my friends really tease me about this, and I've never been able to really defend myself. I know there's nothing new to be seen. I've seen it all, read everything I can.

When *Grease 2* fans tell me they watch it over and over, I really get it. Trust me, if anyone in *Meet Me in St. Louis* was alive and speaking somewhere, I'd get in my car and go see them, because I'd want to hear anything I could about that movie. I guess there's something in the familiar.

Emily: Safety, security, nostalgia, and immersion, feeling like you're part of the story.

Leif: My mother worked, so when I would stay home sick from school, she wasn't with me. Sometimes I would say I was sick so I didn't have to face something at school, like a test or a bully or not fitting in, and my mother knew and didn't fight it. She let me stay home, watch TV shows, and rest, and there would be the 7UP and the saltines. What you're talking about is the 7UP and the saltines of movies.

Emily: That's the perfect way to describe it. When I stayed home from school, I got to watch your movie. *Grease 2* was my 7UP and saltines, and it helped me so much.

Leif: When you watched it over and over, did you ever pause it and rewatch a musical number?

Emily: I was pausing to watch the choreo to learn it in my house to all the numbers, especially "Back to School Again." I set up kitchen chairs, used pom-poms. I had to play all the characters, so it was exhausting, but I had to get it perfect. It was a lot of rewind and pause. I had the soundtrack on cassette tape, but then I also recorded the whole movie on cassette tape on audio so I could listen to it at school.

Leif: I know what you mean. I love *Meet Me in St. Louis* that way. Vincente Minnelli knew what he was doing with that one. The costume and set were incredible. Costume history is one of my passions. One of my parlor games is telling a friend to pull up the internet on their phone, type in the word "fashion," and then type in any year from 1780 to 1980. Find a picture from that year and make sure it's the actual year. If it just says "fashion of the 1920s" it could be anything. But show me a fashion of a specific year and I will be able to guess it within a two-year grace period. I have freaked people out like crazy.

Emily: Did you study this formally or are you self-taught?

Leif: Self-taught. There were these two costume historians on YouTube. One made up a test for the other one, and I scored better than she did, and they both have degrees in it.

Emily: That's amazing!

Leif: So now you have to try. Do you have your phone?

Emily: Yes.

Leif: Type in "fashion," then anything from 1780 to 1980. A bunch of images will come up. You're gonna have to look and make sure it tells you an exact year so we can play this right.

Emily: Okay, I'm ready. I'm gonna cover the date so you can't see the year. [I show it to him over Zoom.]

[There's a short pause as Leif looks at the picture and considers.]

Leif: 1926?

Emily: Oh my goddess, yes! Like EXACTLY [both laughing]. That's a complete mic drop situation. How did you do that? Like how did you know it was 1926 instead of, say, 1922?

Leif: In 1922, the skirt length was almost to the ankle bone. Over time it really rose and got the highest in 1927. If it's skimming the knee, it's 1927. If it's just below the knee and fuller, it's 1926. Hats help, and drawings help. Drawings are so idealized like the perfect way to look in 1926. Most women didn't look that way, because they weren't like eight feet tall or whatever the drawing depicted.

Emily: Do you ever make costumes?

Leif: I sew; that's one of my hobbies. I sew clothes for myself and other people. Mostly children's clothes I like to do and doll clothes. It's really fun. I'm SO gay.

[We both laugh.]

Leif: Every stereotype I fit, except I can't cut hair; that's the only one I can't do. But everything else, yes. Flower arranging. I make aprons and purses for all my girlfriends.

I found an apron pattern at a yard sale from 1954, and I bought it because it was all intact, and I started making it and found out how to make it a little bit bigger and smaller for my different girlfriends, so I might even have like a hundred of those aprons I've made over the years.

Here's a doll whose clothes I made [he shows me]. She's supposed to be from 1838. The back is a bow I made out of a placemat. I even did her underskirts and pantaloons.

Emily: Awww her pantaloons. This is so freaking cute. Very detailed.

Leif: It took forever so I messed it up and started over again.

Emily: I can tell the time you took, the detail, I love the flowers. Just beautiful.

Leif: If you look at 1838 you can tell right away that is just what fashion was.

Emily: Thank you for sharing that with me and everything you shared with me today. You're amazing. I loved everything we talked about and your gay parlor trick is a dream. What an honor.

Leif: You're so welcome. This was really fun.

Cool Rider
An Interview with
Maxwell Caulfield

"If you really wanna know what I want in a guy . . . " I pipe out while applying fire-engine-red lipstick in the bathroom mirror. I'm getting ready to see the Cool Rider himself, Maxwell Caulfield, at a sing-along screening of *Grease 2* at the Castro Theatre in San Francisco in 2017. Thankfully, it's within walking distance from my apartment, because I've had a few glasses of Chardonnay already.

"One fine night, I'll be holding on tight . . . ." My half-sister Stacey (who is visiting for this event) jumps into view just in time to join the chorus: " . . . to a Coooooooollllll Rider, a Coooooollllllll Rider; if he's cool enough he can burn me through and through . . . " (we turn toward each other and throw our heads back) "whoa oh oh whoa."

She spins 180 in a quick, slick move and pops her Pink Ladies jacket collar, using our round hairbrush as a makeshift mic. I attempt the same turn and bump my nose into the bathroom door. "Good move, Rhonda," she laughs, throwing a line from the film into the air at just the right comedic moment.

"Shit, we better shake a tail feather; we are late. Stace, how do I look? You know, just in case I get to talk to Maxwell?" She looks me up and down, considers my black top and capri pants, Mary Janes, Pink Lady jacket, and polka-dot red neck scarf and nods, "You're good. I mean, well, as good as you can get, I guess. It's not *too* embarrassing." She rolls her eyes; we both laugh. She takes a swig directly from the La Crema bottle, and we head out the door.

The line to get into the *Grease 2* sing-along is superlong. I mean, the place is gonna be packed! Hundreds of fans await the opening of the doors, and we are all fabulously gay as hell. In addition to Pink Ladies of all genders, the patrons have 1960s era pencil skirts, vintage sweaters, and bobby socks, and cafeteria ladies hoisting trays with plastic fake food. Sexy dykes on bikes butches show up in motorcycle-gang cuteness with leather jackets and grease on their sleeves.

Sister and I meet up with our little group of queers, eat some quick Cheetos I had stashed in my backpack, and we are ready. We run to find a group of seats together in the midcenter section for perfect film-viewing optics. As the lights go down, I'm so excited that I already have to pee (probably also thanks to the excessive Chardonnay), but there's no way I'm going to miss this pregame show Q & A.

A drag queen dressed as Miss McGee (the principal of Rydell, played by Eve Arden) takes the stage, and her banter warms up the crowd. She introduces Maxwell Caulfield . . . and then we hear it. The song chants out "C-O-O-L-R-I-D-E-R," Maxwell's entrance music. Stacey and I waste no time standing up and spelling out the COOL RIDER letters with our arms, such as in the vein of "YMCA." A standing ovation greets him, and he takes a seat across from Miss McGee.

We very quickly discover that this Miss McGee queen gives no fucks. She unabashedly talks about how she's in love with him and how fine his ass is in *Grease 2*. "I used to masturbate while watching you in this film," she says. She looks out at the audience. "Clap if you did too." Wow! Okay, so it's an audience-participation moment. The gay men in my entourage applaud wildly, and so does the majority of the theater; whistles and catcalls follow.

"Wow, that's brazen of her," I whisper to Stacey. "Eh, he can handle it," she shakes me off. I'm really not sure how this is going to go and of course feel protective of Maxwell and my *Grease 2* baby—what if the whole thing implodes and he storms off stage? It doesn't; sister was right. Maxwell is totally unshaken by this. He even seems used to this kind of queer attention. He is good spirited, cracks a few jokes, and is humble in his responses. Thank goddess.

The Q & A is cute, short, to the point. My friends and I love seeing him in person, and I feel sad when he says goodbye, heading offstage to his wife, Juliet. Ms. McGee gives us her sassy parting words: "Okay, there's some previews first; then the film will start. Don't jack off in the theater while you watch. This is a sing-along, so you better fucking sing. Oh, and there are no subtitles, but you bitches know the lyrics anyway. Bye—eee!" She exits, royalty waving.

As she leaves, so do I. My bladder can no longer wait. I race to the lobby bathroom, piss as fast as possible, and wash leftover orange Cheetos powder from my fingers. I don't want to miss the "Back to School Again" opening-credits song. I hurry back into the dark theater, climb over poodle skirts, and find my middle seat. I'm relieved that the previews have just ended and the film is about to begin.

I get comfortable and pull out a Snickers for a light snack. Then my friend Anthony, returning from peeing from too much tequila, whispers from behind, "Hey, Emily, if you want to meet Maxwell, you have to come now; he's in the lobby." I don't think twice. I shoot back up, grab Stacey's arm, and take her with me. My heart is racing. Stacey and I microscream/squeal as we head to the lobby. I'm completely sure there will be a line to meet him or that we will have just missed him, knowing my luck.

But no. There he is. Finishing up selfies with a gay quartet, he looks even more gorgeous in person. He is wearing a designer black suit, gray collar shirt, and red tie. Stacey and I approach him asking for a picture. "Sure!" he says, putting his arms around us on either side. Man, does he smell good.

I throw my purse at Anthony and hand him our phones to take the pics. Shaking and nervous laughing, I pop an Altoid to mask my Snickers-and-wine breath. My lipstick is all askew from the Cheetos. *Dammit, why didn't I reapply when I was in the bathroom a few minutes ago?*

But at the same time, I don't care. I'm just over the moon to be

in his presence. Pics are snapped, and as we are about to say thank
you and let him move on with his life, I somehow find the ovaries to
show him my tattoo. The adrenaline has beat the Chardonnay at that
point, so it wasn't liquid courage. I just thought, Fuck it. I'm here, I'm
wearing capris, I have a Neo Traditional portrait of this guy on my leg.
Let's do this.

My color portrait of Michael Carrington lives on my left calf. He
is clad in a gold, full-body motorcycle suit à la the infamous dream
sequence "Love Will Turn Back the Hands of Time." He sits atop his
bike, reaching longingly for Stephanie (Michelle Pfeiffer), who we can
only imagine is lurking somewhere nearby me at all times. He is framed
by pinks and purples, and it's just a gay dream. Shout to Brandon
Huckabey, awesome tattoo artist in Denver @brandonhuckabey.

While there are quite a few *Grease*-inspired tattoos out there, there
are not that many *Grease 2*-specific tats I'm aware of. If you have one,
please contact me ASAP. I really wanna see it. Wearing Michael on my

I met Maxwell dressed as a Pink Lady and even showed him my tattoo.
(Photo courtesy of Em Marinelli)

leg is me commemorating and lifting up this magical film. Wearing it, I get to carry with me the cult spirit of the story, keeping it alive and well and forever inked.

Thanks to my friend Anthony, who just keeps hitting the camera button on my iPhone, there are a series of pictures of Stacey and me in motion to show off said tat to Maxwell. Stacey is repeatedly finding ways to unnecessarily touch Maxwell's shoulders in these pics. In doing so, she blocks his facial reactions to my ink, which of course we laugh about later. In one very exciting shot, I'm holding up my pants leg and Maxwell is fixing my collar (yes, he is actually touching my Pink Ladies jacket!)—and yes, Stacey again is blocking half of the pic. But I will still have this forever etched in my memory.

When he first lands eyes on the tat, I can see his shock at coming face-to-face with a rendition of himself reflected on my body. "Darling, that is a bit extreme, don't you think?" We both laugh and I say "Yep!" He smiles, brushes off a hair from my shoulder, and straightens my neck bandana. He is a good sport about it, and I'm aware of how freaky it must be to have someone show you a tattoo they have of you.

When we really do say our thank-yous and goodbyes, sister and I daze our way back into the theater. We sink into our seats, high from meeting Maxwell, fingers shaking, hearts racing. We keep looking at each other and mouthing, *What the fuck just happened?* and *I can't believe this!* Michael on the big screen, as if to respond to us, says our favorite line, "Yeah, I know," to Didi Conn on the football field, perfect timing.

Distracted, we turn to our friends to gossip-whisper about our time with Maxwell until the T-Birds and Pink Ladies yell, "Shoot the ball, shoot the ball, shoot . . . the . . . ball!" As "Score Tonight" begins, we immerse ourselves back in the film. With Maxwell's energy running through our veins, along with the sugar high from the devoured Snickers and white wine remains, we stand up to do the dance moves at the bowling alley. Of course we mark the turns so as to not hit the people next to us and join in the rest of the queers for a sing-along we will truly never forget.

***

Not in my lifetime could I imagine that five years later, I would have the chance to interview Maxwell Caulfield, aka the Cool Rider, aka Rex Manning himself. (The latter reference is to the cult film *Empire Records*, which, if you haven't seen, you should, immediately). When I emailed him to ask for an interview, he wrote back quickly and agreed. He then dropped off the map. I didn't hear from him for a long while.

It took Chris McDonald (after my chat with him) to hit him up and gently nudge Maxwell to call me to make our interview happen. Just another moment of Goose sidekicking to the gang leader and T-Birds helping T-Birds. I love so much that that happened; it still makes me all giddy inside.

Thankfully, our interview is over the phone, so he doesn't have to see my shirt turn from lavender to dark purple rings in my armpits. How is that I'm talking to the blue sweater-wearing, British lead of my favorite movie musical, whose song "Charade" enchanted me so many years ago? It's real. It's happening.

Right away, he apologizes for making me wait, explaining that he got COVID, which knocked him out. He says he's happy to speak with me about *Grease 2*. His voice is soft and pleasant, his demeanor professional yet down to earth. We discuss his theater background and stage acting. He has been in countless off-Broadway and West End shows and on national and international tours, including some of my favorite plays; *Sweet Bird of Youth*, *Cactus Flower*, and *The Elephant Man*.

My favorite unexpected parts of our chat involve his theories about Alec Baldwin, the horrors of climate change, and his deep respect for Tom Cruise in the sequel *Top Gun: Maverick*. We talk about being in love and the key components to a long-lasting marriage (he has been married to Juliet Mills, sister of Hayley Mills, since 1980!). Our convo flows so well, at one point he jokes that I'm his psychoanalyst, and I lose it.

He doesn't shy away from his saltiness over *Grease 2*, which he believes resulted in typecasting that hurt his film career. I appreciate his honesty. I feel his longing for the film career he didn't get to have. I also feel the way he has learned to love and accept the cult passion *Grease 2* has garnered over the years.

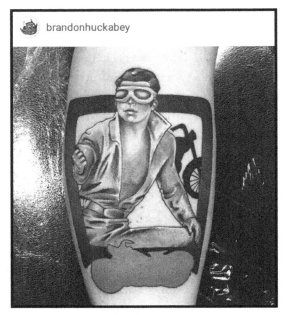

brandonhuckabey

My Cool Rider portrait tattoo.
(Photo courtesy of Brandon Huckabey)

Here is the Cool Rider himself, Maxwell Caulfield:

Emily Marinelli: In 2017, I met you at a *Grease 2* sing-along at the Castro Theatre in San Francisco and showed you the tattoo portrait I have of you on my calf from the movie. You were so sweet but probably understandably freaked out.

Maxwell Caulfield: That was a great event up at the Castro. I got to feel like a rock star. Sure, why not have your fans getting a little ink as long as you don't let the side down [British for disappointing or letting down friends] and they need to get it removed [laughing]!

Emily: I love *Grease 2*, obviously, but critics did not. Why do you think it didn't do well when it came out?

Maxwell: In defense of *Grease 2* and why it was a box office failure, stupidly we opened on the same day as *E.T.*

Emily: No way.

Maxwell: There's been so many juggernaut movies since that people don't realize that *E.T.* truly came and leveled everything in its path. We got obliterated, and *E.T.* is like a massive, massive hit. *E.T.* played at the Cinerama Dome, and my wife and I were there on opening day, standing in line eating Reese's Pieces and having no idea that *E.T.* was going to eat our lunch. But that was Paramount's fault; they should never have released this film not only on the same day as *E.T.*, but with the opening number that is "Back to School Again" when all the kids were just getting out of school for the summer.

Emily: Damn, yes, that's a really good point.

Maxwell: A complete disconnect. If they released our film at the end of the summer and given the kids something to go into school tapping their toes to, snapping their fingers to, it could have been a hit! And the rest would be history. Certainly my career! Because I went down with the ship on that one, let me tell you! Michelle rose like a fabulous phoenix because there was no denying her talent and her beauty. I definitely paid a heavy price for that, because I naively put my mug front and center.

Where I really blew it was that I got offered to do a film that ultimately got called *Reckless*, and it was still in that post-*Grease 2* production period. I got approached by a then very, very top Hollywood film producer about appearing in a movie about an American high school boy with a motorcycle, and I thought, I've just done that, I can't do that. And I should have; that was a big mistake. It was that little tiny window that at the time you don't realize is your shot. It's like trying to join the major leagues and the door opens and you don't only have to go in and through it, but you gotta make damn sure you don't get tossed out again. You somehow just got to stake your claim, and the best thing to do is have backups.

Michelle got to do *Scarface*, and as a result she was able to follow up the failure of *Grease 2* with a smash. A great deal of good fortune is involved in this business. I mean, people say you make your own luck. It's true; you do. We are all architects of our own story. We write the book of our lives, but the film's failure to ignite at the time sent me sprawling across the canvas; it really did. Plus, it was so derided that it didn't help. But the original *Grease* got slammed at the box office by critics. But at the same time, they had a big insurance policy, John Travolta. He wasn't a star at the time; he was a planet already.

Emily: Yes, and so was Olivia Newton-John.

Maxwell: Of course! They are so delicious together. I did my screen test wearing John Travolta's jacket.

Emily: What?!

Maxwell: I know it was his because of the stuff I found in the pocket. They just fished it out of the wardrobe at Paramount.

Emily: How did you get involved with *Grease 2*?

Maxwell: I was doing a play called *Entertaining Mr Sloane*, a Joe Orton play, a very black comedy, and it became a cause célèbre off-Broadway and attracted a lot of the movers and shakers down to the West Village to see it, and a lot of really cool people came to see it; Andy Warhol, Mikhail Baryshnikov, Tennessee Williams, Allan Carr, and eventually Robert Stigwood.

I took the bait. William Morris sent this very young, charismatic agent to see me at *Entertaining Mr Sloane*, and he said, "I'd love to take you out to dinner after," and I said, "Well, listen, you happen to be coming the same day I've got a whole bunch of friends coming to see the show tonight." He said, "I'll take them all out! Where are we going?" They were all out-of-work actors, so I said, "Yeah, sure," and named some speakeasy or something 'round the corner from the theater, and he picked up the tab for everybody—supper and liquor bill for the night.

So they got me! And the next thing I know I was being positioned to be in *Grease 2*, and I did have to get the part; it's not like they just gave it to me. There were a lot of really standout candidates for the film, genuine teen idols at the time: Rick Springfield, Shaun Cassidy, I think—guys that already had huge female fan followings. So I still don't know how I ended up with the part. But it was obviously a bit of a dream come true, as an English boy suddenly living some sort of American high school fantasy and getting crossed-eyed looking at Michelle.

Emily: There's so much chemistry between the two of you!

Maxwell: Well, that's ironic, let me tell you. We saved it for the camera.

Emily: You did! Well if there was tension, it comes across as sexual tension, in a good way.

Maxwell: Well, good, good, good! Well, I still maintain she's the best screen kisser I've ever had.

Emily: You play Michael Carrington, who is a dreamboat. He is quiet and a bit shy, but he's cool, really funny, and doesn't take shit from the T-Birds. He earns their trust and gets money from them to pursue his dream. What parts of Michael's character do you identify with in your own life?

Maxwell: He's got a bit of an edge to him. He's from London and he's a bit of fish out of water but he's definitely going to hold his own ground. He's not a nerd; let's put it that way. They shot a scene where you actually got to meet the family Michael was staying with, but they cut that out of the film, and it's a shame. In the Blu-ray edition or whatever, they make that available.

Emily: You mean his homestay family?

Maxwell: Yes, the American family that was hosting him. And I'd done that. I came over with the Boy Scouts when I was fourteen, and

I stayed with a wonderful family in the suburbs of Philadelphia. The son was the star of the high school basketball team, and I had a really wonderful American experience for those two weeks. I even went to an American high school for a week. It was part of the cultural exchange. It was fascinating, and it was just like *Grease 2*! It was boys and girls, and everyone wore whatever the hell they wanted to wear. They talked back to the teachers. It was outrageous, and I was a straightlaced British public school boy—you know, school uniform, all male, very strict—and then suddenly I was in this unbelievable scene, just rampant hormones. Names were given I had never heard of, like called social studies. I remember going, "What is social studies?"

Emily: I know the movie was shot at a high school. What do you remember about filming there and what it was like?

Maxwell: I remember it was a schlep to get there. It was on the other side of Disneyland in Norwalk. I don't think the school functions as a school anymore. When they shot the first one, they shot it at Bennett High School, and this second one we shot at Norwalk. I don't know why we had such total access to the place. But I do remember it was a heck of a drive to get there every morning. I was being driven by a teamster, so I had no complaints, I think I just rolled out of bed into the station wagon, walked up to the set, got my hair teased by Elvis's hairdresser from all his big movies.

Emily: Wow, AMAZING! And your hair is just everything in this movie. Did you love what he did to your hair?

Maxwell: Of course I did. I remember saying to him, a veteran guy, one of the reasons the film looks so good is because it was all veteran guys from the golden era who apprenticed with the best of the best. I remember saying to him, "Gosh, you did Elvis's hair, the King's hair for all those movies," and he goes, "Yep, sure did," and before I started plugging him for stories I asked, "He had hair my color, right?" It wasn't that famous blue/black that we all associated him with, and at that time he's like teasing my pompadour into shape and he said,

"Yep, that's pretty much his same color. Of course, he had twice as much as you do." [Laughing.]

Emily: Burn! [Laughing.]

Maxwell: I mean, he didn't say it in a bitchy way, I was plugging him for information, and he gave it to me. He said, "Yep, you're right; he did. He had that sort of mouse-brown color, and guess what: he had a really lustrous mane."

Emily: I know you've done stage musicals after, but did you do any musicals before *Grease 2*?

Maxwell: My introduction to show business in British public school was in a production of *The Boyfriend*. I was just in the chorus, but I got my first taste of being in a 1920s musical. I got my first taste of being in a production with lots of pretty girls and having a live orchestra and all that excitement that generates in an auditorium. But I hadn't done anything since, and when I finally got serious about it was when I did *Chicago* in the West End playing Billy Flynn which is a bulletproof part. That started me going *Oh man, I gotta do this*. You certainly remember what got you into the business in the first place, and it's the most fun to be had in the theater.

A lot of theaters have really paid a terrible price for the COVID shutdown, and live performances are coming back. But the principal audience for the theater is over fifty-five, and they are leary for good reason, and they are the only ones with money to buy musical theater tickets.

Emily: I know; it's like taking calculated risks all the time. It's exhausting. It's in our minds all the time.

Maxwell: I know. The world has become so dark. It's hard not to be cynical or pessimistic. I should say not so much cynical; we start getting cynical, then it's over. But at the same time, look at the politics of this country. I mean, are we going into a civil war this summer? I'm sure your patients or your clients are voicing their deepest fears.

Emily: Yes, absolutely. And climate anxieties, lots of things. It's across the board; there are so many things going on.

Maxwell: Oh, yes, the farmers in San Joaquin Valley are getting 5 percent of their water supply this year, 5 percent. And 25 percent of the world's wheat harvest is locked because of the unnecessary war. So you're right; all the more reason for escapism.

Emily: Yes, and art.

Maxwell: Getting lost in great entertainment like fun miniseries, as we used to call them, now these streaming series. But I'm sure Tom Cruise is gonna knock it out of the park on Memorial Day with *Top Gun: Maverick*. Now there's a sequel people can't wait for! Enough of these Marvels and these endless Batmans and what have you. I'll be really impressed to see Tom pull that one off. I mean obviously we're contemporaries; he's one of the last of the major movie stars. Another contemporary of mine is also taking it on the chin, Alec Baldwin. That was just horrible. Bad luck.

Emily: Horrible. It's so upsetting.

Maxwell: Personally, if you ask me, I think it was a setup. I'm not a conspiracy theorist, but my gut feeling was— as soon as I read and heard about it, I was like *Uh-oh, who put that gun in that guy's hand who's been lampooning Donald Trump for the last four years. You know?*

Emily: Yep, I thought the same thing exactly! But no one talks about that.

Maxwell: And it's never been entertained by the media and has never really gone there. They keep pointing to the shoddy work of the armorer, who is the daughter of a famous cowboy, which is no excuse, and who knows, but it's gonna be tough. He can be so funny.

Emily: He's hilarious.

Maxwell: And it will be hard to laugh at him or with him again. But it's a funny game, and you know going into it the odds are long, but it does require hitting home runs or at least RBI singles. I mean, Chris McDonald got *Thelma & Louise*. Chris has always been very intelligent about advancing his career, but it sure helped to be in a hit film. It makes all the difference in the world.

I can chart the successful period of my career to when I was with a strong agency because they have the clout. They package; they get you to the head of the chow line. They insist the actor be given a script with an offer, not to stand in front of their cell phone and try to get a part along with forty others. But I don't want to come across as bitter. I'm frustrated. I find it a very frustrating career. It didn't quite materialize the way I'd hoped. But maybe I would have messed up my marriage or something, and that's the best thing I've got in my life. But before we got into this shrink session, you must have had some pertinent questions to ask me? [Laughing.]

Emily: I love this conversation, thank you. What was it like to work with Pat Birch, who directed the original *Grease*?

Maxwell: She's a lovely woman. She took it on the chin too. People thought she didn't direct *Grease 2* well, but actually she did a fabulous job. The camera moves marvelously, the colors in the film, the performances she coaxed out of us all. I can't say enough about Pat Birch. I wasn't being called on to dance in the film. All my stuff was dancing on the motorcycle, as it were, so I didn't go to the dance classes that they were conducting, I probably should've. I probably should've learned some choreography and they might have incorporated some into the finished product. So I think I let myself down by doing that. But I would've had to get out of bed even earlier to get to work in Norwalk, and I couldn't face it!

Emily: That's right: you're not doing a lot of dancing in the film. You're singing and—

Maxwell: And smooching! I did a lot of smooching in the film and motorcycle stunt car jumping.

Emily: Who are some of your favorite movie stars?

Maxwell: All my favorite movie stars have been able to maintain a state of innocence. It's part of what makes them so compelling. With that innocence comes a certain vulnerability.

My favorites were all actually antihero, rebel hero actors: Marlon Brando and James Dean, Montgomery Clift, Paul Newman. After James Dean died so young, Paul Newman ended up in at least two of his parts; *Somebody Up There Likes Me* and *The Left Handed Gun*. Both of those were roles Dean was signed on to make.

Emily: As you're talking about these actors, I'm thinking that part of what is appealing is that there's a softness to their masculinity too. These people we see in these larger-than-life roles, but there's also an antihero vulnerability, a softness to how they present themselves on-screen.

Maxwell: That's true. You know, Emily, frankly the thing about them is they've got it. The camera loves them. They absolutely crackle on screen. Maybe that's the big difference. You can be a very competent actor, you can retain your looks, you can put a moderate string of successes together, but do you set the pulse racing? Do you make even heterosexual men have a man crush on you? The girls are like *Oh my God, he's my dreamboat.*

Think about Clint Eastwood. When he was young, he was one of the most handsome men that the cinema's ever produced. Now the guy's like ninety and he's still doing it. Clint Eastwood turned into a really gnarly old dog, and yet he's still riveting. And that's it: just the ability to have the screen catch fire. Only certain people get to do that and actually have what it takes. As a result, I'm very grateful for what the theater has given me to not so much fall back on but to affirm that I wasn't completely misguided when I thought I could become a movie star.

Emily: Well, I have to say I have never met anyone, men included, who did not have a man crush on you in *Grease 2*.

Maxwell: They weren't just homosexual? [Laughing.]

Emily: No, straight men too! My friends, women, everyone. You name the gender, yes. That's that. You have that crackle. What is it like watching *Grease 2* today?

Maxwell: I resisted doing *Grease 2* because at the time I aspired to be regarded as a more serious actor, and I was leery about trying to follow in the footsteps of John Travolta; I couldn't dance like he could; I couldn't sing as well as he could. And the film was called *Son of Grease* originally, and it was gonna be a much grittier picture, so I kinda went along with it. And the closer we got to the film, the more they tinkered with the script and kind of turned me into a male Olivia Newton-John and Michelle into a female John Travolta, so they softened the picture. It's still a charming film, a lot of really lovely performances in it.

Adrian Zmed is just fantastic as Nogerelli, and the boys around him, the goon squad around him, I mean my buddy McDonald, obviously. Goose McDonald! He's just amazing. I mean he walks into a party that he hasn't been invited to and he's suddenly the life and soul of it. At Sundance, we walk in, they say, "Is your name on the list?" and he goes, "Oh, it's bound to be," and he just blew by the door and we were just tagging along behind him. Within three minutes we were suddenly at the head table; he's telling all the funny stories and cracking everybody up. And we weren't even invited. He's a hoot and a half, that guy.

Leif and Peter, they were just such a great combination. And the chicks were just fab! And we were all on such a high. We couldn't believe our good fortune. I wish it wasn't the only thing I'm still talking about all these years later. It's like someone talking about *The Silver Chalice* and you're going, "But what about me in *Cool Hand Luke*?" No, I'm still talking about the Cool Rider.

Emily: This book is about movie sequels that were comforting to me growing up. For me, they provided more comfort, more familiarity, more of the same but different.

Maxwell: Yes, I understand where you're coming from. There is some pleasure in revisiting characters that you fell for and also seem to still be around. The one thing you go on is a hardcore retread where they basically replicate the first one, but it doesn't have the originality or the inherent charm of the first one because it's a formula they're reproducing. It's hard to top the original, but once in a while the sequel does actually, and they grow. They have an idea, and they take it further. They take it to the next level, and it potentially is more profound. Now, I'm not suggesting that was the case with *Grease 2* [laughing].

Emily: Of course it was! It'll always be number one in my book.

Maxwell: In terms of sheer entertainment, and because of the star power of Travolta and Newton-John and of course that incredible soundtrack, a lot of the people who were in *Grease* had done it on Broadway, so it's in their DNA . . . The one thing that we really did have over them was that we were much closer to the age of the characters, and we appeared to be too.

But I must say, I've come to appreciate *Grease 2* over the years. I've since seen it two or three times. I've been invited to see it at a film festival screening or whatever anniversary screening, and every time I see it, I feel it did succeed in making a very worthy sequel, and it was really a great film that was derided at the time.

They talked about a third *Grease* at one point, and Kylie Minogue was gonna do it. You know each new female pop star that comes along, they talk about her playing a version of Stephanie, but they've all fallen by the wayside. But the one that is finally seeing the light of day is *Grease: Rise of the Pink Ladies*, which is supposed to be a prequel and is supposed to predate even the first *Grease*. So we will see if it comes to pass, and maybe they'll have me play the toothless old owner of the bowling alley or something [both laughing].

Emily: What do you think makes *Grease 2* so comforting for audiences?

Maxwell: Now as you know, *Grease 2* was set in 1962, so it's not in the fifties; it's just before the end of innocence, before the assassination of JFK. There's the reference to the nuclear fallout shelter, that wonderful song with Maureen Teefy and Peter Frechette, that at the time was sort of mocked and dismissed, which is not only very pertinent but is actually a charming scene about a girl trying to avoid being deflowered by a horny high schooler [laughing]. At the end of the day, all of these guys loved these girls. It's not all animal lust, it's all . . .

Emily: Genuine.

Maxwell: Yes, genuine. They're so well matched. What is comforting about *Grease 2*? Well, all the boys get the girls. I know it's formulaic, but it's an enchanting concept. Our daughter right now is back together with her boyfriend from high school, and she's having her first relationship in a very long time. So it's a lovely thought. They say the first time you fall in love, it's never more powerful. You can have a more profound relationship of course in your adulthood than in your adolescence, but there's something about that. I always say hormones make the world go round. But I think there's something about that release of hormones that's just extraordinary. Your brain gets stimulated in a way it has never felt before. Of course it does open up other aspects of your brain as well. It can get turned onto other aspects of your psyche that you didn't know. Love comes with responsibilities, because you've got somebody's soul, you're intertwined with someone on a really cellular level, if you're lucky to have a relationship that goes the distance.

At the end of the day, it's all about finding respect for each other and your commitment, faithfulness, and somehow maintaining your innocence if you can. And that is what I think it represents—the very next year after *Grease 2* is set, some murderous monster decides to blow the head off the president of the United States.

Emily: And it changed everything in the country.

Maxwell: And Martin Luther King, who was literally a living saint. So that's one of the reasons your love of our film is well-founded.

Emily: What other movie sequels or TV shows or art do you find comforting?

Maxwell: My greatest comfort is watching English Premier League football. I love the zen aspect of it where you're just completely consumed with the game. The game now is played with such grace and speed. I'll be honest with you: that is my go-to relief.

Emily: Love that. Thank you for all the time and all you shared.

Maxwell: Best of luck with your book and finding a receptive audience. I look forward to reading about your book in the *New York Times*.

Emily: Awww, well, I don't know about that, but thank you! [Laughing.]

Maxwell: Hey, positive projections!

Emily: Yes, positive projections!

Dream A Little Dream 2

"Joey, we're gonna go out to the hot tub now. Smell you later, asshole!" Even at age twelve, Deena talks to her dad like he is just another annoying boy at school instead of the mountainous, game-hunting, Confederate flag-sporting, monster truck-racing enthusiast that he is.

Deena's dad Joey, is my dad's good friend. As Southern white men do, my dad and Joey met at a National Rifle Association meeting, and it was love at first rifle. They attend monthly gun club meetings together, shoot skeet, tell racist jokes, smoke cheap cigars, and eat at Olive Garden on special occasions like they are some kind of working-class fancy.

They get along for these reasons and also because Joey is a single dad with a daughter the same age as me. My dad doesn't know what to do with me on the every other weekend I stay with him, so I often end up hanging here, at Deena's double-wide trailer. That is totally fine by me because Deena is . . . well . . . hot.

Deena is the exact opposite of her good ol' boy dad. She's a tall, curvy, loud culturally Italian but southern to the core girl who reads Joyce Carol Oates and smokes Marlboro Reds. Often suspended from school or in trouble at the principal's office, she is brilliant and radical.

When a history teacher refuses to talk about the Tulsa Race Massacre because it "isn't in the textbook," Deena calls her a "fucking fascist bitch." Sexy. I'm not totally sure what a fascist is, but I know that Deena knows, and that is all that matters. I love her brain and her badassery antidote to her dad's racist bullshit.

I awkwardly shuffle out the back door of their mobile home with a "Thanks, Mr. Moretti," and I guess I'm thanking him for letting me have a slumber party with his daughter, for the pizza he bought for us earlier, and for the use of his aboveground hot tub in the backyard. He doesn't look up or acknowledge us as we open the screen door and step into the cool September night.

Deena and I have arms full of beach tote bags stuffed with towels, beer, water noodles, and sunglasses, like we are going to float on the river instead of a hot tub in West Tulsa in the middle of autumn. I watch her olive skin rounding into half moons around the bottom of her one-piece purple swimsuit, fat and muscle bubbling out into little moon slices from under the spandex. It makes me feel less self conscious as my baby fat moves into curves underneath my bikini. My boobs have only recently moved from gymnast flat to sixth-grade-dance padded bra, and I'm not sure what to do with them yet.

Two huge shepherd mutts bark at us, herding us toward the hillbilly hot tub across the yard. "Hurry up, bitch," she laughs at me for having shorter legs than hers. It also takes me longer to climb the ladder over and into the water of the second-hand tub. Found at a junkyard, the tub miraculously works, and the water jets pop on rippling water reflected by moonlight. A makeshift privacy fence covers the whole thing, and it's quiet back here. Just me and Deena.

Even though we are both only twelve years old, this isn't our first alcohol rodeo. She pops open a can of Bud Light using her index finger as the opener, chipped black-fingernail polish flaking as the tab cracks. We "Cheers," and she undoes her high bun. Long, thick, dark-brown hair shakes out over her shoulders.

I try not to notice how certain movements make her curls glow in the light. I try not to notice my swimsuit feeling good between my legs or that my head is a little looser from the beer. I look around to make sure we are really alone. And we are. It's safe to be ourselves.

Clueless had just come out in theaters, and we talk about what characters we would be in the movie. "You're totally Cher and I'm

Dionne, obvi, cuz I'm your BFF," I say to her. But secretly I know that next to her, I'm really the uncool Tai, trying to roll with the homies and destined to fall in love with a loser skateboarder. "As if!" she says back. We both laugh, and I tell her to "talk to the hand, 'cause the face won't listen."

We talk about what we want to buy at Suncoast Records and Hot Topic at Woodland Hills mall and make a plan to go there next week. I have my eye on flowery Doc Martens I could never afford, and I want the new Skee-Lo album even though he's probably a one-hit wonder. Deena says she wants that one T-Shirt from *The Crow* because she's in love with Brandon Lee. She will likely steal a peace sign choker from Claire's, and I will be stressed out the whole time that we're gonna get caught. But I'm not gonna think about that right now, in this hot tub, in this moonlight.

"Truth or dare?" she asks. "Truth," I say, and she rolls her chestnut eyes. She knows I'm always gonna pick truth because I'm afraid of whatever dare she is gonna make me do. "Okay, truth. Have you ever French kissed someone?" Her dimples pop out as she smiles at me. Whew, that's easy. "Yes, you know I have, bitch," I say and laugh, my cheeks turning rose.

"Truth or dare?" I ask, and in a turn of events, she picks truth.

"Okay, what base have you been to?" I finish off the crappy beer, and she hands me another, like clockwork.

"Second rounding into third."

She looks away, then dips her whole body under the water. I pause, waiting. Finally, she emerges and is quiet, wrings out water from her hair like Grandma squeeze-dries towels. The night is completely ours except for the cicada orchestra playing several notes over and over and the occasional deep, groveling barks from the German shepherds. Light drops of sweat wet my face. I'm hoping she will say more about third base, or any base really, but she doesn't. She just looks at me and says, "Truth or dare?"

Maybe it's the beer, maybe it's Deena and the dance we do each time we see each other before we can start making out, but this time I tell her, "I'll take dare." With a sly smile, she swims over to the tote bag and pulls out two pairs of sunglasses. She puts on one and hands me the other. "Wear these," she tells me. Ridiculous because it's nighttime but, of course, I put them on. I wait. This can't be the whole dare, I think. This is too easy.

"Now, when you wear these, you will do as I say."

OMG, hot.

So that's it. I'm her puppet. The sunglasses are pulling the strings.

OMG, very hot.

"Put one hand on your hip."

I nervous laugh. "Okay."

"Put the other hand on your shoulder."

"Are we playing Simon Says now?"

She laughs and splashes me. I move my hands to block the chlorinated water slapping my face.

She floats closer to me. "Stay in the position I told you to." Her voice is softer, like a whisper. I put my hands back to my shoulder and hip. I'm at her whim. Her hand goes to my hair and pulls a fine, thin strand back behind my ear. One finger traces the line of my cheekbone. The sunglasses stay on. She straddles me, her inner thighs wrapped around my middle. Now we have graduated from *Clueless* and are the girls from *Foxfire*. She's the fearless girl gang leader Legs (played by Angelina Jolie) and I'm Maddy (Hedy Burress), the brown-haired basic girl, following in her footsteps and totally in love with her. Legs makes Maddy do adventurous things, pushes her out of her comfort zone, gets her into trouble rebelling against authority, because fuck authority.

Forgetting Deena's authority over me for a moment, I break the rule of the sunglasses game as my hands climb to her back and dig into the straps of her bathing suit. In a quick motion, she jerks my arms back in place and goes deeper into my mouth. I'm already afraid this will end. Inside my head, I'm willing Deena to keep kissing me for hours, to do things to me. Maybe if I keep imagining it, it will happen.

But it doesn't. A scratch on my forearm from Deena's neon waterproof Swatch snaps us back into the night, and she checks the time. "Shit, we should go in. The movie's gonna start soon." Her words barely register as I come back from a daze of water heat, crisp air, fire inside. "You're gonna love *Dream a Little Dream 2*," she says and pulls away from me.

Fuck. The bubble between us deflates, but I can't say anything. I'm not even supposed to clock this as actually happening. We are living in a secret, sexy dream. A secret we share only with the night and the hot tub and the dogs lying next to us, who lift their heads occasionally to bark at a passing pickup truck.

***

Back inside her trailer, we tipsy-trip over the clutter all around Deena's house. Empty beer cans, open boxes of ammo; Deena's old, childhood plastic toys that were meant to be taken to Goodwill but never made it; cans of green beans and corn; and lots of rolled-up Winchester posters that are meant to someday hang on the empty walls.

"Chester, there you are!" Deena pulls out her teddy bear hamster in a clear ball that has been rolling around the house for a few hours since we had lost sight of him. "Aww, hi, little cutie," I say and touch my water-pruned finger to his air hole. His tiny claw kisses my fingertip, and his eyes look into mine. Deena sets him carefully back down on the carpet, and he begins rolling again, this time toward the kitchen, and I know in a few minutes he will get stuck again in a cluttered corner.

We take off our suits and hang them in the bathroom. I watch her brush her hair in sections to work out the tangles as I put on the Lisa Frank matching PJ set I got for Christmas a few years back. Deena sports a long Guns N' Roses T-shirt that was obviously Joey's and is full of holes. Why is she so much cooler than me, even in her nightwear? Legs to my Maddy and Cher to my Tai.

Snoring echoes through the mobile home, and the almost-empty bottle of Bacardi on the coffee table tells us Joey will be out for a while. Deena takes a swig of the remaining rum drops and hands the bottle to me to finish off. I do because she tells me to and because I have a feeling where this night might be going.

"Okay, let'sssssssss . . . "

And I join her to finish the sentence " . . . DO THIS," a catchphrase we use for whatever reason. She turns on the TV to HBO, a channel she accesses through the "courtesy" of the neighbors, since her dad has rigged their cable box. We grab an open bag of off-brand potato chips from the dollar store and arm swipe a bunch of shit off the couch so we have a place to sit. We turn out the lights.

I'm cross-legged, and Deena sprawls out. One of her long legs, splotched with some cuts and bruises, is close enough for me to still feel her fire but far enough away that I still yearn for her skin. She lights up a Marlboro Red, and Chester rolls by in his hamster mobile home. On the TV, a camera pans over a fake city, into the night sky, waking up the neon letters "HBO Feature Presentation," and *Dream a Little Dream 2* begins.

Sense Transmission: Dream a Little Dream 2 Recap

In my preteen years, I used to stay up late for *Red Shoe Diaries*, *Dream On*, and other soft-ish porn shows on HBO and Showtime. I would turn the volume all the way down so no one would know I was awake. I didn't even trust the remote control to work fast enough, so I sat right in front of the TV on the floor just in case I needed to reach up and change the channel super quick. I was worried someone might get up in the middle of the night for a snack and catch me watching something naughty.

As *Dream a Little Dream 2* (*DALD2*) starts, I soon realize this film falls just shy of this category of HBO shows. It doesn't have nudity or steamy between-the-sheets moments with a saxophone backdrop. It's a PG-13 flick with more implication than giveaway but is full of kinky escapades I'm quietly hoping for. It's *Exit to Eden* (one of my favorites) meets *Cool World*. Sexy.

DALD2 is set almost six years after the first film was released, and unlike *Dream a Little Dream*, this comfort sequel went straight to HBO. Though I saw the first film I barely remember it, but I love Corey Haim (Corey H.) and Corey Feldman (Corey F.) (whom I will henceforth refer to collectively as the Two Coreys, as did their short-lived reality TV show), so I'm excited. I could seriously watch *License to Drive* and *The Lost Boys* all the damn time.

As I watch with Deena, I learn that the *DALD2* plot is WAY more convoluted than it needs to be for a direct-to-HBO film. WAY

MORE. Here's the simple version (I hope): The Two Coreys receive a pair of sunglasses and discover that one person can control the other when both pairs are worn. Ahhhh, so this is what Deena was doing to me in the hot tub. Got it.

A thriller-light story ensues in which the Two Coreys dream what is to come: 1) that a beautiful, mysterious, and sexy woman (Lena) will attempt to steal back the shades, 2) that they will be pursued by scary mob-like guys whose motivations are never fully explained, and 3) that things will come to a head when forces make Corey F. try to kill Rachel (Robyn Lively) but instead he uses his free will to make a different choice and save the day.

We aren't hippies, but Deena and I like Corey H. as a smoothie-drinking, meditative, energy-sensitive dude in *DALD2* (similar to River Phoenix's Devo in *I Love You to Death*). Next to Corey F.'s type A suit-wearing businessman, the Two Coreys are polar-opposite best friends, living together, a nineties Felix and Oscar.

I look over at Deena lying on the couch, engrossed in the film, laughing as Corey F. makes Corey H. deep clean the house under the power of the shades. I try not to notice the tiny windows of skin peeking through the holes in her Guns N' Roses nightgown or the way her left cheek dimple sharpens when she opens her mouth to laugh.

A powerful spiritual process occurs at the end of the film in which Corey H. and another prisoner (who are incarcerated for reasons that don't matter except to separate the Two Coreys) use what they call "sense transmission" or "soul sharing" to communicate telepathically to Corey F., repeating the mantra "Know your heart, know your will."

It is because of their sense-transmission mantras that Corey F., under the influence of the mind-control sunglasses, is stopped from shooting Rachel. The sense transmission taps into his internal sense of right and wrong to fight AGAINST the power of the sunglasses, which are telling him to kill her. It works: all is well in the *DALD2* landscape. See? It's kind of unnecessarily complex, with just the right amount of holes to keep me struggling. Even as I rewatched as an adult to write this chapter, I'm like, *Damn, what happened in that writers' room?*

But also, who cares? The movie is hot.

"Ready when you are honey" Power and Sex

It's really the female leads who make the movie. Lena (Stacie Randall), the sultry villain, and Rachel (Robyn Lively), are the fierce and powerful deuteragonists to the Two Coreys. They demonstrate how power and sex can be both harnessed for good and also wielded for evil. These two women are brave, outsmart men, and save the day. And the film.

Rachel is the third housemate to the Two Coreys. We meet her at the beginning of the film, in the kitchen, eye-rolling the Two Coreys, who are just being bonehead guys talking some BS. As Deena and I watch, it becomes clear Rachel is also the love interest for Corey F. But that is hardly what she's about. Sporting red curls, a killer crop floral vest, and hot combat boots, she is a fierce feminist academic.

As the Two Coreys argue about nothing, she quietly reads Susan Faludi's *Backlash*. Sick, right? The book is a feminist classic, discussing the 1980s popular culture backlash that came in response to the second wave women's rights advances of the sixties and seventies. Without saying it, she's saying this film is not that. She's saying, *My character is a badass bitch who doesn't take shit from men*. In fact, she sees right through them and doesn't need sunglasses to do so.

How did political commentary make its way into this straight-to-HBO flop? Amazing. I won't read *Backlash* until I get to college, but watching with Deena that night, I can see so clearly that Rachel is powerful and brilliant. Her wisdom ends up saving the Two Coreys on multiple occasions. Her clever antics single-handedly solve the major crimes and dilemmas in the film. She's actually the ONLY one in the film who is brilliant enough to stop the bad guys. In a patriarchal world, where men are on top and know best, Rachel answers Corey F.'s big-dick energy with a skillful saving of the day.

She also outsmarts Lena, the beautiful, mysterious villain in the film. Lena is tall and slender, sandy blonde with bangs, and wears purple thigh-high stockings underneath her purple power suit. She's stunning in high heels, feminine and strong, radiating an archetypal ballbusting CEO-type energy.

While technically Lena's seductive power is wielded with manipulative intentions, she is powerful in her scheming, holding agency in her desire to get what she wants. She infiltrates dreams, entices men to do her bidding using the shades, and uses her position to gain control.

While watching the movie at Deena's, I don't understand this feminist analysis or the larger commentary on power, sex, and gender roles in the film. I'm sure Deena does, but we don't talk about it. On this night, with Deena, my head swirling from the booze and the hot tub, I'm just here, taking it all in. Having seen *DALD2* the week before, Deena gave me a hot tub taste of Lena. The sunglasses, the scheming, the seduction. Sneaky bitch.

When Corey H. puts on sunglasses to mind control Corey F., we both jump off of the couch, take rum swigs, and attempt our Micheal Jackson moves like Corey F. He is REALLY good at dancing, and we aren't. We are also kinda drunk, so I end up hitting my shin on the coffee table and fall on the floor laughing.

Deena keeps going: her hips gyrate; she grabs her crotch, pulling it so hard she's on her tippy toes with a tilt of her pretend fedora. Somehow she has gotten the sunglasses back on, and she throws the other pair at me. I don't hesitate to put them back on. I freeze, waiting for Deena to lead into whatever is next.

She's in her own world and keeps dancing even when Corey F.

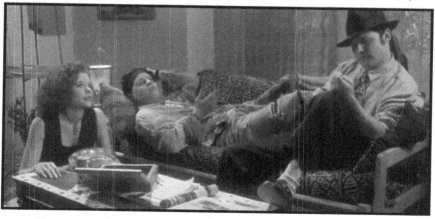

Dream a Little Dream 2 cast always make me think of Deena's couch.
(Photo courtesy of New Line Cinema)

stops. My leg hurts like hell; my head is spinning, but my attention is peaked when I hear Lena tell Corey F. that she, in fact, was part of the team that developed these power sunglasses. She says the goal is that "one conscious mind would completely control the other." All of the sudden she's seducing Corey F. by telling him she is conducting sexual experiments and needs the shades. He says he left them at work. She smiles. "First, I'm going to teach you to make love like a man," she says and dangles a pair of handcuffs from one finger.

Deena stops dancing and watches closely. My stomach jumps into my throat. Next thing we know, Corey F. is blindfolded and handcuffed to his bed, moaning in delight. "Ready when you are honey," he says to Lena, then eek-laughs like an annoying excited kid who is about to eat chocolate cake for the first time.

Please do that to me, I think, and I carefully sit up. The room stops spinning, and I lock eyes behind sunglasses with Deena, who I know is looking at me. The pause is so long I wonder if I'm so drunk I'm making it up. *Ready when you are, honey*, I think to myself, and the booze is making me almost bold enough to say it out loud. Would she like that? Would I be too presumptuous? Would it turn her off?

Thankfully, I don't have to figure that out, because she says sternly, "Who told you to get up?" She jumps on top of me, pinning me back down. We don't have cuffs, but she uses her hands to hold me in place. She touches me in ways I could only dream, bites my neck, and leaves magenta teeth marks I will have to cover later.

She's completely in charge, and I love it. She won't let me kiss her like, earlier in the hot tub; in fact, she won't let me move at all. The shades stay on. Sometimes they scrap a little against my cheek as she works her hips against mine.

The movie continues above us. Lena grabs his car keys, rolls her eyes, and walks out the bedroom door. Corey F. is left in his bedroom handcuffed, unfulfilled. A Green Day *Dookie* album poster, just like the one I have in my room, is revealed from behind the door as Lena walks out. I register it at a quick glance from the corner of my eye on the screen, but return my gaze to Deena on top of me.

The torture of her being so close and in control is electric. A bead of sweat rolls down her chin; her face looks more tan than usual through the shades. I can only really see her nose and mouth, her lips pursing together like she's focusing. Occasionally her bottom lip tucks behind her front teeth, and it makes me excited. Her breathing becomes shorter and shorter, and it seems like she wants to let out a moan but doesn't let herself. The heat between my legs is on fire. And I can't put it out.

And then.

All of the sudden.

Like Lena, she peels off of me.

I'm Corey F., left behind with aching, unrequited desire and a Green Day poster.

"I love this movie," she says, laughing, and returns to her spot on the couch. Some potato chip pieces bounce off the cushion and sprinkle to the floor. Chester rolls by in his ball, oblivious. This is our game. She always leaves me wanting more.

"Know your heart, know your will"

It's about three months after that drunken mystical night at Deena's. I stand by my father in the kitchen as he pops popcorn in a cast iron pot. He listens closely to each kernel so they don't scorch. His huge belly comes close to the stove, and I wonder how he doesn't accidentally get burned from the flames. Butter turns bubbly in a small pan on the adjacent burner, and he signals to me to grab the orange-and-green marbled melamine salad bowl that fits all the popcorn I could possibly want.

He drizzles butter slowly over the top of the Orville Redenbecker and shakes out copious amounts of salt and a pinch of garlic powder too. That's gonna be so good, but I want a specific spice. I stand on my toes and dig deep into the back of the cabinet to find the Lawry's Lemon Pepper Blend. I douse the bowl with it. I use so much that a handful makes me sneeze white and tan kernel bits all over my nightgown.

Dad yawns, says "Goodnight, sweetie," the most he has said all day, and goes to bed. I'm on my own. The house is quiet, and my private ritual of popcorn and HBO begins. I find my spot on the floor mere inches from the TV, pull a Barbie pillow underneath me, and dig in.

My fingers growing steadily more sticky from popcorn, I try to communicate with Deena through watching *DALD2*. This comfort sequel is my "sense transmission." *Deena, can you hear me across the miles? Can you feel me?*

When Corey F. does his MJ moves, I join him, having mostly memorized them by now. When Corey H. does his meditation mantra, I do it with him. *Deena, can you feel me through these actions? Can you find me telepathically through this movie?*

As the movie goes on, time makes the salted butter turn the fluffy popcorn pieces a little stale. I lick my pointer finger and circle the bottom of the bowl to collect bits of the artificial lemon seasoning and black pepper flakes. I place kernels on my tongue one by one and suck the flavor from my finger.

With each kernel, I try to manifest our way back together, to the sunglasses game. I will myself to dream her, so I can give her messages about what I want from her, her lips, her thighs, her watermelon Lip Smacker goodness. I want her to hear me from across the miles through my dream states, through my obsessive watching of this ridiculous movie, through my mind communication with her. I long to once again be the uncool *Foxfire*-Maddy bottom to her *Foxfire*-Legs top.

But it doesn't happen. We don't hook up anymore after that. I call her sometimes, but she is never home or too busy to talk. Our dads drift apart too. Friendships change.

Over time, Deena and I just stop hanging out. We both move on. Me to my nerdy theater friends and her to another, rowdier middle school. A life I was never invited to. By high school, we lose all contact, and I never get to really say goodbye to her or to her herding dogs or to sweet Chester rolling around in his hamster ball.

The last time I see her is during a brutal Tulsa summer a few years after our hot tub night. She seems bored, so we smoke weed from a pipe in her living room and play Skip-It in her front lawn for nostalgia sake. I get chigger bites all up and down my legs, and she tells me about some boy she is going out with. I don't ask what "going out with" means; I don't want to know.

The afternoon sun catches her in a rainbow light prism, and her face is hazy. Could be the weed, but she seems to be fuzzy. Could be my desire, but I seem to be sad. Could be the circumstances, but we both seem distant.

I pull out a lighter I bought for her from Spencer's. It's covered in peace signs and mushroom characters with bloodshot eyes. It is atrocious, but I know she wanted it. I tell her I stole it, just to sound cool, and she says, "Oh. Thanks." Indifferent.

We stand close together; I can smell her Bath and Body Works freesia spray, and I stare at the faded henna on the back of her hand. Her fingernails glitter, the dark blue and pink alternating. I look at my own hand, bare and empty, no polish, the cuticles bloody from biting them.

She stares far away but talks a mile a minute about some monster truck rally she went to and how she started watching *Dazed and Confused* and wants to mastermind air raids on freshmen when she becomes a senior. As I half listen to her droning stories, I repeat the phrase in my head—know your heart, know your will—over and over. I want us to find each other again like we did watching the film.

And just as I think that, Deena, out of nowhere, breaks her nonstop monologue and says, "Hey, remember when we danced like Michael Jackson like in that one movie?" She starts moonwalking and stoned laughing. "Oh yeah, I remember," I say and join her. We hold hands for support as we stumble on the grass, and our Sketchers get mud and grass stains on them.

For a brief moment, it is like old times, and I catch what I think is a glimpse of her desire. A side glance through weed-slit eyes. Out of breath, we sit next to each other on the scorching cracked sidewalk and smile. I light a cigarette for her with the mushroom lighter and she shakes hair away from her face. As she opens her mouth to exhale, I notice shiny pink gloss on her lips, the color of Molly Ringwald's from *Pretty in Pink*. Kiss imprints make parentheses on the tan Marlboro Red filter.

But the flicker quickly fades. She seems distracted and uninterested. She reverts to talking about some buff dude named Billy and what kind of Chevy truck he drives and where they go off-roading and other acceptable Oklahoma chatter. I wonder what happened to that feminist shit-talking bitch I once knew?

Walking over to the hose attached to her dad's mobile home, she fills up water balloons to chuck at some kids who live down the street. And that's that.

As fast as it starts, it stops.

***

I loved and still love *Dream a Little Dream 2*, for reasons that are simple. It's sexy (it's a late-night HBO movie, after all). It's about fierce and brilliant women who don't allow men to dominate them. It stars the Two Coreys (I really miss Corey H., who died too soon). Mostly I love it because it's not that serious. I needed and still need movies like that.

Aside from the creepy nonconsensual factors of mind control, the overly complicated plot is rad. As a concept, sunglasses that make people do what you want them to do is really cool. What teen doesn't want that? What would YOU have willed with magical, sexy shades at the age of twelve?

This comfort sequel reminds audiences that power in the wrong hands can be destructive. It also reminds viewers of the power of love to overcome negative forces. *DALD2* is about willing our desires into consciousness and existence. At the same time, the story showed me that some things are just not meant to be.

As I write this as an adult, I think about Deena and wonder where she is now. Is she married to Billy and struggling to make ends meet? Is she a feminist activist? Is she the CEO of a big company in San Francisco? Over the years, I've googled her and looked for her on social media, but I can't find anything. Guess I'll never know.

I wonder if she remembers our sleepovers, our preteen sexcapades, our tipsy dance-offs. I wonder if she remembers our games of M*A*S*H where I often ended up living in a shack, working as a surgeon, and married to Devon Sawa with seven kids. I wonder if she remembers that hillbilly hot tub on a crisp moonlit night with a game of truth or dare and a six-pack of Bud Light. I wonder if she remembers me at all.

Ghostbusters II

It's 1991, and I'm nine years old. Mom takes me across town to my aunt and uncles' house to watch *Ghostbusters II* (*GII*) on VHS. I'm already super-jealous of my cousins, and I haven't even stepped in the door. They have both seen *GII*, and I haven't. Plus Bryan (my cousin who is a year older than I am) has the coolest *Ghostbusters* toys: a Proton Pack and a Ghost Trap. He can put on his very own pack, zap ghouls, and then contain them safely in the trap before they cause more destruction. How cross-the-streams rad is that?

When I ask to try on his pack to take over ghostbusting duties for the afternoon, he is generous and patient and shows me what button is for what and encourages use of a PKE meter to find said ghost before busting. I instantly LOVE it. I suddenly transform into Venkman (Bill Murray), saying, "Come in, Ray." I turn into a badass, taking no Slimer prisoners in the Sedgewick Hotel.

I catch Slimer while yelling "Don't cross the streams" to my cousins, who become my ghostbusting sidekicks. I ask them all about *GII*. They love it and say I will too. I'm excited but a little nervous watching it for the first time, as the first film truly scared me. But I soon learn it's all pretty PG-ish fun. It's actually really hilarious, and we laugh out loud, especially over Janosz (Peter MacNichol). Bryan does a great impression of him in an accent that is possibly Hungarian

The Ghostbusters are intrigued by the psychoactive pink slime.
(Photo courtesy of Columbia Pictures)

but definitely some kind of Eastern European, which makes us laugh more.

GII doesn't take itself too seriously. The pink slime plot is ridiculous and kind of beautiful. The story is simple and a bit cheesy. And it knows it is. That's why it works. It is my kind of comfort sequel. Of course I want to rent it to watch again, but more importantly, I need pink slime in my life. If you know *GII*, you know why pink slime is important.

"Mom, can we stop at Toys"R"Us on the way home? I need to get some pink Gak." "Some what, sweetie?" "Don't worry about it; just swing by there and I will handle it." I figure Nickelodeon Gak will make a perfect pink slime alternative and won't be so messy.

So with pink Gak in hand, back at the small, single-family home Mom is renting, I continue living inside the *Ghostbusters* world. I throw on a short red wig I have from a dance costume and a pair of lensless black cat-eye glasses to transform into Janine (aka Annie Potts: the fiery, sardonic *Ghostbusters* secretary). Booking ghostbusting appointments is an important job, which obviously falls to my sassy little theatrical self. I sit in a makeshift office desk on the back patio and take fake emergency ghost calls. I pick up a beige rotary phone, which of course is not plugged in, and twirl the curlycue cord in my fingers.

I hold the receiver between my chin and shoulder while learning that New York City is in peril. I jot down notes in a legal pad. Hubba Bubba pink gum hangs from my mouth, and I loudly project my lines in an exaggerated New York accent. "Ghostbusters, what do you want?" "Okay, and how big was this ghost exactly?" "Sir, can you please calm down?" "Ma'am, I need you to tell me on what street you first saw the ghost."

I use my pink Gak as a slime prop, imagining it's seeping through the firehouse and onto my desk. I dramatically slam down the phone receiver, push a huge fake red button on the picnic table, and yell, "WE GOT ONE!" (BTW, I really nail this line just like Annie Potts in the movie, but no big deal.)

"One what?" Mom replies, pushing the sliding glass door open to come outside and check on me.

"Mom, I'm Janine right now," I whisper, slightly agitated at the interruption.

"Okay, baby, but dinner's almost ready; see if you can wrap up soon."

I look down to see that my Gak had fallen on the dirty concrete when I slammed the phone receiver down, and my tape-dispenser bubble gum quickly follows.

Two pink slimy, stretchy substances lie next to each other on the ground. I'm defeated. I knew my rendition of *GII* would fall apart without a Ghost Trap or Proton Pack. Oh well. I pick up my pebbled, indented, dirty Gak, now adorned with a feather and possibly bird poop imprinted into its tackiness. I consider what to do with it, then decide to just put it back in its case for later.

"Your Love Keeps Lifting Me Higher" Ghostbusters II Recap

There are so many reasons to love the Ghostbusters. I have loved seeing these supernatural crime fighters "cleaning up the town" again and again, from the original *Ghostbusters* in 1984 to 2024's *Ghostbusters: Frozen Empire*. What's better than seeing the good guys prevail and be total doofuses while doing it? Their nerdy humanness is refreshing. They are just like me, but you know, fighting ghosts for a living.

GII comes out at a very specific moment in time. It's 1989. New

York is a pressure cooker. People are mean as hell. Reaganomics is alive and well. It's bleak out there. Audiences are looking for a reminder that humans can in fact be good and loving people. *GII* has that simple message. Be kind to each other. Kindness is what matters most.

And it all starts with pink slime.

A marble mix of rosy and watermelon pink psychomagnatheric ectoplasm (try to say that three times fast) oozes through a crack in a Manhattan sidewalk. Flashing across the screen: "5 Years Later," indicating it's been this long since the original film's release. Dana (Sigourney Weaver) pushes her baby carriage down a Manhattan street. Every New Yorker she passes on her way home is over-the-top yelling and exaggeratedly rude. Even her building's doorman is peeved at life, and he barely agrees to hold her groceries while she searches for her apartment keys.

Another day of sorrow and irritation in the Big Apple soon becomes eerie and paranormal. With no obvious explanation, Dana's baby son, Oscar, begins to inch away from her, slowly, then a little faster, then—*bam!*—his baby carriage takes off into oncoming traffic! After he is back safe and sound in her arms, she goes to Egon (Harold Ramis) to procure his help in determining what might be going on.

Dana finds Egon heading an ethically questionable research study on human subjects. He's looking at the effects of the environment on emotion and discovers that temperature and other environmental stressors can in fact create emotional distress in people. So when it's the heat of summer and I'm hangry and I'm fighting with my partner, I'm experiencing emotional distress? Okay, yep, that makes sense.

Egon reunites with Peter (Bill Murray), Ray (Dan Aykroyd), and finally Winston (Ernie Hudson) to detective their way back into ghostbusting and to solve the case of the baby carriage mishap. They discover pink slime underground that they trace to Dana's place of employment, the Manhattan Museum of Art. A creepy-ass painting of Vigo the Carpathian (Wilhelm von Homburg) comes to life and puts a spell on Dr. Janosz Poha (Peter MacNicol). Sidebar interesting fact about von Homburg: in real life, he was a boxer and drug dealer and the son of a Nazi. Oh—and a total asshole apparently. Sounds like a case of perfect casting.

Dana calls Vigo a "lunatic and a genocidal madman." In the 1500s and 1600s he was known as Vigo the "cruel, the torturer, the despised, and the unholy" and was murdered multiple times and in many ways. Yeah, he was a scary dude. According to Ray, before he died Vigo said, "Death is but a door; time is but a window. I'll be back." And the foreshadowing abounds. Another sidebar: Vigo's character is actually based on real-life scary dude Vlad the Impaler, the inspiration for Bram Stoker's *Dracula*. Cool, right? But I digress.

The Ghostbusters discover that the pink slime running under the city is psychoreactive and responds to both negative and positive emotions. As Winston says, it "feeds on bad vibes," and there's nothing more bad vibey than New Yorkers' attitudes. So as expected, Vigo's reign of hellfire ensues, ghosts are set loose from the slime, and the city succumbs to the darkness. Turns out Egon's research on environment and emotion was spot-on.

Vigo plans for Janosz to kidnap Oscar (Dana's baby). Vigo wants to use Oscar as a vessel to come back to Earth for his evil reign. Super-weird idea. In a Wicked Witch, *Wizard of Oz* moment, Janosz flies in on a bicycle and basket, steals Oscar from a high-rise apartment building, and takes him to Vigo. In a plan to rescue Oscar, Dana and the ghostbusting foursome meet at the museum, which is now covered in a pink slime cloud of doom. We are set up for a Vigo vs. Ghostbusters showdown.

The only way to stop Vigo's return is to use the pink slime against him. Obviously. Pink slime must then be repurposed with "good vibes" so that the good guys can win. But how will the Ghostbusters convert a city of annoyed and irritated New Yorkers into a positive, loving, and caring energy force field? You guessed it: by spraying the Statue of Liberty with pink slime and blasting Jackie Wilson's "(Your Love Keeps Lifting Me) Higher & Higher" from atop her crown. It's the only logical way to do it.

In a nod to the Stay Puft Marshmallow Man in the first film, Lady Liberty, a beacon of pure love and joy, comes to life. She walks through the Hudson River, across midtown, and to the museum. And the plan works! Lady Liberty, with her Jackie Wilson soundtrack, overturns the shitty New Yorker way of being. The love among people grows;

everyone sings "Auld Lang Syne" and sways together. The pink cloud surrounding the museum dissipates. Love prevails.

Vigo's hope to be reborn through Oscar falls apart, and he gets sucked into the vortex of his painting. The art piece is replaced by a new oil work of the Ghostbusters, angelically dressed in togas, surrounding Oscar, who lies peacefully and safely in a baby manger. It's an over-the-top, tacky painting, and I love it.

Peace is restored in the world of the Ghostbusters. New York is as safe and sound as it can be. Well, at least it's free of unruly paranormal activity for now. I can't speak for the long-lasting effects of the positive attitudes of New Yorkers.

Transitional Objects

For me, as a kid growing up in a working-class family in Oklahoma in the eighties and nineties, TV and movies were babysitters—movies were, effectively, my caretakers while my single mom was working long days. I felt safe watching cartoons, sitcoms, musicals, comedies; they were predictable. I wanted to take the shows with me wherever I went, carry the characters in my arms, relive the magic and the adventure, take all the risks my beloved characters took while maintaining a sense of safety, of comfort.

At night I curled up with my Rainbow Brite plush doll, her red-yarn hair getting caught and frayed each time I attempted to brush it. Her silver-and-rainbow skirt the coolest, galactically hip suggestion of her superpower. She was strong and liberated the Sprites from the drab, black-and-white world of Shadows, making everything colorful again. If I could just hold her, I could be close to her and take in her world of color and wonder, I could be transported.

I had a Talkboy from *Home Alone*. I sneakily hid behind the living room couch and recorded my cousins, aunt, and mom talking. I was being a Kevin McAllister little shit. When they least expected it, I would play back their conversations in slow motion and then at high, chipmunk speed. We all laughed until we damn near peed our pants.

Then there were the My Little Ponies. These were the OG ones— way before Netflix made *Friendship Is Magic*. These were the Saturday-morning cartoon ponies that I loved so much. I had a My Little Pony lunchbox that held my very nutritious lunch—PB and J on Wonder bread, an apple, a Squeezit, a ziplock bagful of cheese balls, and the My Little Pony matching thermos that warmed my Campbell's chicken noodle soup. Gobstoppers topped off the lunch meal and I was set.

I owned maybe twenty My Little Ponies, many of them hand-me-downs with marker marks on them and other gross, sticky gobs matting the pony hair. They all fit in a carrying case that was made to look like a stable. I carried them around everywhere—to the store, to my friends' houses, to family gatherings, to dance class—my traveling suitcase of plastic ponies.

One day I made the bold choice to take them to school. The whole stable. Sadly, it didn't fit in my locker, and my mom had already left after dropping me off. So I was stuck carrying them all day and got strange looks from teachers and classmates.

I didn't care. The Ponies gave me the courage to make it through my school day. They gave me protection, joy, and distraction. These objects I could count on. They got me through boring teachers and mean kids in the hallway and being away from what I loved most. They connected me back to the show that made me feel safe.

These transitional objects were a lifeline. The concept of transitional objects comes from D. W. Winnicott, a therapist who worked with kids. He discovered that as kids reach milestones in their growth, they need a link between a parent or caretaker and the big, scary outside world. In this way, objects can help children soothe the anxiety they experience when they are separated from their parents.

So transitional objects like blankets or pacifiers or My Little Ponies symbolically replace the primary caretaker and provide a link between the caretaker and the outside world. I felt safe at home with my mom and my Ponies on the screen, so if they can leap off the screen into my portable stable, lunchbox, and thermos, I can take that sense of comfort with me wherever I am. If I can play with my dolls, Talkboy, and Colorforms and sleep in my Strawberry Shortcake nightgown, the world of pop culture objects can travel with me and help protect me as I venture out. These objects are a bridge between fantasy and reality.

As an adult, I have plenty of transitional objects. I have my own version of My Little Ponies in a stable that connects me to the comfort of the world of sequels. Things like my Falkor doll from *NeverEnding Story* and my Gizmo lunchbox from *Gremlins 2*, my disgusting pink Gak that I STILL have to this day from my childhood in an homage to *GII*, all make me feel connected to the movies I love, no matter where I am. They soothe my nervous system.

Fans of shows or movies might collect objects, action figures, artwork, toys, bobbleheads, and games and engage in an online world with other collectors to share stories and finds. Bryan Johnson and Peter Mosen are living examples artists and fans who immerse themselves in the *Ghostbusters* world. They know more about the franchise than I could ever imagine and have shared their stories, their obsessions, and their transitional objects with me in this book. The next two chapters are interviews with them, and they share the objects that have kept them emotionally anchored to *Ghostbusters* for years and likely will continue to do so for many years to come.

Think back to when you were a kid.

What were some of your transitional objects?
What are some of your transitional objects now?
How do they make you feel safe?
How do they bring you joy?

"You the weird guy that buys strange old things?"

It's 2024. I'm forty-one years old. I'm in Pensacola, Florida, visiting Mom for a few weeks. Recently retired, Mom is balancing finding her new identity after fifty years of teaching and dealing with her short-term memory loss. She's becoming more and more, with each passing day, an unusual blend of Southern, Golden Girl sass tinged with the ditzy forgetfulness of, say, Dory in *Finding Nemo*. I now have a fully remote job as a therapist and professor, so I spend as much time with her in Pensacola as I can.

It's a northern Florida chilly March day, and the humidity is hibernating. *Ghostbusters: Frozen Empire* has just opened in movie theaters, and I can't wait. We buy our tickets in advance and get there thirty minutes early to get good seats. I'm stressed we will be in the very front, necks craning to see. But we are the first ones there and get perfect seats in the center. I'm expecting tons of kids and preteen boys, loud adult fans, and overall opening-weekend blockbuster chaos. Turns out only about ten more people trickle in, and the theater is quiet overall except for me. I can't contain myself.

I add about twenty extra pumps of artificial AMC butter to the small popcorn we share, and the butter grease seeps through the bottom of the bag. While Mom is entering a new life stage that will likely be years of cognitive decline, some things, like my love of chemically engineered "butter flavor" at movie theaters, never change. What also hasn't changed is my love of going to the movies, my love of watching movies with Mom, and my love of movie sequels, especially when it comes to *Ghostbusters*.

I'm not sure how Mom will handle what I assume will be the loudness of the movie, the grossness of the ghouls, and the fastness of the plot. But she is a champ, laughing and washing down peanut M&M's with sips of her Coke Zero. She loves *Frozen Empire* as much as I do, especially seeing Aykroyd, Hudson, and Murray all back together again (Ramis passed in 2014). I'm that person in the theater who literally LOLs and pumps my fists in the air in excitement, yelling "Yes, get it!" and other obnoxious interjections during pivotal moments. I love watching Phoebe in the gunner seat in the Ectomobile, and the actual Ghost Trap, the replica toy I always wanted, opening up to catch unruly aberrations. I'm actually on the edge of my seat for the last forty-five minutes of the film. I can't help it.

I won't give away the plot because you should see it (and also I'm not trying to ice out *GII*, which this chapter is really a love letter about), but *Frozen Empire* is a sequel after my own heart. There's a scene in which Nadeem (Kumail Nanjiani) enters Ray's Occult Books, unveils a box with his dead grandmothers' relics, and asks, "You the weird guy that buys strange old things?" Ray affirms that he is in fact that guy, and while he is not interested in most of Nadeem's items, one particular artifact does get Ray's attention: an ancient brass orb covered in archaic script.

While the audience is as confused as Ray and Nadeem about this orb, my guess is that it holds keys to unlock mysteries that may or may not be destructive. We soon find that this powerful object holds supernatural history within and will soon be an integral part of the story. A "strange old thing," it connects one dimension to another and comes back for important reasons, none of which I will spoil here.

Another object in the movie, a match, becomes an emotionally charged anchor for another character, keeping her tethered to a certain world. She holds on to the match, an object representative of her trauma, in a repeated pattern, striking it over and over, trying to heal what has not been emotionally resolved. While serving different character and plot needs, the two objects are links between worlds, ties that open and then close intergenerational and transpersonal portals, objects of transitional importance.

Mom and I wait out the epic end credits of the film. The only ones still in the theater, we smile and say "aww" in sync out loud at the mini Stay Puft postcredits scene. I want to see *Frozen Empire* again as soon as possible. In the meantime, I want to take the movie with me. I want something tangible to hold, to look at, like I did with the pink Gak years before; I want something to help me always remember seeing this film with Mom. I'm aware that our time going to movies and being able to really talk about them afterward might be limited. This feels important to me.

We head to the lobby, where something strange catches my attention. Right by the register, next to four bored teen AMC employees, is a bright purple cone on top of what I can tell is a pretty awesome-looking Ghost Trap replica.

"Mom, I know I'm forty-one, and this is ridiculous, but I think I kinda need that Ghost Trap. I recognize it's a toy, but it's calling to me."

There's no one in the concession line, and I look around to see if anyone is coming in the front doors racing to get Sour Patch Kids and pretzels.

"Sweetie, let me buy that for you. I want you to have a toy, and I never get to treat you to anything because you live so far away."

"Really, Momma?"

I can't help wondering if this request is excessive on my part—but then it occurs to me that maybe, just maybe, it's okay to accept this

Climbing up to the top of the Statue of Liberty makes sense to me.
(Photo courtesy of Columbia Pictures)

gift from her. I can tell it would make her as happy to get it for me as it would for me to have it.

Or I'm kidding myself and trying to justify accepting a film franchise toy as a keepsake at this age. Either way, I'm in. I soon learn that the purple cone on top is meant to hold popcorn, as the teen tries to give us a large popcorn that comes with the purchase. We don't need it; we are full from the heart attack-level fake butter I added to the popcorn we got before the film.

The acne-faced AMC teen with a Southern drawl hands the Ghost Trap toy over with an apathetic "Here you go. Y'all take care," and my eyes widen with childlike wonder as I hold it in my hand. It feels like old times with my cousins, only this time I don't have to play with Bryan's toy and wish that it were mine. This time (yes, at age forty-one), I have my very own.

On the way home from the movie, we call Bryan (who is still a *Ghostbusters* superfan) to debrief, and he shares all kind of fun *Frozen Empire* BTS facts and prop intel. I remind Mom that she saw *GII* in theaters with Bryan when it came out in 1989 and tell her about the pink slime and the Statue of Liberty. She laughs, remembering how absurd the plot was and how she thought the movie was as funny and lighthearted as we did. And still do.

When Mom and I get back to her apartment, I decide to rewatch *GII*, and while Mom has had enough Ghostbusters for one day, she's glad that I have my new toy and that we had this time together. I play with the Trap while *GII* starts, the pink slime oozing underground, making the New Yorkers angrier than ever—all the while knowing the anger will soon morph into kindness.

I decide then and there that the AMC Ghost Trap, my new transitional object, will be a centerpiece at my book release party for *Comfort Sequels*. Yep, I have no shame in my Ghostbusters toy game. It lights up and rolls around and everything. Seriously, it's awesome. I embrace my inner kid, who adores having objects that link me to the things I love. I become Venkman and catch a ghoul that I imagine has been haunting Mom's seashell-themed guest bathroom for years. Yes, it's over the top; yes, it's superfun; yes, it makes me smile.

And yes, just as satisfying as it was thirty years ago.

Story Is Everything:
An Interview with Prop
Designer Bryan Johnson

In addition to being a Ghostbuster enthusiast, Bryan Johnson is a well-known artist and award-winning props and special effects designer, artisan, and technician for theater, opera, film, and television. He was the lead props and special effects technician with Blue Man Group-Las Vegas, where he fabricated, maintained, and operated the long-running hit show and was a puppeteer for it as well. Bryan has taught prop design at the university level, and no joke, his list of professional credits could fill this whole chapter.

I'm proud to say he is also my cousin.

Being so close in age (he's a year older than I am), we played all the time growing up. He introduced me to David Copperfield and would perform magic shows for the whole family. I was always impressed with his paintings and charcoal drawings and his incredible toy collection, including Ghostbusters-themed toys we chat about in the interview that follows.

Fast-forward and years and geography pull us apart, but we stay social media connected. After leaving Blue Man Group, he moved back to Tulsa, where he has designed and built twenty operas and now designs and illustrates gorgeous movie posters. Seriously, his *Die Hard* poster is the most creative storytelling, and his *Dahmer—Monster: The Jeffrey Dahmer Story* poster will haunt your dreams. Check them out on bryanjohnsoncreative.com.

I was in Tulsa for a visit last year. He invited me over to his house. I had no idea what I was walking into. A perfect rendition of the Audrey II plant from *Little Shop of Horrors* greeted me in his foyer. I soon found out that he had spent years filling a room in his house with the most incredible prop replicas you can imagine.

From the Christmas tape from *Die Hard* that made me smile to a life-size Cryptkeeper from *Tales of the Crypt* that made my skin crawl, his collection is outstanding. I looked over at Gizmo from *Gremlins* and felt giddy. I saw an Auryn and felt transported back to watching *NeverEnding Story II: The Next Chapter* on repeat as a kid.

Each piece was carefully displayed in glass cases, and the lighting was perfect. It was warm and inviting, nothing at all like a sterile museum. You want to hang out for hours and never leave. He took the time to answer all my questions and told me stories of where all of the pieces came from, how he found them, and how he restores and enhances them. Mad props, literally.

The MOST incredible part of his collection is his Ghostbusters corner. It's clear he's spent countless hours collecting, crafting, and curating it. He has a Terror Dog cast from the original mold and a life-size Slimer replica made of fiberglass and metal. I couldn't stop looking at it; Slimer IRL is so damn cute.

I felt goosebumps seeing Billy Bryan's actual white marshmallow gloves from his Stay Puft latex suit. I wanted to reach right in the case and grab the P.K.E. meter, slide on the pair of Paragoggles, and hoist the proton pack directly onto my back and just start ghostbusting right then and there.

Then I saw something in his Ghostbuster corner that I couldn't quite place. I asked him about it, and he looked at me and asked if I've seen *Ghostbusters: Afterlife*.

"No! I planned on it. Then COVID happened, and I didn't know if it was gonna be released in theaters after that. Did it come out already?"

"Yep." He answered with a smile.

"And it's awesome," he continued.

"I won't tell you what these props are until you see them in the film, because I don't want to give anything away."

So after my three-plus-hour tour, he was kind enough to invite me over the next day to watch *Ghostbusters: Afterlife* on his sixty-five-inch 4K TV in his living room. With his sound system and huge screen, it was like I was in the movies. He was not exaggerating. The movie is awesome. I was blown away.

Filled with nostalgic Easter eggs and musical homages to the first film, *Ghostbusters: Afterlife* is the extremely well-crafted story of a wacky scientist passing on his gifts to his granddaughter. It quickly became another comfort sequel. Bryan, of course, knows behind-the-scenes fun facts and was kind enough to share details with me. I cried like a baby at the end of it. As for the props I didn't know about before? I'll let *him* tell you about those.

In our interview, he shares his love of the Ghostbusters movies and what they mean to him. We reminisce about Ghostbusters toys from childhood, and I learn that he first saw *GII* with my mom when it came out in theaters. I just love that. We chat about props and his process for finding, designing, and creating replicas. He shares his thoughts on how props can act as transitional objects, linking us from the safety and containment of a movie to the outside world. I'm just in awe of his artistic brain, and soon you will be too.

If we learned anything from *GII*, it's that we know our environment does in fact affect our mood. Where we live, who's around us, the items with which we surround ourselves—all these impact our emotions and well-being. The time Bryan spent with me cracking jokes and sharing the intricacies of his art was pure Pink Slime bliss.

Each prop in Bryan's collection is a story, a memory, an object that brings this franchise to life. "Detail tells the story, and story is everything," he says to me. Bryan has made his home a place filled with stories that he loves to share with others. I'm so lucky to have his stories in this chapter.

Here's the magic of Bryan Johnson:

Emily Marinelli: Why do you love the Ghostbusters?

Bryan Johnson: They were identifiable, relatable saviors. Superheroes have a back story about where they're from, a different planet, or they were bit by a spider or they were just rich millionaires, like Batman. But Ghostbusters were scientists. They brought an intellectual side of things with science and math. Basically, they were nerds. The whole concept of their flight suits and all their equipment, they were essentially plumbers and exterminators, blue-collar service workers that happened to save New York. They showed that anybody could save New York. You didn't have to have powers to do it.

Emily: Who was your favorite Ghostbuster growing up?

Bryan: It's probably Peter (Bill Murray), because he's the mouth. Although of the action figure line, the only one I ever owned was Winston (Ernie Hudson). He's the everyman. Then Egon (Harold Ramis) brought the technology in. The spirit of the Ghostbusters is Ray (Dan Aykroyd), with his family history with the farmhouse up in Canada. He's the heart of the story.

Emily: Growing up, you had a Ghost Trap that I was jealous of. Tell me about that.

Bryan: It was made by Kenner. It wasn't from the movie. It was from *The Real Ghostbusters*, the animated series. With the trap, the only thing that opened the doors was stomping on the pedal. That sent air through that little hose that popped open like a party blower, and that was the whole mechanism. They were blue, plastic, but it was the closest thing you could get to "Oh my gosh, I'm a Ghostbuster."

Also, I remember my dad went out in the garage and actually built me a proton pack. It was basically a plastic toolbox. He just opened it and just started finding stuff to make it. The hose coming off the pack to the wand was a wooden dowel rod wrapped in duct tape, and it was tied to a piece of yellow nylon rope from a tetherball pole. He just tied it to the backpack, and I thought it was the coolest thing. I felt like I had a real proton pack. I wish I still had it. Later I got the proton pack from Kenner. I saved up for that. As a kid I thought, "Oh, I don't need that other one anymore." But now I would almost display the one my dad made more than I would display the best screen-accurate prop.

Emily: That's so innovative and sweet of him, knowing how much you loved them.

Bryan: Do you remember the felt things that Grandma used to make us?

Emily: Oh my goodness, yes!

Bryan: She had a felt board and would trace and then cut felt characters out and display them on the board. I had a Ghostbusters bedsheet set, and she took Polaroids of the images and basically copied all the characters off the bedsheets and cut them out of felt pieces. When I hung up the blank felt piece, I could stick the Ghostbusters on there to make a scene out of them.

Emily: What do you love about *GII*?

Bryan: I love *GII*. When it came out, I was probably seven. I saw it with your mom. Then I took my dad to see it again in the theater.

I remember sitting and watching the Preview Channel TV, where the cable schedule would scroll constantly. A trailer tape would be on loop at the top of the screen, and I would sit there because every hour, on the hour, they would play the commercial for *GII*. I would just watch the Preview Channel in hopes that I would get to see it because I loved it so much in the theater.

When Janosz says "So why are you came?"—that might be my favorite part of the movie, actually, or when he talks with Dana and you can start to see what kind of a creeper he is. She's got glasses on and she's restoring the painting, and he's messing with her hair, and he just picks off a little white, fuzzy thing. What's amazing is that a props person had to come in and set that every take.

Statue of Liberty Walkman from
Bryan's collection
(Photo courtesy of Bryan Johnson)

Emily: Wow! That's just something I wouldn't think about. So cool. Do you have any *GII*-specific props?

Bryan: I have the Walkman that they play in the Statue of Liberty. I would like to build a Slime Blower to hang on the wall, but they're enormous. I just don't know if I can do it. I had a Slime Blower toy when I was a kid. I begged and begged for it. The day I got it, I remember it was so hot out. My dad showed up after working a whole day, and he had gone to Toys"R"Us to pick it up. He came in with this big box with the Slime Blower in it. His work dress shirt and tie were drenched in sweat. I even remember how hot the box was. It was a gun that was spring-loaded. I mean it was extremely phallic. You should Google it right now.

Emily: [I Google it.]I'm looking at it now! [Laughing.] Oh no!

Bryan: I mean, it's pink. If it buzzed, it'd be from a full-on different toy store, let me tell you.

Emily: [Laughing.] That's the slime? This plastic pink phallic thing?

Bryan: So you push down into the wand, and when you hit the button, that pink phallic thing just pops out. I mean, they wanted children to use this thing and scream "Bustin' makes me feel good" at the same time.

Emily: [Dying of laughter.] Bryan, stop, you're killing me!

Bryan: All that stuff is based on real life, things that they repurpose, that Egon rewired. One of the things I love to do is figure out what model that was and then try to replicate it visually in a way that looks like it's from the movie.

In the first movie, in the scene at the hotel, they all have walkie-talkies. That's the only time they ever wear those radios.

In *GII*, they are replaced with a yellow box called a Lifeguard. It's made for firefighters, where basically if you collapse and are still for a length of time, it starts to send out an alarm so your firefighter friends can come rescue you. There again they're taking real-life search-and-rescue items because they're blue-collar workers. I have one, and mine is actually from a retired actual firehouse. On the back, it actually has the stamp "property of," and it has real smoke stains on it.

I've almost bought the toaster, but then I was like, *It's just gonna sit there as a toaster.* Some fans out there have rigged it to dance and jump around. It's air powered, and the cord is an air hose just coming out the end.

Someone's operating it, pushing air into it to make it go up and down. And that's what is so magical about it. It's not CGI. An actual person is operating it and making it go. I love that.

Not that CGI artists aren't doing amazing work, but it was just completely different.

Emily: How did you start prop, collecting, and recreating?

Bryan: Being a magician. I got into magic because of storytelling. I had this soul-searching moment a year and a half ago when I started making a bunch of life changes.

I was trying to rediscover my purpose. I started to ask, *What is it? Why am I so attracted to prop making and to the right piece of music, to art in general, and now to posters.*

It's the storytelling aspect of it. As someone that has tattoos all over your body, you get it. You're not just picking them because you're bored. They mean something—not only the story of the tattoo, but there's a story of when you got that tattoo. It's going to be a story that changes because now having that tattoo has redefined your story moving forward.

For me, props are that. They're tangible. As a prop designer working in theater and entertainment, I found that an actor just wants to be seen at the end of the day. They don't really care what the lighting looks like on them as long as it's on them. They don't really care how they sound as long as they're heard. But the costume people and props people, we are handing them something, and it's for them. And there is a connection.

In operas, specifically, they're given rehearsal props, a stand-in prop for the real one. In footage of rehearsals, you can see they kind of believe it. But when you hand them the real thing, they transform. The audience may not see the sword or pistol that is scratched and rusted a certain way, but the performer does. If the performer believes it, then the audience believes it. So for me, that's my draw to props. The storytelling.

Emily: Ghostbusters fans collect action figures, artwork, toys, games, and engage in an online world of other collectors to share stories and finds. Curious to hear your thoughts around *Ghostbusters* props as potential transitional objects between the parental comfort of the film franchise and the real world?

Bryan: I always imagined what it would be like to hold the actual wand or roll an actual Ghost Trap, not the cheap plastic toys. I never got that opportunity as a kid. So now, as an adult, to actually have things that are from original movie molds or scans, there's a lineage to them. You hold it and imagine, *This is what it feels like on set.* It's not even about wanting to bust my own ghosts. It's more about what it feels like to be part of the Ghostbuster experience. Not so much *I'm a Ghostbuster,* but more, *Oh, this is what Bill Murray experienced.* That's the story I'm drawn to.

You're talking about the psychology of reliving a moment, reliving a memory, and how it made them feel. It's that draw of people wanting to go back. That's why *Ghostbusters: Afterlife* was so important and so amazing. Every single person on that set was a fan.

In fact, when they filmed in Alberta, they had Alberta Ghostbuster fans come in. Imagine that thirty or thirty-five years after the movie was out, to be a fan of such a franchise, a kid who saw the movie and wanted to be a Ghostbuster, who owned the plastic proton pack and played the song over and over again, now as an adult who is part of a group that gets dressed up and goes in and fundraises for the community and spreads the same joy that you found. All of the sudden you get called to say, "Hey, we want you all to come in as consultants because you're local, and you know the lore as much as we do."

That's why in *Ghostbusters: Afterlife*, you can feel the magic. You can hear it in the music. You can see it in the shots. You can tell that they got all the new cast on board, and they actually believe in it.

Emily: Tell me about your *Ghostbusters: Afterlife* props and how you made them.

Bryan: In the Ectomobile, there's a box that holds the wand for the gunner seat that swings out. In the first movie they showed a sort of quick connect attachment to the handle of the wand, and the hose would come up and lock into something and latch in. In the other movies, it was all one piece, the hose, the wand, the pack; all of it was one thing. I think it made sense as they grew and Egon designed equipment to be serviceable.

To service it, you don't want to take the whole thing apart. You just want to take off the piece that broke and replace it. There was a spare wand that lived in that box next to the gunner seat. You can see it in one scene for maybe one second. On the top it says "Neutronawand" on it.

Just before that, Hasbro came out with a replica wand, and I wanted it. It was made from 3D scans of the original wand, so it's literally exactly a one-to-one replica. I completely repainted and weathered it as if it was used. I wasn't making scratches exactly like in the movie. It was more *How would this be used if it was mine?* So I made it my own.

I watched a video on YouTube about it, and they interviewed Ben Eadie, a member of the *Ghostbusters: Afterlife* props team. They had the screen-use prop next to their replica to show how close they were. They styled the packaging to look like that box, and they had the screen-use box there as well. I didn't even see the movie yet and didn't know how this box was being used. But I thought, *I want to build that box.* There is so much story in that box, almost as much as there is in the wand.

Again, I don't know how it's being used. I don't know how prominent it is, but I knew there might be a chance it's in the movie a lot. I replicated the box as a display stand to set the wand on. Because I'm replicating it from that screen-use piece, every bit of rust is exactly where it was in the film. I needed to make a stencil for the top, and that font I couldn't find anywhere. So I took a screenshot from the YouTube video and scaled it up, made a stencil out of it.

What's cool is I then connected with the prop master Ben Eadie from *Afterlife*, and he asked me how I got it off the set. I'm like, "What do you mean?" He was like, "Wait, wait a second. You made that? I thought you got that from an auction from the set. That looks exactly like what we had."

Emily: Wow, that's an incredible compliment.

Bryan: I also have the coin from the 1964 World's Fair in New York at Flushing Meadows. I actually have two of them. It's the postcredit scene when Egon goes off to fight Stay-Puft. Janine wanted him to have it for good luck, and Egon goes, "I don't know if I should take it. We may not be coming back," and Janine says, "Don't worry. I've got another one at home." It's such great, *SNL* writing.

The coin has a globe on it, and the only way you know is that last scene, when she's sitting there with Winston in his office. I took a photo of it on my 4K television to try to find it. Once I found the date details, I could find it. And when she says that line about having another one at home, I'm like, *Well, I need hers too.* I had to have the set. They're like wedding bands.

Emily: What's your process for finding objects? What happens for you when you're looking?

Bryan: It's the coolest treasure hunt. In the first movie, when Venkman is in Dana's apartment, he pumps the stick with the little bulb to look for ghosts. That item is actually equipment used to detect gas leaks in real life. They just had a props table and all these props lined up, and they just said, "Pick out which one is funnier," and that's how that prop was selected.

They have random scientific equipment. So then I basically become curious about what it was probably used for. Then, honestly, eBay is huge. I can figure out the years, and then I can start figuring out what it was used for. That's a ton of fun to figure out.

Just the radios alone from that Sedgewick hotel scene: it's actually a Motorola MT500 radio. Now, Emily, there are so many things in this life that I just don't know and I can't remember. I can't remember how to do CPR, but I will remember the Motorola MT500. It's something that will stick with me forever [laughing]

Emily: [Laughing.] You have your priorities straight.

Bryan: They sold that same model in a long body and a short body. They had long antennas and stubby antennas and then three switches, three button tops, and two buttons, then different channels depending on what you wanted. That iconic scene when there's a close-up of Bill Murray and you just see the radio come up and he says, "Come in, Ray." I can do that now.

Emily: What's it like to have these objects in that amazing room in your house?

Bryan: The room has energy. It's the stuff in it, and it's the whole story. If I move out of my house, the room in my house is just another bedroom to somebody else. But surrounded by that stuff, you go in there, there's an energy about it.

I'm reminded almost overwhelmingly of the amount of stories. I remember that scene that made me cry or that made me laugh hysterically. I wanted to have that. That's what it's like to own them.

What I love is seeing people go in there for the first time. I've spent four hours there with somebody before. I've watched a grown individual turn into a kid. It's really something. It's the same thing as being a magician. It's a sense of wonder again. They're discovering it like I discovered it or rediscovered it. And what's really great is when they're like, "Wait a second, I know what movie that's from!"

Or they will ask what movie it's from, and I won't tell them. I'll have them explore it and figure it out, and then it clicks. All of the sudden they say, "Oh my gosh, yeah." All of the sudden, that entire story comes back for them. With Ghostbusters in particular, I have so much in there, it's really the feature of that room. I think if I were to sell that entire room, the Ghostbusters stuff wouldn't go anywhere.

Emily: Is prop creating and collecting a magical art form?

Bryan: Well, especially with props you're a prop designer and a props artisan. You're creating something that may not exist. So, what's a proton pack? Someone had to figure that out. That's a magic trick. There's a "ta-da" moment, and as a props designer, I loved to go into a production meeting and sit down with the director and figure it all out.

I did a production of *Cabaret*, and every table needed an old candlestick telephone. I was young, and I didn't know what I was doing yet, so I went to eBay thinking that's where old phones would be. I saw that they were $500 apiece. I had to do the entire show on a small budget. So I went on Amazon and found replica phones, but they were $120 a piece. I needed ten of them, and it was too expensive.

I thought, *How do I do this?* So I just broke it down into shapes. I was like, *Well, that looks like a pipe, and that base could be made out of wood, and the little cup that you would talk into looks like a condiment cup you would get ranch or ketchup in.*

I built a mock-up out of a circular piece of wood attached to a triangular piece of wood with a PVC [polyvinyl chloride] pipe coming down into a round piece of wood. I used rope and an actual wooden candlestick from the craft store, and I put a little eye bolt through it. I put a teacup hook on the back of the thing so you could hang it up. I did it in two days and went back into the production meeting the following week. The director said, "Did you figure out the phone thing?" I brought it out of the case and said, "Like this?" and she was so happy and said, "Yes!" I said, "These are eight dollars apiece." The look of the room was pure amazement.

It's the equivalent of a magic trick. There's a "ta-da" moment in them, and that's the same with poster illustration. These poster reveals are so exciting for me. No one sees the process until I want them to. I don't let them in on the secret, and all of the sudden it's just "ta-da." Not everyone is amazed, but those that are, it's really powerful to see.

Emily: I feel that way every time I look at your poster art now, and when I walked into the room in your house I felt like a kid. I couldn't believe it. My eyes first gravitated towards the Slimer, and then I slowed myself down because I got too excited. I wanted to stop and take everything in one thing at a time. It was like a perpetual feeling of joy upon joy upon joy upon joy, like it just kept building. I don't even know anything about props, and I was just asking you questions. And you were telling me stories.

Bryan: The prop sparks the memory. The biggest thing about storytelling is the series of memories, and that's what a prop triggers. For me, it's not about the prop; it's just about the memory. I think the same way about the movie. It's not about *Ghostbusters*; it's about the memory I have of *Ghostbusters*.

In *Willy Wonka & the Chocolate Factory*, they wouldn't let the kids see the chocolate factory until the door opened. They didn't want any acting; it had to be genuine. So they captured them walking in as kids actually seeing a chocolate factory for the first time. For me, the room in my house is exactly that.

Emily: What other art pieces are you working on?

Bryan: Right now I have three gallery releases. Several pieces are being released in a book on Ultraman, a Japanese sci-fi superhero from the sixties. And then I have several other really fun projects, but I can't talk about them yet.

Emily: This was so wonderful. It was exactly what I was hoping for, all these connections, all the things we talked about, how everything is interrelated. Your voice is exactly what was needed in this chapter, I'm so glad to be able to chat with you.

Bryan: Thank you for letting me share it.

Slimer in Bryan's magical prop room.
(Photo courtesy of Bryan Johnson)

Get Ready to Be Slimed:
An Interview with
Ghostbusters II Cast Member
Peter Mosen

It's 1984. *Ghostbusters* movie posters are everywhere. On them, Harold Ramis, Bill Murray, and Dan Aykroyd stare up into the sky with their Neutrona Wands aimed high, proton packs charged and ready. Notably, Ernie Hudson, the fourth Ghostbuster in the film, is missing from the shot. The iconic symbol of the white ghost with a red circle and line through it is behind them. "They're here to save the world," the tagline reads. Soon audiences will know how these nerdy, ordinary men will become extraordinary heroes.

Peter Mosen saw this movie poster and knew he was a "Ghosthead" before it was even a thing. From the poster reference, he created his own rendition of the ghost-fighting uniform. The film had not even come out yet! But he nailed it. He won a convention costume contest and tickets to the opening-night screening of the film. His life was forever changed.

Since then, Peter has devoted his life to the world of Ghostbusters. He makes Ectomobiles and is featured in the documentaries *Ghostheads* (2016) and *Too Hot to Handle: Remembering Ghostbusters II* (2024). He was hired by Columbia Pictures to travel around the country and perform as the official Ghostbuster at themed kids parties. How cool is that? In fact, when Winston and Ray dance at a kid's birthday party in *Ghostbusters II*, they modeled what they did after Peter. As the official promotional Ghostbuster, Peter has, over the years, attended fan conventions, led reenactments at places like Knott's Berry Farm, and made appearances at children's hospitals.

When *Ghostbusters II* came out, the studio finally got it right and put Ernie Hudson on the promo posters. Thank goodness. AND Peter got a cameo in the film. I know, so cool. He is uncredited but not hard to find.

In his scene, Dana and Vankman are on a dinner date. Egon, Winston, and Ray run into the restaurant in their long underwear, covered in pink ooze. They implore Vankman to leave immediately to come help them. An overexcited Ray points in the direction of the museum where the slime is headed. In doing so, he slimes a woman and her date at another table. That man, covered in pink slime in a close-up shot, is Peter.

In our talk, he tells me how he got involved in *GII* and what he remembers about filming the restaurant scene. We discuss how his life's passion has evolved over time. He tells me story after incredible story about his lifelong experiences working in the film industry and his sweet connection over the years with Dan Aykroyd. He tells me he is the puppeteer of the gremlin singing "New York, New York" in *Gremlins 2*. Amazing.

After our talk, he takes the time to send me a huge packet of Ghostbusters memorabilia. It arrives in a regular priority-mail envelope, but there are vintage Ghostbusters stamps in different colors splattered on the outside. Inside there's a double-sided folder filled with newspaper and magazine articles and pictures and a sticker of the Ghostbuster logo. In one picture, he's dressed to Ghostbuster perfection, standing in front of the Ectomobile.

I keep thinking about our shared devotion to the things we love. Peter commits his life to making fans happy. He's so devoted to his prop recreation and reproduction craft. The time he takes to intricately detail his wardrobe, his proton pack, and his Ghost Trap, makes the end result just astounding. He transports me and anyone around him to the Ghostbuster universe. He actually creates what *Comfort Sequels* is all about: an immersion into the films we love.

The best part inside the packet is an official Ghostbusters fan badge. Ghostheads and others in fandom know that it's not an everyday occurrence that someone gets a personalized Certificate of Anti-Paranormal Proficiency. Without knowing it, Peter has given me my own transitional object into *Ghostbusters II*. It hangs in my hallway, and every time I walk by, I think about Peter and smile.

Oozing with pink slime kindness, here's the pure joy of Peter Mosen:

Emily Marinelli: When did your Ghostbusters fandom begin?

Peter Mosen: It started two weeks before the [first] movie was released in 1984. I was at a convention, and they ran this contest to win a pair of passes to this supernatural comedy. And there were the boys standing in their gear on the poster. I thought, *Hey, this looks good: Dan Aykryod and Bill Murray, two of the funniest guys on Saturday Night Live.* I'd like to see this movie. As I was standing there looking at this poster, I was like, *Wait a minute-three weeks ago, a friend of mine gave me that exact jumpsuit!*

Emily: What?!

Peter: I thought, *This is fate, I gotta do this.* So I put this costume together with a patch with my name on it. And I won! I went to the screening in the jumpsuit. There were all these executives from Columbia Pictures hanging out at the screening looking for reactions from the audience. They looked at me and were like, "Where the hell did that guy get that jumpsuit? He looks an awful lot like Dan Aykroyd, doesn't he?" I loved the movie, and I knew it was the next thing, so I was like, I'm on it. So that's where it all started, from a competition to go see a movie.

Emily: How did you become the official promotional Ghostbuster?

Peter: I got introduced to the people in charge of merchandising and licensing. Next thing I know, they start using me for everything. When they did *The Real Ghostbusters* (animated TV series spin off after the original film aired), at the Ambassador Hotel, they had me listed there as their "promotional Ghostbuster," I have all these pictures from that time.

I did theme parks too. I made an appearance at Knott's Berry Farm, I had a guy with me doing Venkman, another guy doing Spangler, my wife was doing Janine, along with Mr. Stay Puft. I had the car, a big green Slimer. I had a guy make a big sign that had the Ghostbusters logo on the left and said West Coast Ghostbusters Headquarters.

I got to do a birthday party for Barbra Streisand's niece and nephew. I thought my mom would be so freaking proud to know her son performed for Barbra Streisand. It was unbelievable.

Emily: Wow, that is really amazing. I would've been so starstruck.

Peter: I did a convention a while ago, Hudson Valley Ghostbusters, and they go out and set up for people to make their own slime. You can take pictures on a green screen, and they put things in the pictures with you, and they do all of this to raise money. This particular fundraiser was for suicide prevention. Some pretty dedicated people. Anything that helps people and creates positivity is a good thing.

Last year I had these cards printed up. One side has pictures of my Ectomobile; the other side is a replica of the original fan club ghostbusting certificate of antiparanormal proficiency. I went to Spirit Halloween and gave them the certificates to see if anyone wanted them. I put a small stack on the table, about an inch thick. I came back a few days later and they were like, "Oh, everybody loved those. You got any more?"

I'm a fan, but it's way more than that. I'm a fan who turned it into something. I was able to create this little niche for myself.

Emily: Tell me about your Ectomobile.

Peter: I got the plates in 1984. A friend of mine had a store called the

Dan Aykroyd and Peter Mosen, "king of the Ghostbuster fans."
(Photo courtesy of Peter Mosen)

Hollywood Dream Factory. He calls me and says, "You'll never believe what I got," and I'm thinking movie posters or something, and he says "I got a 1966 Cadillac ambulance." And I say, "Well I have the Ecto license plate," and he says, "Well, we gotta get you two together."

So I fly out to Toledo and trade in like five hundred six-feet-tall *Vampirella* posters for the car. I made my own logos and brought them with me and set them up and drove the car home, put my plates on it. Later on I took the '66 and made it into *GII*, so it became the Ecto 1A.

Emily: How did you find your way to the industry?

Peter: When I was a kid, my mother was the secretary to the president of Paramount Pictures, doing the legal contracts, and she met all the talent who came in to sign their contracts. She met all kinds of people, I have a picture of her and Ray Milland and his wife. My mother passed away in 1984, and my father had passed long before. We sold the house, and in 1987 I moved to LA to live out my dream to work in the movie business. I brought my Ectomobile with me.

Running around in costume for the Ghostbuster franchise is not all I ever did. I've done a lot of films and been on *The Morning Show* with Regis Philbin. I worked on so many different shows. I built for *Terminator 2*, and *Stargate*. I was even a puppeteer for *Gremlins 2*. I had my hand stuck up the tail of a gremlin singing "New York, New York."

Emily: No way! I love *Gremlins 2*, and that's my favorite part of that movie. How did you get into design and costume and props?

Peter: All from the conventions, hit or miss. Can I win a hundred bucks? Cool, let me try to make a costume. Every time I entered I won. I always won first, second, or third. Most of the time I won first. I did an *Alien* costume, all kinds of things. Later on I got involved in building sets for shows and building sets for *SNL*, and until I retired I was working at Hudson Scenic. They build Broadway shows. I was working on *The Lion King* and *Aladdin*, *Hamilton*, you name it.

When *Conan the Barbarian* came out, I went with six people in costume to Studio 54 for the premiere party. I had made a copy of the sword, and Arnold Schwarzenegger comes in and sees the sword sticking up over my shoulder like a sheath. He has all the cameras on him, all these lights, and somehow spotted this thing over my shoulder. He comes running over to me, pushes everyone out of the way, and says "My sword, my sword." I pull it out, hand it to him over my wrist, and he says, "Now there's a man who knows how to handle his sword." It had the ruins in it, and it was carved. That's how I do my work: it's in the details.

Emily: How did you become a part of *GII*?

Peter: It was 1988, the last two weeks of shooting *GII*. I knew I had to find out where they were filming. A friend of mine who was a stuntman was doing the Ghostbusters parties with me. We went down to city hall to find out where they have a permit to shoot.

Turns out they were shooting at the Firehouse (FDNY fire station). All the exteriors were done in NY, and all the interiors in LA. So we go to the Firehouse, and I have my arms full of posters I have for Dan to sign. Dan knew who I was and what I had done. Of course there were two armed guards waiting to see what I would do and cameras rolling at that time.

I went in with posters for Dan to sign, and he said, "Okay, come over to my trailer," and I said to myself, *Say something now or forever hold your peace.* "So, Dan, what do you think? Maybe I can get into the movie?" He said "Hmm, yeah, maybe you can be one of the cops. Here's the phone number; tell them I told you to call, and see what happens."

I called the production office and got them on the phone. They said, "Call this guy over at central casting." Well, this was a guy I had already been calling, asking him to put me on the show. But this time I called and he picked up, and I explained that production wanted me on the movie, and he said okay. I mean, he was a little pissed, you know?

I go on the bus to Silverlake. That's where Armand's Restaurant is. I'm sitting there between the extras and the production crew, and I put myself a little closer to the production crew because I wanted to know what was going on in the scene. I'm just listening and listening, and I hear, "We are gonna need somebody to get slimed," and once again that little buzz in my ear said, *Say something now or forever hold your peace.* "I'll do it!" I yelled, and I'm surprised no one broke anything, the way their heads snapped around. Someone said to me "You WANT to get slimed?" I said to myself, *They don't waste slime on people in the back of the room.* I said, "Absolutely! Let's do it."

Most of these people knew who I was and the things I had been doing. So I was in. I'm sitting at the table with Judy Ovitz [the other slimed restaurant patron], waiting for things to start rolling, and I feel this tap on my shoulder. I turn around and look up, and it's Sigourney Weaver. She says, "I understand you're the person I gotta talk to to get an 'I've Been Slimed' button." I say, "Sure! No problem. I've got one right here." I gave her the button, and this is what she wrote on my *GII* poster: "To Peter: Get ready to be slimed. Best, Sigourney Weaver."

When they did the birthday party in *GII*, I got a call asking for a copy of a video of me doing a birthday party. I sent it to them and found out they want to use it for the movie as a reference. Felt like a tip of the hat to all I had been doing.

Emily: What was it like for you to be there, in the scene with all those people in real life?

Peter: It was sort of like floating on a cloud. I couldn't believe I was with everyone. And Danny has always been on my side. When they had the double casts on Jimmy Kimmel [the original cast and four women from *Ghostbusters: Answer the Call*], they were talking about fans. Danny said, "My friend Peter Mosen, he's the king of the Ghostbusters fans." He gave me this big shout-out. It was really cool.

I was working on *Coneheads* only because I was one of the only people who knew how to operate the interior of an F-16 fighter. I asked where Danny was, and they told me what soundstage he was on. I tried to get in, but all these people were piled blocking the door. But I know soundstages, and that there are other doors.

Emily: Sneaky.

Peter: I walked to the next door on the right-hand side, looked behind the curtain, and there's Danny standing there, and we talked about *Coneheads*. Every day I would go to Danny's trailer, give a quiet knock, if he came to the door, I knew he was there and wished him luck for the day. One of the last days I was there, I came up, knocked on the door. He said, "Peter, come in, sit down. I'll be with you in just a minute." He picks up the phone and makes a call and says he put me in for the commercial. When you see the Conehead devouring the sub in the Mass Quantities Meal Deal, that's me.

Emily: That's so awesome! It's so amazing to hear about your work and also your ongoing relationship and support from Dan over the years.

Peter: Anytime he's nearby, I always go see him. I went out for the *Answer the Call* premiere in 2016, he got out of the car with his family, passed like three hundred Ghostbuster fans in costume, and walked directly up to me. He's just like that.

Emily: This book is about why these sequels are so comforting and predictable and make us feel good. Why do you think *GII* is so comforting?

Peter: The first movie made you realize these guys are there to help out. They've been told you can't do this, you can't do that. They've been stopped from doing anything to help. But their friend has got this situation, and they gotta do it anyway. And after the first movie, we started to trust these guys, so I think it's the fact that these familiar characters come back again five years later. We are putting our trust in them to save the day. It might not be predictable in terms of the exact story, but it's familiar. They do the things that most people would do.

Emily: Yeah, their humanness comes through.

Peter: They show their human side. They are citizen superheroes. You do what you do. This is their portal of expertise.

Emily: It's also the backdrop of angry New Yorkers and how pink slime can be repurposed as a reminder we can be kind to each other.

Peter: That's the way New Yorkers are. You hit them as hard as you can, and they find a way to bounce back.

Emily: I'm so grateful for your time and for all the stories you shared with me. I want to thank you I've learned a lot.

Peter: No problem. You're most welcome.

Karate Kid Part II

"Hey, wouldn't a flyswatter be easier?"

The Guy-My-Mom-Married drinks Jim Beam and Miller High Life. Mom cleans up the empty bottles and cans during the middle of the night. By the time I head out the door for high school, the kitchen and living room look straight out of *Good Housekeeping*. Well, if *Good Housekeeping* featured a working-class single mom and their teen kid living in a rented home on a limited budget with an emotionally and physically abusive alcoholic man. More like the cover of *Shitkeeping*.

I saw the recycling in the garage and could smell the alcohol on his breath when he would brush by me. I knew what was up. I rarely see or talk to him, except for when he is drunk yelling, name-calling, breaking shit, and tornado-ing around the house.

This is my mom's second marriage, so technically he is a stepfather to me. He and Mom were high school sweethearts, and Mom never gave up on the dream of being with him forever. I couldn't believe this was the forever she wanted. I was forced to go to their wedding, so I wore all black and openly expressed my objection. It didn't matter. No one listened. He came home with us.

Depressed and untreated, he is a Vietnam vet with severe post-traumatic stress. Green army fatigues cover his 6-feet, 7-inch frame, a hefty, menacing presence. He towers over us, and, for fun, calls us "stupid little bitches." Playing his favorite Sadistic Hallway Game, he casts his long limbs out, a spider net, blocking the hallway with his body. We try to run into the bathroom or my bedroom to hide, but he follows and blocks the doors each time. "Where you gonna go, huh? You better not even try it." And we don't.

This goes on for what seems like an eternity, or until he finally gets bored, tired, or passes out. When he does, I retreat to my room and wait. After a while, I peek out to see if the light in their bedroom is out. Then I tiptoe down the hall to the kitchen to get my go-to snacks of Cool Ranch Doritos and Little Debbie Zebra Cakes for the night.

Who knows what he does all day when he leaves for "work." My guess? Drinks with his buddies at hole-in-the-wall bars by Promenade Mall. Maybe he shoots pool downtown? Or loses money on horses at Fairway Meadows?

Sometimes when he comes home from "work," he plays another of his drunken pastimes: breaking Mom's nautical knickknacks against the wall. After he's done and gone out for the night, I help Mom pick up the ceramic pieces. We see if we can puzzle together a white seagull or reconstruct a periwinkle blue conch. Mostly they go into the trash, where the evidence of abuse is piled on top of McDonald's wrappers and oily, empty Pop Secret bags. I squint my eyes to make the blue, silver, and white fragments melt together and turn into sea glass.

Tears mix with black mascara to create calligraphy brushstrokes on Mom's face. Her cheeks, already pink from L'Oréal Tender Rose blush, brighten into a darker maroon from embarrassment and shame. Mom looked tired before, but living with this man ages her even more. Skin divots and folds around her eyes. I can tell she doesn't sleep much. I know she is afraid. Afraid of him getting into a car crash and dying. Or worse, of him living and coming home.

Yet she stays with him year after year.

I usually drown out the fighting by blasting musical soundtracks in my room; *Rent, Miss Saigon, Falsettos, Guys and Dolls*. I dance and sing as loud as I can. I play all the male protagonists in each, vying for the love of Mimi, Kim, Trina, and Sarah. I like to imagine I'm the guy hero to these fierce heroines who are powerful and actually don't need men at all when it comes down to it. Still, I feel powerful playing their sweethearts. I create my own choreography to the songs, quick pencil turns, sharp rib cage isolations, long turn leaps. The ritual of dance grounds me and changes my focus. I sweat out what I don't want to hold in.

Today I hear their bedroom door slam. I hear my mom trying to calm him down, pleading, explaining, reexplaining. I want to get out of here. I can't drive yet, and my friends don't either, so I can't really go anywhere. If I took a walk around the neighborhood, that would mean I'd have to walk through the house to the front door and get caught in their crossfires. I refuse. I'm trapped.

Earlier in the week, Mom and I had made a Blockbuster trip, and as I look at my VHS stack now, I realize I have already watched *Coneheads*, *Twenty Bucks*, *Gilbert Grape* and *Like Water for Chocolate*. The only film left in my Blockbuster loot is *Karate Kid Part II* (*KKII*). I know that the third film in the Karate Kid franchise is coming out soon, and I'm behind in my viewing.

I pop this soon-to-be comfort sequel into my VCR, getting ready to watch on the small white Magnavox TV in my room, hoping there will be a loud fighting sequence like in the first film, to compete with the noise in my house. A light knock on my door interrupts the drum and flute playing over the Columbia Pictures's woman holding the lighted torch. I sigh, having to pause the film just as it starts.

"Come in, Momma," I say, frustrated at the interruption but also wanting to make sure she is okay. "Sweetie, I'm gonna go to the grocery store. Do you need anything?" *Do I need anything? Is that all? You're not going to say anything about the shitshow you married? About his yelling all morning? Do I need anything? Yes, I need something.*

"I need you to stop fighting and kick that fucking guy out," I say, unapologetically. My heart is racing, and my palms are moist and sticky. I take a deep breath to try and come back to earth. "I'm sorry, sweetie." My mom's voice is tiny. She looks defeated, a scared child who, like me, doesn't know how to leave. She holds back tears and says, I-will-be-back-soon-and-will-bring-some-cherry-cheesecake-for-us-and-maybe-we-can-watch-The-Golden Girls-later-and-not-to-worry,-he-is-gone-for-a-while.

Just a while. A while is not long enough. I ignore her as she shuts my bedroom door. Adjusting the pillows around me on my bed, I yell "FUCK!" as I hit one of them. Anger inside me boils over, then subsides to a simmer. I unpause the remote and watch as Mr. Miyagi (Pat Morita) tries to catch flies with a pair of chopsticks. "Hey, wouldn't a flyswatter be easier?" Daniel (Ralph Macchio) asks, to which Miyagi responds, "Man who catch fly with chopstick accomplish anything." I smile; it's cute, lighthearted. The story of a loving father figure teaching his chosen son how to protect himself begins. I soften, enter their world easily, finally escaping mine.

Karate Kid Part II Recap

Ever since seeing *The Outsiders*, I have been a fan of Ralph Macchio's. In the first *Karate Kid*, his character, Daniel (soon to be Daniel-San), resonated with me; we were both poor, lived with single moms, felt like outsiders, and were picked on at school. When he defeats Johnny (William Zabka) at the karate tournament at the end of the film, he proves heart and skill can triumph over brawn and bully. He is stronger and more confident not because of the win, but from what he has learned from his sensei, Mr. Miyagi.

As the VHS plays, the sound slightly warped because the video had been played so many times, I see that *Karate Kid Part II* is Daniel-San's continuing story, a true sequel. Released only two years after the first film, *KKII* starts right where we left off, at the tournament at the end of the first film. Daniel walks out of the event carrying his huge trophy, and two young boys approach him asking for his autograph. This moment, illustrating Daniel's influence on youth, has a meta feel to it, given the gargantuan response to the first film and the way it boosted Macchio's career.

KKII then goes into a montage of clips from the first film just to make sure we are all caught up on the story. Dammit, I love a good montage! When I'm held by the story this way, I feel safe. It's reassuring. There are no questions or confusions about what led the characters to where they are now. I know how to build on what was before and what is to come.

This comfort sequel takes a geographic turn when Miyagi gets word that his father is dying, and he and Daniel-San head to Okinawa, Japan. I laugh out loud when, on the plane, Daniel reads an entire book on Okinawa and becomes an expert on the culture overnight. Literally.

As Miyagi and Daniel fly into this next chapter, the trauma in my house becomes more and more distant. *What will I say to Mom when she gets home? What mood will Guy-My-Mom-Married be in when he comes home?* Thoughts float in but don't grab hold of me. The afternoon of tension is fainter in my psyche. I'm fully immersed in the story of this father/son sweetness as their new adventure begins.

Miyagi shares his backstory: years ago, he fell in love with a woman, Yukie (Nobu McCarthy), who was set to marry his best friend, Sato (Danny Kamekona), a rich guy who owned most of the village. When Sato got wind of this, he challenged Miyagi to karate to the death, and instead of fighting him, Miyagi escaped to the US, leaving the love of his life and his best friend behind. Returning to Japan after all of these years is a big deal for him. What will he find there?

Once they arrive, Daniel and Miyagi are threatened by Sato, who still wants the karate fight he never got to have. Sato's pupil Chozen (Yuji Okumoto) threatens Daniel too, so we have a teacher/student rivalry set up. In preparation for what's to come, Miyagi shows Daniel his ancestral dojo and the secret of his family's karate, a handheld drum. The drum is small and double-sided, fastened to a rod with pellets held by strings on either side. When held just at the right center of balance and turned back and forth, the pellets hit the drum, igniting sound.

Miyagi reunites with Yukie, and she just happens to have a niece Kumiko (Tamlyn Tomita) who just happens to be Daniel's age, so naturally, love blooms. Kumiko is stunning, and Daniel falls quickly for her. She shows him around the village. They go to a sock hop, and they have the most sensual scene in the form of a green tea ceremony. In the ceremony, Kumiko shakes out her long, gorgeous hair and reaches over the table to kiss Daniel, and I can't believe how beautiful this moment is. I love them. To top it all off, they fall in love set to Peter Cetera's "Glory of Love" as a backdrop. Amazing.

The apex of the film comes when Sato challenges Miyagi to a duel to the death, to which Miyagi finally agrees. Right before the showdown is scheduled to begin, a hurricane stops the fighting before it even starts. Sato and Chozen are asked to put ego aside for the greater collective and work together with Daniel and Miyagi to save villagers. Sato has a change of heart, and the next day he deeds the land back to the community and helps them rebuild after the storm's destruction. A good old-fashioned bad dude turning good overnight. Sweet.

At the Obon festival, Kumiko's dance gets interrupted by a karate fight between Daniel and Chozen. Everyone in the audience beats their handheld drums in unison and the sound grows louder and more energizing. Surprise, Daniel wins, and not because he kills Chozen but because he lets him go to the beat of the pellet drum. Brains over brawn. Strength of focus and determination, over strength of body. As the film ends, I yell "What?!"at the screen, pissed that Kumiko and Yukie aren't returning to the US with their love interests but instead opt to stay in Okinawa. Okay, maybe they want to stay and rebuild the village? Maybe Kumiko will build a career as a dancer there? Still, I want them to be together. As much as I love the male protagonists, Kumiko is my hero. Is she in Karate Kid 3? I hope so.

Peter Cetera's "Glory of Love" plays again over the credits, bringing me pure eighties joy. I belt out "Just like a knight in shining armor, from a long time ago . . . " and then mumble the next few lines because I can't remember the lyrics, but come back in with " . . . castle far away." The credits finish, and I immediately get up and press stop and rewind. I listen as the tape whirls. The quiet brings awareness of the stillness in my house, which I know won't last. As soon as I hear the double-click finish, I consider ejecting the film. Instead, I press play to watch it again.

Kumiko's Dance, Daniel's Drum

I spend three or four days a week after school at the Peggy Lanik Dance Studio learning tap and ballet and have been since age three. I take both solo lessons and group classes with other girls my age. The owner and dance teacher, Peggy, is in her seventies and wears sweatpants with matching sweatshirts, the kind that have a soft butterfly-flower pattern in the center and a doily collar. She holds her shoulder-length thick gray hair with amber plastic clips, the kind with the hard plastic claws that if you aren't too careful could end up poking you in the head.

An L&M cigarette is forever held in her wrinkled fingers, the ash growing into a speckled log, and when she demonstrates a tap step for us, it falls to the floor. When she thinks of it, she ashes into her small McDonald's coffee cup, and I wonder how it doesn't burn through the Styrofoam. Peggy coughs and hacks instructions, warm-up routines and plays warped vinyl records that have dust and ash collected on the sound waves.

Peggy is kind and patient. She's perfect for a scared little kid like me, whose gay over-the-topness happened mostly behind closed doors. I needed a gentle teacher. When she gives me the nickname Auntie Em, I know how much she loves me. I run to the corner store to buy her smokes, and sometimes the store clerk gives me a butterscotch toffee for free at checkout. It's the only thing I ever see her eat, and I wonder how she can smoke and chew that thing at the same time.

Peggy's studio is a safe place for me. When things are hard at home, I know I can go to my second one. The studio is a place I can go to just be. I don't have to worry about anything else, just keeping time to the music. Staying in line with the other girls in my class.

Peggy teaches me how to properly do a series of turns. With Chaînes and Piqué turns, the key is that you prepare first. Preparing is a pain in the ass because it involves sitting in my core, bending one leg slightly, sticking the other out in front with a pointed toe, and waiting for Peggy's cue. Ab and butt muscles I never knew existed catch fire. One arm in front, the other to the side. It takes time to get it all right before I can make a turn, and even then sometimes I put weight on my pointed foot, begin the turn, and Peggy calls me out for losing focus. Then I have to start all over again.

The most important part of preparing is where to look. I set my eyes on a place across the room that will be easy to spot each time I whip around. That one spot is my focal point, the place I keep coming back to with each turn. "Spotting" helps me not get dizzy and keeps my goal in sight. Only when all of these preparing and spotting systems

Kumiko teaches Daniel the Obon dance.
(Photo courtesy of Columbia Pictures)

are in place can I do a turn or series of turns. Each turn brings me back to center after whipping around.

After seeing *KKII*, I rewind and pause the movie many times in an attempt to learn Kumiko's Obon dance. She is focused but smiling the whole time. The dance tells a story, an intergenerational tale of connection to spirit, culture, and ancestors. Obon is a time-honored dance that is part of an annual Japanese holiday commemorating ancestors. The specificities of the dance and the celebrations vary according to region, but the intention behind the dance remains. It's part of a larger festival that often involves sending lanterns into the air or through water, helping ancestor spirits return to the grave. Mr. Miyagi does this in a beautiful scene with Daniel, looking out into the water and sending a lantern off to honor his father, who passes in the film.

I never master her grace or elegance. I mean, she's Kumiko; she's perfect. I try spotting, but with this type of dance, the turns operate differently. The spot changes as you go. The movements are precise, but fluid. They feel organic but are automatonic.

She weaves in and out, crossing her hands in front, then bringing one through and back to the other side. The turns are in opposite directions, back and forth. Gentle yet exact. One arm follows the other as she turns from one side to the other. It's hard! I try again, and this time I prepare by breathing, concentrating, centering my body. It helps, but this is going to take a lot more practice.

Kumiko teaches Daniel how to do the Obon dance, and he actually gets it pretty quickly. How does it learn it so fast? Dammit! But he does. Daniel says the dance is "just like the handheld drum." The drum, Miyagi's family karate secret, represents the human body and how to move it, with the handle as the legs and pellets as arms. The dance, the drum, and karate all seem simple but are extremely hard, with half-turns left and right, intricate hand movements, all while the core stays centered.

Every week in dance classes, I have to use my left and right brain in tandem to hit the marks, to spin and flap, to shuffle and Maxi Ford. I have to stay present, dodging gravity's urge to slip and fall on my ass. Music and dance are ways I learn to stay completely present in my body and also transcend to another place. I get lost in the songs; the rhythms, and the lyrics help take me there and lift me like a lantern to the sky. I never studied traditional Japanese dance or martial arts, but I see that dancing, like karate, is both an art and a sport. They are both creative and athletic. Form matters. They are about keeping your core strong, your mind sharp, your body in alignment.

KKII reminds me of the importance of using my body to heal, to move energy out, to channel energy forward, to stay rooted in my core. *KKII*, and the first film as well, shows the true art of movement as defense. Miyagi shows Daniel the connection to an inner center, which Daniel must achieve in order to fight back from a solid place.

One time Peggy called me out in dance class, "Auntie Em, if you don't stop looking down on your turns, you gonna hit Julie. Then she gonna run into Becky. Then she gonna fall on Margie. Y'all wanna fall down like dominoes?" I didn't want to fall down like dominoes. I had to learn mind, body, and spirit connection. I had to learn to find my focal point and breathe into it. I had to learn to spot my turns. Not just spot once and be done, but spot each and every time. I had to learn that once I found connection, my work wasn't done. Spiritual practice is called practice because you have to keep doing it. It's a lifelong journey.

Dance and martial arts help repair the soma and the spirit. They are about balance, finding a focal point, rooting to the ground, centering energy. Without centering, the dance won't work. The drum won't sound. The hero will lose in karate. I will fall on my ass in dance class.

"No Breathe, No Life"

During my rewatch of *KKII*, I get a call from my crush. "Hey, Britt, wuzup?" I try to sound casual and not like a freak who just watches movies on repeat. Britt is a year older than me; her family is wealthy and owns a big house in Midtown. I can't tell if she wants to be friends because I'm queer too or if she's interested and wants to hook up. Either way, when she says she's coming to pick me up and to bring a jacket, I'm in.

Britt is tall and skinny compared with my curvy 5 foot 2, and when I get into her SUV, I see right away that seemingly overnight she has cut off what was once long, sandy hair. Serving tomboy hot, she has an androgynous chic vibe, and I like it. When I ask where we're going, she smirks and says, "You'll see" and turns up her Le Tigre cd.

When she pulls into a big parking lot, it's a fully pitch-black night. One barely operating pole light illuminates a dumpster and some empty parking spaces. It's 8:00 p.m. on a Sunday in the Bible Belt, where almost everything is closed. "Uhmmm . . . where are we?" She says nothing, smiles, and grabs a huge sack in the back seat. "Hold this," she tells me and gets out of the car.

I follow her, confused and wondering what is going on. Standing ten feet from the green American Waste Control ten-foot dumpster, she tells me to pick something from the sack. I'm even more confused when I pull out the first thing I see; a Precious Moments girl figurine, wide eyes, pastel colors faded, she is kneeling in prayer and looking to the heavens above. WTF.

"When my parents fight and I feel like shit, I always come here," she tells me. So her parents fight too. "You come here? To this . . . parking lot? Why?" I ask. She pauses, looks down at the figurine, and then yells "AHHHHHH!" as she chucks it at the dumpster. Prayer girl breaks into tiny pieces that fly everywhere, on the pavement, on the ground next to a tree nearby, ricocheting off a Reserved Parking sign. I survey the area, thinking for sure someone is gonna see us and we are gonna get in trouble. Or worse, the God of Precious Moments is watching us, and we are going directly to hell.

Either way, I'm freaking out. "Don't worry; my dad owns this building. We won't get in trouble," she tells me. "Here," she says, handing me another ceramic figure. It's my turn. Images flash in my mind of Guy-My-Mom-Married playing his breaking-Mom's-nautical knickknacks game, and I shudder. My eyes glaze over, I seem frozen in place, and I'm despondent. I'm somewhere else. "Hey, what's wrong?" "Oh sorry I . . . um . . . nothing"

I look down at the chipped Shawnee Pottery poodle and carriage in my hand. The ceramic glaze sits cool in my palm. I trace my pointer finger around the baby-blue wagon wheel, coated with gold painted trim. I think about Mr. Miyagi and Daniel taking time to breath in and out before making karate moves. Miyagi says "When you feel your life is going out of focus, always return to basic of life. Breathing. No breathe, No life." I close my eyes and try it. Breathe in for four counts, then out for four more. My heartbeat slows. I see Guy-My-Mom-Married's face, his jungly eyebrows, pockmarked skin, flaring nostrils, slits for bloodshot eyes. It ignites the rage in my stomach, and I scream "GO TO HELLLLLLLL!!!" I fastball the chipped poodle into the dumpster, and it breaks in half. I feel like a badass.

"Nice," Britt says, and I can tell she's actually impressed. I feel high, a release. "Go again?" she asks, and we do. "It's a buffet from Everything's $1 store; ceramic bells, a terracotta swallow head she found on the street, a thrift store ashtray, all go flying into pieces. I get a little nervous when she pulls out a beautiful porcelain woman's-head vase, but she says her mom has hundreds and won't notice it's missing. We laugh and break and break and break until we no longer feel broken.

I walk up to the dumpster and take a little piece of the poodle's head that has chipped off on the ground below. I place it in my thrift store Levi's jeans pocket, a little souvenir of this catharsis. A reminder that it's okay to feel angry and that I don't have to hold it in. I don't have to be afraid. I don't have to be part of his game. I don't have to be just stuck in my room pausing and rewinding and replaying my movie. As we head back to Britt's car, I realize that whatever has brought us here, to this night, to this parking lot dumpster, has dissolved into the night air.

"Live or Die Man?"

Britt sticks a personalized mixed CD in my hand as she drops me back home. She says goodbye and quickly peels off. Okay, maybe she wants to be more than friends? I look at the playlist, and it's full of what I expect; Ani DiFranco, Bikini Kill, Sleater-Kinney, Bitch and Animal, but then inexplicably there's some David Gray and Sonic Youth.

I'll be reading into every song and lyric later to see if she likes me or not. If that was in fact a date, it was the best I've ever had. I'm smiling and feel calm for the first time in a long time, a steadiness that coats my insides. I'm not seething with rage or wanting to scream. A stillness settles over me, warming me.

I take my shoes off in the foyer and head toward the living room. The house is completely silent, but they are home, I can feel it. My spidey senses tell me something is very off here.

I tiptoe into the living room. It looks normal: couch and pillows, shell-filled see-through lamps, seafaring fare on shelves, and beachscapes hanging on the wall. As I round into the kitchen, I see them. His massive military body hovers over her little tanned frame. Mom is frantically doing dishes, and tears shake out of her eyes with each sponge wipe. He is silent, but he doesn't need to say anything to terrify her.

"Get away from her!" I remain calm. He slow motion turns toward me, his quizzical face making each of his thicket of eyebrows turn in a different direction. "What did you say, you little bitch?" I can smell his boozy breath from across the room. I stay a tranquil sea. "I said, 'Get away from her.'" I touch the sharp edge of the ceramic poodle in my pocket.

When he comes toward me, I know this is it: the Daniel/Chozen showdown at the Obon festival. I tell my body to be a tree, the branches swinging with intention in the wind. I put my body in position, keeping my core strong, preparing for the dance of what's to come. I find a scratch on a cabinet above my mom's head, perfect for spotting.

Somewhere in my consciousness, I hear Mom cry-yelling, but I can't register anything she says. "Mom, go call 911," I break her sob. "Honey I . . . " This is serious, "Mom, do it now!" She nods and goes toward the living room phone. He tries to stop her, and I trip him with my shoe, yelling "Stop!" This only pisses him off more. A weighty, standard-issue military boot stomps on my foot. I can feel the screaming pain of my big toenail stabbing into my other toes.

I think about Miyagi, pulling the handheld drum from his belt and playing it. A call to the other audience members to drum in solidarity. The beats that remind Daniel he is strong, he can fight, and he is not alone. It's what Daniel needs to bounce back, to punch Chozen from the left, then the right, then the left, and back and forth until Chozen loses his footing.

The drum makes the most even sound when the drummer holds the center straight and upright. Despite my foot screaming and my adrenaline coursing, I have to stay in my spiritual practice of rooting in balance, my feet on the floor. He starts to leave again, to find Mom and stop her from calling the cops. I find the nearest thing next to me to throw: a ceramic spoon rest. It bounces off of him, hitting the floor and breaking apart.

I grab a Shawnee Corn King cookie jar lid. "I will throw this. You have a choice." He comes toward me, tired, head spinning from booze, weak. As he gets closer, I can see he's got wild eyes, but I know enough to know he's too fucked up to do anything more to me or Mom. At least this time. He mumbles some bullshit as he runs out the back door, gets in his pickup truck, and speeds off. I put the cookie jar back on the counter and breathe again.

In the film, Daniel says, "Live or die, man?" Chozen looks at him with disgust. "Die," he says, and Daniel, face bloodied, out of breath, his ribs and foot broken, calls in the family secret to karate. "Wrong," Daniel says, and instead honks Chozen's nose, pushing him away and ending the fight.

I don't cry; I just go blank. The police come ten minutes later, and I don't remember what I say to them as my mom ices my foot. This isn't the first time the cops are called on him, and it won't be the last.

There was a time before when he took a baseball bat to the windshield of Mom's Mazda while we were in the front seats. Covered in bits of glass, we walked up the street to McDonald's and called Grandma and Grandpa's from a payphone. We stayed there to be safe. We go there again tonight; it's our place of refuge.

I wish I could say that this moment was the breaking point for Mom, that it pushed her over the edge and she finally kicked him out. I wish I could say that we never saw him again. But he comes back, and the cycle continues for a while longer, until one day he just leaves and doesn't return. I don't trust it. But time passes, and we move to a new place, a condo, another promise of a cheaper place, a new chapter. As far as I know, he doesn't know where we are.

Until one day he shows up. He stalks us for a while, lurking around the parking lot. Yelling things at me as I drive to school in the morning. I ignore him, but my blood goes cold when I hear his voice. The day he gets through the gate to our front door, thankfully I'm not home. My mom's new boyfriend is there, however, and they have an altercation. Some furniture breaks; a lamp, a table, and the police are called. My mom's new boyfriend punches him in the face. Damn, I wish I was there to see that. There's a restraining order against him. FINALLY, I think. And this time it sticks. We never see him again. It's actually over.

Comfort Food

Thirty two years after *KKII*, the TV series *Cobra Kai*, the newest entry in the Karate Kid franchise, comes to Netflix. It's a true sequel to the sequels, and it's fabulous. It imagines Johnny (William Zabka from the first film) today, starting up a dojo and finding new ways to compete with Daniel, who is now a car salesman. It's easy to watch, funny, campy, and sentimental. AND *Cobra Kai* starts with a montage sequence from the first film, just in case you need a reminder of the story. Dope. I love a good montage!

In an interview with Jimmy Kimmel, Ralph Macchio calls *Cobra Kai* "comfort food," speaking to its nostalgia. Macchio is speaking my comfort-sequels language. I love watching the actors return and relive the rivalries and the lessons of karate as a defense, not an attack, lessons that we could all benefit from.

Kumiko returns in this Netflix TV series. Thank goodness! Where was she all along? I'm so happy she's back. She's amazing, beautiful, talented, fierce. She's Kumiko, okay? Turns out she joined the Hijikata Tatsumi Dance Company and traveled around the world and since has been teaching dance in Okinawa. Daniel, feeling lost, visits Okinawa to conduct a business deal and meets up with her. She hands him a box of love letters between Aunt Yukie and Miyagi. The last letter he reads is from Miyagi, written the week of his death. He writes about how proud he is of Daniel and how he was lost until he found him as a "guiding light." Amazing that even in death they can find each other this way.

Before Daniel returns to the US, Kumiko introduces him to a friend of hers. Turns out she is the little girl Daniel saved from the typhoon in *KKII*! I know, right? She's an adult now and just happens to be the senior VP of the company Daniel needs to do business with to save his car dealership. Okay, I'm all waterworks during this scene. The kind of crying where I can't catch my breath and snot runs down my nose. I just love Kumiko and all she adds to the *Cobra Kai,* the perfect sequel to my comfort sequel. I'm so glad we see her again.

Cobra Kai has some modern-day updates that I appreciate greatly. In *KKII*, many Japanese cultural expressions in the film are less than accurate. The actor Tamlyn Tomita (Kumiko) is of Okinawan and Filipino descent. In *KKII*, she was just starting her career and had no influence on the authenticity of Asian representation in film. She told Karen Robes Meeks in a 2020 *SF Chronicle* article that in part she decided to reprise Kumiko in *Cobra Kai* because the producers gave her "permission to bring Okinawan language, to bring Okinawan behavior, props and costumes to the set, and we were able to integrate a little bit more of an authentic Okinawan flavor to the piece."

Yet there is much more work to be done, even in *Cobra Kai*. In a 2021 article, LA Times staff writer Jen Yamato called out the lack of diversity in the series, pointing out that even though the young character Miguel Diaz is played by Xolo Maridueña, a Latinx actor, most of the protagonists are white. She goes on to say that sending

Daniel back to Okinawa in the third season (and having him reunite with Kumiko and Chozen) was a step in the right direction, depicting the martial arts not just as a way white people learn how to fight but also in the context of its broader cultural and historical context and history.

As a white American teenager watching this film, I would've never known that Kumiko's dancing in *KKII* was not a true Japanese Obon dance. As an adult with consciousness and access to more information than in the early 2000's, I can see how it was more about the cinematic aesthetic. Now I understand how systemic racism and Asian erasure create the circumstances under which restorying and whitewashing cultural traditions happen all too often in Hollywood.

In her interview with Yamato, Tomita says she was told by the choreographers of *KKII* to turn and face the camera more than the Obon dance originally calls for whereas ". . . in Obon dance, you just face the person in front of you." Okay, so check out what she did next (this is how much I love Tamlyn Tomita.): in preparation for *Cobra Kai*, Tomita got the script ahead of time and translated "things from Japanese to Hogen, or Uchinanchu, which is the Okinawan dialect." Tomita went to the Okinawa Association of America and asked "for the correct Okinawan choreography to 'Tinsagu nu Hana." How incredible is that? Tomita and her husband have also founded the Outside In Theater, telling stories of underrepresented populations, seeking "to invite them in, to know that they all belong."

Despite its representational challenges, *Cobra Kai* is a solid, modern, continuing story of the *Karate Kid*, and I love it. But my "comfort food" nostalgia is and will always be *KKII*. Although it too has representational issues, I couldn't love this film any more than I do. It's simple, slow, but exciting and sweet. A love story between Daniel and Kumiko, between Miyagi and Yukie, but mostly between Miyagi and Daniel. I have never seen such a tender father/son love depicted on-screen, and it's especially affecting here, in a film that could easily be hypermasculine and annoying. It's not. The love between a teacher and his chosen son is beautiful: a father/child relationship I longed so desperately to have.

For years to come, I will think about Miyagi and Daniel. I will

Daniel comforts Miyagi after his father's death.
(Photo courtesy of Columbia Pictures)

think about the way they look at each other and just know what they are feeling without using words. I will think about the scene after Miyagi's father dies. They sit together looking out into the ocean at sunset. Miyagi cries quietly, and Daniel gently puts his arm around him. Rays of dwindling light shine on a bonsai tree, peeking out between waves. A reminder of inner peace and balance, the bonsai tree is a symbol of both karate and of their relationship, withstanding years, wind, and ocean swells.

Mostly I will think about the beauty of the Kumiko's dance, the gentle swerve from left to right, the intricate hand motions, an ancestral dance that tells intergenerational stories. I will remember the handheld-drum rhythm and how being in the dance of the drum saved me during a time when I didn't think I could fight back. I will remember Britt, who helped me channel my anger, and my Mom, who did the best she could in a fucked-up situation. I will remember my own power to move from side to side while holding a focal point for every turn.

Teenage Mutant Ninja Turtles II: The Secret of the Ooze

Ted is a scientist. Or a geologist. Or an environmentalist. Actually, he's all of the above. He is also a gentle and kind teacher. Ted's hands are leathery from working outside, his fingernails crusted with soil, his skin, a brandy tan. I was three years old when my parents got divorced. From that time until I was a preteen, my mom dated lots of guys. Out of all her love-capades from this time, I liked Ted the most.

A scientist at heart, Ted loves conducting experiments to teach me lessons about the world. I'm eight years old. The snow is up to my kneecaps in Tulsa, which is a rare winter event. I trudge through the white mounds in the front yard of our rented duplex. I use my mittened hands to shove little balls of ice into my mouth. The arctic cold of the snow hits my sensitive front teeth and blasts my tongue numb. But I love it, and I crush the snow bits between my fingers to form shapes before crunching and swallowing the flakes.

While hanging my *A Christmas Story*-esque red padded jacket to dry in the garage, Ted asks me, "Do you know what snow is made of?" "Well, I mean, it's water that's frozen?" I respond, unsure of myself next to Ted's smart science brain. "It is. But it's much more than that.

It's actually bad for you to eat because of all the dirt and chemicals it contains."

He proceeds to explain why eating snow is not the fun adventure I think it is, using words I can't really understand like "pesticides"and "carcinogenic." I had heard of "pollution," and when he tells me this is all related to the "toxic way humans are destroying the earth," I cling to his certainty about the future of our planet. I believe him when he tells me that the earth is heating up at dangerous levels, but I have no idea what any of this has to do with my delicious snow snacks.

"Okay, but why can't I eat snow? Because it has this bad stuff in it?" I look for any way to hang on to my nature slushy. "I tell you what: you eat as much snow as you want today, but we are going to do an experiment overnight. And if by tomorrow morning you still want to eat snow, you can." He then proceeds to put a ball of snow in a beer glass and leaves it on the living room table. *Fine*, I think, *I'm sure he's right, and I won't want any snow tomorrow, but at least I have today.*

The next morning, I wake up to find that the snow has melted, water filling the cup. A few condensation drops constellate around the rim, dampening the coaster, which is made of cowrie shells. At a closer look, I'm mesmerized by the swirl of brown and black inside the glass. Debris fossils, suspended in water, chunks of all sizes floating. And it smells bad, like something earthly rotting. *Ugh, it's so gross*, I think, and vow to never eat snow again.

He does the same thing with Coke. Mom and I drink Cokes and Diet Cokes all day every day. This concerns Ted, who is kind of a crunchy hippy, before that was a thing. How, in Oklahoma in the late eighties, he is aware of the health risks of high fructose corn syrup is baffling. But he knows these things, and that leads to another experiment. He pours a Coke into a glass, puts a penny in the bottom, and leaves it on the Formica kitchen table overnight.

The next day, bam! The penny has almost completely disintegrated. "If pop does this to a penny, just imagine what this is doing to your insides," he says, and it makes me nervous. I look at my mom, and she just shrugs. It's then that I know we are and will forever be a Coke family. In fact, when I was a toddler, I could have Coke and Diet Coke in my baby bottle, along with sweet tea. Pop and iced Lipton are pretty much all we have flowing at the house on any given day. The penny experiment is a good try though, Ted.

His house is a picture book come to life. We drive over an hour to his geodesic dome cabin in the woods outside of Tahlequah (a small town southeast of Tulsa). The custom-designed cabin is well crafted from locally sourced lumber, with lots of windows. Chipmunks and red squirrels devour buffets of acorns, and hummingbirds are tipsy on honeysuckle. He takes me on walks through the acreage in his backyard, pointing out the trees along the path; Oak, Maple, Magnolia. "That's a scissor-tailed flycatcher," he says, pointing to a bird with a long tail. It looks like a blue jay, but he says it's even more special because it's the state bird.

It's exhilarating to venture outside of our small, rented, single-family duplex in the city and actually see lots of land! And space! And animals! There's a whole underground world of plants and life that I never knew before. It seemed like a land from another time, before Coke disintegrated pennies. Before snow was too dirty to eat.

Once we had a sleepover. I'm ten years old, cuddled with my Popple stuffed animal, snug on the living room floor in my New Kids on the Block sleeping bag and matching pajamas. Ted and Mom sit on the couch behind me, and we watch *The Incredible Journey* (a live-action Disney movie from the sixties, with two talking dogs and a cat that get lost and travel three hundred miles through the wilderness back home). I tell Mom I want a dog just like Chance. "We'll see, sweetie," she says, and takes a delicate sip of Beringer white zinfandel.

I can tell they both like *The Incredible Journey* but don't have the bandwidth for a double feature. I'm determined to watch *Teenage Mutant Ninja Turtles II: The Secret of the Ooze* with or without them, so when they leave to clean the kitchen and talk grownup talk, I ninja forward into my evening.

Until I get hungry.

The opening scene of the film involves a van full of pizza boxes, and when the turtles chow down in April's apartment, I can't hold it in anymore. "Mom, can we order pizza? Please please please?" We had just had dinner that Ted made; brown rice, steamed vegetables, and sauerkraut. I was starving.

"Honey, we just ate, Ted made us such . . . a nice dinner," and I can tell by her voice she is hungry too. I remember that she has some peanut M&M's stashed in her purse for emergencies like this, so I would be okay. But I won't give up.

"Okay, but Mom, it's Saturday night, and I wanna eat like Donatello."

"Who is Donatello, honey?" She's completely confused. I sigh in frustration and hunger.

"The best turtle, the purple one. Duh, mom!" Purple is my favorite color, and Donatello is the smart one. I want to be him. I don't know how we convince Ted to call Domino's, but when the large pepperoni arrives, I say "Thank you so much," give Mom a slice, take the rest of the pie into the living room, and return to my teen green ninja friends.

TMNT II Recap

Teenage Mutant Ninja Turtles was adapted from the Mirage comic book series and rose to fame with the late eighties TV cartoon. *Teenage Mutant Ninja Turtles II: The Secret of the Ooze* (*TMNT II*) is the second in a live-action series from the nineties and is a wonderfully terrible film. I knew it was terrible at age ten, and rewatching as an adult, I can safely confirm this to be true. It's terrible because it was written and shot just a year after the original, and it feels rushed. It's terrible because there is nothing groundbreaking about the sequel compared with the first film, and yes, let's face it, its people in turtle costumes fighting to save the world from the dangers of ooze. But that's also what makes it great. It doesn't try to be anything other than what it is: a throwback, with more cowabungas, more Shredder (who I thought died in the first film), and more pizza. Lots more pizza.

But there are things that are impossible to look past. The film starts with a fatphobic joke. When I first saw it, and each time I watched it growing up, I just didn't notice it. It was the nineties, and fucked-up jokes were a part of the cultural landscape. No one was batting an eye. I was a fat kid and couldn't have known the emotional toll that moments like this would create in my life. At the time, they flew right past me, as fast at Michelangelo's nunchaku.

If you can look past this oppressive remark (and I don't blame you if you can't), this excruciating film is good in all the ways it's bad. It's predictable, a recycling of the first story, which is what makes it comfortable and familiar. Nothing revelatory, and for kids like me who want a repeat experience of Turtle vs. Shredder (the franchise's supervillain), it works.

The sparse plot starts off with the Turtles in New York (of course), eating pizza by the box (of course), and looking for a new home. I wonder how many pizzas were sold in the early nineties to kids like me who were binge-watching the Turtles? Anyway, after their sewer encounter with Shredder in the previous film, the foursome is displaced and temporarily staying at April's apartment. April is the kick-ass news reporter who is a quasi mother to the teenagers, and boy do they need her.

Splinter (their sensei) is there too, a wise elder keeping these teenagers on track. As a young kid, I can tell he is old and wise, and even though he is a rat whose looks remind me of the terrifying Rodents of Unusual Size from *The Princess Bride*, I love his kindness. They soon discover that a green ooze from the TGRI company (headed by David Warner) is in the wrong hands (or the wrong Foot, that is, which is the name of Shredder's ninja crew). The turtles are once again in a

Who can ever forget this headline in newspapers across the country?
(Photo courtesy of New Line Cinema)

fight with their rival gang, and their mission in this comfort sequel is simple: get the ooze back.

The ooze is the OG toxic, man-made substance from the first film and is responsible for what made the Turtles mutate in the first place. Shredder has his crew find two vicious creatures (Tokka and Rahzar, voiced by famous voice actor Frank Welker) to ooze and become unstoppable fighting machines. As the creatures begin their mutation, they bang on the sheet metal of their cage, and this part made me put a pillow over my eyes. Even though I was a tough kid, I was not above being scared by Jim Henson lifesize Muppets that growl, roar, and attack.

Thankfully, David Warner creates antimutant goo that transforms them back to their original, nonmutated selves: a little snapping turtle and a baby wolflike creature. Aww, cute. This happens right after an inexplicable Vanilla Ice concert that comes out of nowhere, and the Turtles do an awesome synced dance to his unforgettable "Ninja Rap" song with the refrain "Go ninja, go ninja, go!" I pause and rewind the song to perfect the Running Man like Vanilla Ice until I almost knock over a Japanese vase on Ted's bookshelf.

Turns out Shredder has also consumed the mutation ooze and turns into Super Shredder. The Turtles have a showdown with Super Shredder, and it appears he dies again. But then his body disappears, so clearly the franchise is gearing up for a third film and another return of Shredder. A recurring villain is somehow comforting too; at least we know what evil to expect.

As far as I can tell in my rewatch as an adult, there is actually no "secret" to the ooze, despite the subtitle of the film. The ooze makes the Turtles mutant. We know this. They are called Mutant Ninja Turtles. In my research for this chapter, I learned that in the comics, the ooze turns out to be an alien form. Cool! *TMNT II* originally sought to do the same, but for whatever reason, that reveal ended up on the cutting room floor. So the secret of the ooze is . . . that there is no secret? Ominous. What a bold cinematic choice to keep the subtitle of the film anyway.

By the end of the movie, the turtles have set up shop in their new home, an abandoned train car in the New York sewer system.

They seem to have electricity and a never-ending supply of pizza, so I guess they really figured it all out. The Turtles end up on the front page of the newspaper, thanks to their "Ninja Rap" moment. This goes completely against the ninja art of practicing invisibility. As punishment, Splinter makes them do backflips (the ninja equivalent of getting grounded), making me snort into my mozzarella as I finish off the last Domino's slice.

"Never forget who you are"

As the sun begins to peek into the living room the next morning, I notice red sauce stains on my cherub cheeks. A pepperoni is stuck to Joey McIntire's face on my nightgown. "Oh no, Joey! I'm sorry." I peel it off and right into my mouth. I kiss my pinky and put it on his face as a way to inform him through clothing that he is still loved by me despite the accidental pepperoni deposit.

Mom is still sleeping on the couch next to me. She always stays near me when we have sleepovers so I won't be scared to sleep alone. We are surrounded by several bookshelves filled with nature and art books. Sunrays reflect outlines of petrified wood, ceramic bowls, and clay sculptures from Ted's travels around Asia.

I yawn and stretch my arms, noticing little bits of parmesan from a packet stuck underneath my fingernails. I quietly suck the cheese powder from each finger and step over the discarded Domino's box right next to my sleeping bag. I look around. Ted is still slumbering in his room, so I'm the only one up and about. I begin my journey to the bathroom.

At first I didn't notice the slithering on the floor. But then I look down at my feet and see it: a black, scaly ribbon with a yellow paisley stripe curled down the side. Two black eyes, looking right at me. A snake slowly slithering across my path. I freeze. I cup both hands over my mouth to stifle a scream.

I must be brave. I have to think like the Turtles. What would Donatello do? Oh! Donatello would use his brains, of course! I think hard, but nothing comes. Hmm. Just then, the sun reflects a samurai sword Ted has on display on his bookshelf, and in a quick second I become Leonardo, the fearless leader of the Turtles, wielding a sharp and dangerous object to fight his enemy.

I don't know the actual size of the reptile, but to me, it's a ginormous mutated snake the size of Super Shredder, Tokka, or Rahzar. The snake is a monster to be annihilated, and I'm a fearless Turtle, protecting Mom and Ted from Shredder's creation. "Cowabunga!" I loud-whisper and raise the sword above my head. Thankfully, Ted hears me thumping around the oak floorboards and comes running in just in time before I hurt myself and damage his wood floor.

"Whoa!!! What are you doing? That's dangerous, Emily!" His words are gentle as he carefully removes the sword from my grubby pizza hands and puts it on a higher shelf, out of my reach. "I'm protecting Mom from the monster!" I yell. "Honey, are you okay?" My startled mom wakes from her slumber to this disruption. "Yes, I'm fine." We fill her in on the situation, and the commotion makes the snake disappear into the floorboards and far away from us.

"Emily, that was just a garden snake; it's harmless." "Oh . . . I'm sorry. I didn't know." To me it was a Super Shredder Snake, but I guess it's the morning light playing tricks on me. And then Ted proceeds to tell me all about garden snakes and snakes in general. He brings out his big, color picture books detailing reptile origins, scale dimensions, and poison propensity. He explains that garden snakes are helpful because they eat rodents and insects that could be harmful for the garden. They are snakes with an important job, and they don't hurt humans. *What was I thinking trying to murder this sweet snake? What came over me?* I guess I was a misguided mutant turtle, a teenager without the guidance of Splinter and the brains of April.

We shake off the snake incident of the morning with breakfast. We fold blueberries picked from Ted's garden into homemade pancakes. I had only ever had pancakes from a box, so this is very special, and very messy! After breakfast, Mom and Ted take a walk on the trail outside and let me stay in to watch *TMNT II* again. I don't bother changing out of my New Kids on the Block ensemble. I like to think Joey wants to watch it again too.

In my second *TMNT II* watch, I think about my run-in with the snake. I don't like my quick reaction of wanting to kill it. That's not who I am. I get teary-eyed for the snake. I love animals. I have three gerbils at home, Ginger, Cinnamon, and Spice, and of course my trusted bulldog, Snookums. My friend Jennifer has a pet snake, and I like when it slithers up and down my arms. I love all creatures. My snake run-in is confusing.

I watch the beginning of the film more closely this time. The Turtles take out a whole group of thieves attempting to rob a store. They do this in public, not running though shadows like the ninjas they were trained to be. Splinter reminds them of the importance of invisibility. Living as mutated Turtles with superpowers means they are at great risk in this world. Ninjas should be stealth, sneaky, using superlative martial arts skills. He says to them, "Never forget who you are," and he means not even for a moment, lest these teens stray from their paths.

My morning sword stint is me forgetting who I am. I was swept up in the moment. The urge to protect, to be a hero, had taken over. I didn't think; I acted instead. In that moment, I lost regard for creatures. Sure, I was acting out of instinct and fear, but I didn't slow down and map out a plan. I temporarily forgot the importance of nature and all the lessons Ted was teaching me.

The Psychology of Ooze Mutation

Like the mutated gremlins in *Gremlins 2* (who wreak even more havoc than we see in the first film), the Turtles have plenty of company in the pantheon of mutated crime fighters in comics, films, and TV. The Mutants (street gang from DC comics), the Joker (Batman foe), the Thing (mutated from cosmic rays hitting his spaceship), and the Hulk are all examples of characters who were "oozed" into being in some way and became stronger, scarier, and able to fight back.

In comic lore, many mutated creatures traumatically encounter a substance, usually human made, that triggers their transformation. When this happens, the characters often have a choice: will they turn their traumatic experience into good or evil? Sometimes the characters go to the evil side (think Joker's antics or the Gremlins' torturing of Gizmo). But it's not that simple. Vigilantism (like Catwoman's) comes from a place of pain and trauma. Bad and good are not always so simple to determine, and a superhero's or supervillian's life is a much more complicated gray.

The non-secret, secret of the ooze in *TMNT II* is about these mutations occurring and the possibility of the ooze creating mass destruction. Mutations can also be used for good (think Hulk's journey toward being a hero or the choices made by the Mutants who become the Sons of Batman to help fight Gotham crime). During my second watch of *TMNT II*, when I saw the two mutated monsters (who turn back into the snapping turtle and baby wolf), I wasn't scared at all. In fact, I was sad for them, just like I was sad for the snake I almost decapitated. They didn't ask to be made into Super Tokka or Rahzar monsters and forced to fight. They were taken from their natural homes and mutated into fighting machines for Shredder.

Two little sweet creatures were made into monsters. This monster duo represents evil, but the Turtles, having metamorphosed from the exact same ooze, represent good. Both groups are mutants, both were animals/reptiles before the ooze, both are fighters. So what makes one bad and the other good?

Nurture. The Turtles have Splinter, their caregiver and rescuer. Splinter guides, directs, and trains the Turtles to use their ooze powers to help others. The monster duo however, have Shredder and the Foot gang as parents, and thus no chance for good. In this environment, they can't be anything other than what they were created for: evil.

When Tokka and Rahzar emerge from mutation, the first person they see is Shredder, and they call him "Mama." This is funny because, well, he's Shredder and about as far away from maternal instincts as you could imagine. But he did create these monster babies with the ooze, and they morph into beautiful, life-size Jim Henson puppets, looking to be loved. They are true toddlers, looking for the upbringing that the lucky Turtles received from Splinter, the kind of love and care they will never get from Shredder.

Watching the movie as an adult, I can't help but wonder what kind of life Tokka and Rahzar would have had, if they had loving caregivers. What if they had a nurturing and supportive environment? What if they didn't have Shredder as a mama and weren't trained to destroy? Even more I wonder what their lives would've been like if they weren't taken from the natural world. What if they were left to grow and

Cowabunga! The Turtles teach important environmental lessons.
(Photo courtesy of New Line Cinema)

thrive in swamp and forest?

TMNT ooze comes from dangerous man made chemicals in a lab. Green pollution slime is an offshoot of corporate toxic waste. It acts like genetically modified foods do, making things bigger and supposedly better. But we know the huge palm size strawberries we see in the store are not actually good for us as they are not real food. They just look delicious.

The ooze of the twentieth century is the move toward mass agricultural production, GMO's as standard food, burning fossil fuels, and greenhouse gas emissions. It's the deforestation of natural habitats. It's humans having no regard for the natural world and the animals that live there.

Now, do I believe that the writers of *TMNT II* were thinking about climate change and protecting the earth when they wrote this film? Who's to say? I will never know, but whether there is an intentional message or not, *TMNT II* delivers important commentary about the earth and the possibility of creating a generative and protective life force (the Turtles guided by ancient Indigenous wisdom).

The film also reminds us that humans have the potential to destroy nature and one another (Shredder's antics). Things that morph or mutate into other things can be good or evil, but the film instills hope that things can change back to their original form, like Tokka and Rahzar. Is it possible for the natural world to prevail? Is it possible for the destruction of the planet to be stopped? Is it possible for mutated Turtles to carry ninja wisdom and strength to save the world? *TMNT II* says yes.

Cowabunga!

After my second viewing of *TMNT II* at the geodesic house, I go outside to find Mom and Ted. This is a departure from my usual activity of watching a movie for a third or fourth time. I find them sitting on a swing, talking about work and running their feet through leaves. "That's an oak tree leaf!" I proudly proclaim, and Ted, smiling, says that I'm right and tells me more about their bark and how high they grow.

He takes me to his garden and teaches me how to identify herbs. I yell "Cowabunga" in the wind each time I pick basil, thyme, and dill and get the names right. I run the red-and-black soil through my fingers as I listen to him talk about how important it is to garden and grow our own food. He talks about the sun and about watering plants and how we should grow as close to organic as possible. I like hearing his voice, which sounds a little like Kermit's to me. I do the Running Man and sing "Go, ninja, go, ninja, go!" on the walk back to his house. He and Mom chuckle and hold hands, enamored with each other and the blue wild indigo blossoms that sprinkle the front yard.

The following summer, just when I think I'll be back at the geodesic dome soon for more Ted lessons, Mom tells me they broke up. "We are still friends, and we work together, and you will see Ted from time to time. But we won't be spending as much time with him," she says. This sucks. I'm really sad, because I love Ted.

Over the years, I see him less and less. Until one summer in high school. I'm a junior and enrolled in a class at a local community college where he and mom teach. I was trying to knock out some college credits before graduating from high school. Turns out he's the professor of the human ecology class I decide to take. I'm so excited to

Tokka and Rahzar deserve to be nurtured and loved.
(Photo courtesy of New Line Cinema)

see him again. He gives me a big hug, and we talk like the years haven't gotten between us.

The AC in the building makes the outside heat tolerable, but none of us want to be in a classroom. It's summer, after all. I'm supposed to be chillin' at the mall and going to the movies. Instead, I'm at a community college that has seen better days, and waking up early to make the 8:00 a.m. class start time. Ugh.

But it's Ted, and I know he will keep things interesting. On this particular day, he hands out wintergreen mints to the class. They are the hard white circular kind that look like a life-preserver ring. I'm a little curious and kinda freaked out when he turns out the lights to make it pitch-black in the room. "Okay, everyone," he says in his Kermit tone, "We are gonna bite down when I count to three. One, two, three," and right after he adds in a "Cowabunga!"

I see the sparks that emit from our mouths and think, Damn, Ted is still the coolest. A lesson on triboluminescence wouldn't be complete without a classroom-wide mint demo. When the lights come back on, he looks over and winks at me. The fact that he remembers my love of *TMNT II* after all these years and says "Cowabunga" to an entire college human ecology class is exactly why Ted is so rad.

Ted and my mom dated throughout my childhood but ultimately were not cut out romantically for each other. She consumes about twelve packets of Sweet'N Low every day and never recycles. Not a great match. But they remain friendly acquaintances to this day. As an adult looking back, I understand what he taught me. Science can be magical and nature is sacred. From him, I learned to love the wonders of the forest, to identify and respect wildlife.

He taught me, as a young kid, about climate change, and that humans, like the ooze, have the capacity to make dangerous toxic substances that can be used to harm one another and the planet. His teaching planted seeds and has made me conscious of, and committed, to the little things I can do to help the earth sustain. I'm so glad to know men like him exist in the world. In a childhood with so many Shredders in my life, he was a Splinter. I wonder what my life would have been like if he had continued to be with Mom. What a tubular dude.

There is nothing life-changing about *TMNT II*, but the film has had a great impact on me. It's a comfort sequel that reminds me of Ted and Mom and our walks and talks together. I remember his geodesic dome house, the birds, the trees, and the super garden snake in his living room.

I appreciate the puppetry in *Teenage Mutant Ninja Turtles II*, the funny jokes, and the pizza. I like it because when Mike "waxes on and off" while wiping the counter in April's kitchen, he references *The Karate Kid*. I love the messages I see now as an adult in the mutated ooze as it relates to larger-scale topics of good vs. evil and nature vs. nurture. And yes, I still know every word to the "Ninja Rap" Vanilla Ice song that I had on cassette single. You better believe my Running Man dance moves are solid to this day.

The NeverEnding Story II: The Next Chapter

"P.Y.T."

When I answer the phone, I don't have a chance to wipe the Ritz crackers and Easy Cheese from my hands, so bits of them smear into the tiny holes of the receiver. I wrap the beige, overstretched rotary cord around my chubby fingers, just enough so that the circulation begins to cut off. I squeeze it tight, and skin bunches out in pink-and-white clouds around the coils. But I'm aware of none of this. All I know is my dad has just called, and this rarely happens.

"How's school goin'?" His voice is a hint of Okie, twisted with Southern twang at the end.

"It's fine. Math is boring. I love singing in choir. I'm so glad school is almost over, I can't wait to be in fifth grade next year." Silence meets us, and we are unsure of where we go next in this conversation.

I break the awkwardness by inquiring about his thrift store and antique quests. "Find anything interesting lately?" My dad is a walking paradox of card-carrying-NRA-good ol'-American boy AND Depression-era-glassware-and-pottery collector. On my every-other-weekend visits with him, we watch MGM musicals on an old, black RCA TV and sing along to Judy Garland and Gene Kelly. At night when I can't sleep, he sings "Hushabye Mountain" from *Chitty Chitty*

Bang Bang to me, his quiet, baritone lullaby notes washing over my pillow.

With a degree in music, he can play every instrument. He always hums something under his breath as he drives and chain smokes Romeo y Julieta cigars. It's always hard to reconcile these parts of him, the guy who tells racist jokes and works at a pawn shop downtown with the one who goes on for twenty minutes about the Roseville Florentine ashtray he found at an auction in Catoosa.

"Oh yes, I found a little tiny Raymor creamer which is that gray-blue color they only manufactured from about 1946 to 1953."

"Wow!"

"I was in McGillicutys, that little shop in Jenks."

Of course I know the one he is talking about; we go there every-other-weekend, but I say nothing.

"Evelyn had this listed in her booth for four dollars. It wasn't marked on the bottom so she didn't know what it was, and I knew exactly what it was, so I talked her down and brought it home for two dollars."

"Wow, that's great, Dad!"

He goes on to tell me about what he will mark it for in his antique booth, how sales have been slow, and how maybe business will pick up again. I listen, interjecting appropriate laughs and "yeses" and "of courses" and "hmm hmms."

Then it's silent again. We get stuck at some point in time every time.

I look down at my plump little toes, sweaty from a mixture of summer heat and nerves from this call. I dig my pinkie into a dirty yellow-and-white-striped piece of vinyl kitchen flooring that is coming up at the edge. It leaves a scratch mark in the skin fold by my toenail and wakes me up.

I have to ask him.

"So dad . . . " I hesitate as a butterfly garden springs around in my stomach. "I . . . um . . . have my dance recital coming up in a few months, you know, at the Union Performing Arts Center, and I'm gonna be doing my first solo dance." Silence on the phone line. I keep going. "It's to this Michael Jackson song called "P.Y.T. (Pretty Young

Thing)," and it's got a really good beat, and I will be wearing my new jazz shoes, and it's a few months from now. If I didn't already say . . . and . . . and . . . " I keep rapid fire sharing details with him about my costume and a hard dance move I do where I slide to the ground. I'm not sure if he is listening on the other end because I'm met with only continued silence—A silence that gets louder with each phone call we have.

I wind the phone cord even tighter around my hand. The lack of circulation in my fingers, and the bleeding scratch on my toe, become my focal points.

"I was wondering if you might be able to come? You don't have to stay the whole time, and actually I dance at the midpoint, and . . . so . . . you could come at around 3:00 p.m. and probably catch me." Surely, I think, he has time to make it, because it's on a weekend, and he works weekdays at Rose Company Pawn.

"That's great, honey. I might be able to make it. We'll see."

I cover the mouthpiece to squeak and jump up and down in excitement. My dad might actually be coming to see me dance. This has never happened before. I'm a balloon filling up so tight that it could pop any second.

"Well, I don't wanna run up your phone bill," he says by way of wanting to end the call. I'm sure this local call won't actually run up Mom's phone bill.

For years to come, my dad will always try to get off the phone this way. In today's world of unlimited cell phone minutes, he still does this. But in this rotary phone call, at ten years old, all I hear is his "We'll see," and that means that maybe, JUST MAYBE, he will come to my dance performance after all.

After we hang up, I vow to make it worth his time and use discipline to practice my "P.Y.T" dance over and over until it's perfect. And I do. Each day after school, at Peggy Lanik's Dance Studio, in front of a wall of mirrors, I perfect every turn, every toe point, every combination. Then I turn around to face the cement wall so I can't see myself. I get used to doing the moves without watching myself to correct mistakes. I build up muscle memory this way, not relying on the mirror as my guide.

It's time for the girls in my group dance class to pick out costumes for our recital. I love flipping through the thick matte pages of the catalogs, but sometimes when I turn the pages between my fingertips, the cha . . . cha . . . churing sound it makes, are nails on a chalkboard to me. I cringe and shiver inside when this happens and hide my ick feeling from the other girls. They are too busy mice-squealing at outfits they love and earmarking the pages so that they can come back to them and vote later.

The catalog pictures are full-color spreads of thin girls modeling gaudy sequin outfits. The models are stiff, their poses seem forced. They have cheap makeup for days and full smiles with freshly painted white teeth. A scarecrow à la *The Wiz*, pops out on one page, a "one singular sensation" full-gold leotard with tails and a top hat on another. On another, there's a little girl, six or seven, in a yellow polka-dot bikini for the song's namesake, with a fake palm tree behind her. Think *Toddlers and Tiaras*. Totally inappropriate.

None of them look like me.

I want to look like them so badly. I long to be tall and skinny, decorated as a beautiful aquatic bird in a mauve white tutu so I can glide to *Swan Lake* in pointe shoes. Instead, the plus size outfits for my age are few and far between. This is always an awkward moment in group class when the rest of the girls are measured. I get measured last and end up crying because I'm always bigger than the previous year, and sometimes the costumes don't come in my size.

Thankfully, for my solo dance to "P.Y.T.," I don't have to worry about the other girls, because it's only me. My aunt and grandma have fashioned and sewed the cutest outfit: a simple black one-piece leotard and a purple plaid skirt with black, shiny sequins sewn around the bottom. Thicker lines of sequins frame the leotard's neckline and armholes so it will shine from the stage. They made a matching black sequin scrunchie to wrap around my high ponytail. I strut around in it at home and feel so cute and powerful.

When I wear it at the studio to practice my dance, the sequins cut into my underarms, leaving red marks in my fat folds. I expect this and pick out a black sequin stuck with sweat in my armpit and fling it to the floor. Underneath thick sheer panty hose, red fire alights my sweaty inner thighs, rubbing together with the dance moves. The leotard rides up my butt a little, but the skirt covers it, so I will be fine on stage.

As the recital gets closer, I imagine sparkling at the performing arts center filled with people, all looking at me. The spotlight. The cheers. The inner thigh chafing.

I think about my dad being one of the many in the audience. At 5 foot 6 inches and three hundred-plus pounds, he won't be able to fit in the wooden seats, so I imagine him standing toward the back, close to the door. In his everyday uniform of shorts and T-shirt, he will shift his weight from side to side, his flip-flops squishing with his body weight.

Will he be excited to see my very first solo performance? Will he come early and take pictures with me? Will he bring me flowers like Mom does each year? Will he be glad he came? Will it be worth his time?

And then, finally, it's here.

It's the afternoon of the recital, and my solo is quickly approaching. My nerves are volcanic. Despite having perfected "P.Y.T." to the point of Mom saying she really can't hear that song anymore, I have to keep running to the backstage bathroom, having come down with a case of diarrhea. Getting in and out of that leotard costume quickly requires Mom's help to undo and then refasten about twenty safety pins.

"Mom, did you see him out in the audience?"

"Not yet, sweetie, but I'm sure he will be there."

She answers sweetly, her drawn-on CoverGirl dark-brown eyebrows turning inward with concern for my stress. Her white watermelon-print dress with matching belt, stretches over her gorgeous tan arms and stands out against my pale and now even paler baby skin.

"You're gonna be great. Now let's get you a sip of Diet Coke and then go back to the wings. Peggy wants you to start lining up."

I spot my forehead with cold water and take one last look in the bathroom mirror. A high pony sprayed tight with Aqua Net, encircle the hair tie by sequins, stands high on my head, and a million bobby pins surround the hair tie. Magenta rouge rings circle my doll cheeks, matching Wet n Wild lipstick covers my little mouth, and dark eyeliner and turquoise eye shadow create a gaudy haphazard makeup look that will be perfectly over pronounced from stage.

In the wings, my dance teacher, Peggy, gives me a gentle nod of encouragement, calling me by her nickname for me.

"Go get em', Auntie Em!"

Michael Jackson's "P.Y.T." starts up. Writing this as an adult, I realize it is perhaps not the most appropriate song for a preteen, but it was the nineties, and no one was trying to win politically correct contests. We just picked songs we liked and did what we wanted; no one gave a shit.

I travel onstage with an eight-count entrance and already the sequin/sweat mix has cut rash lines in half circles around my armpits, making me self conscious about lifting my arms all the way up during certain moves.

By the time I hit the first chorus, "I want to love you, P.Y.T., pretty young thing," which is a kick-ball-change, step-slide, prepare, fan-kick sequence, the sequins have already rubbed me raw. I squeeze my arms a little tighter to avoid getting more scraped, and as a result the steps are muted, looking like I'm marking the steps instead of full-out performing them.

Where is my dad? I think. Knowing the steps by heart, I do my best to look out into the audience's darkness to find him. The seats are all full, so I think it's impossible, but then, I actually see him. Just as I suspected, he's standing, backlit from the door that leads to the lobby of the auditorium. He is exactly as I imagined, wearing his usual ensemble of comfy elastic band shorts and alligator collar shirt. I'm overcome with joy and adrenaline. He came to see me.

And in my moment of elation and overwhelm, I lose what I'm doing. I just come to a complete . . . stop . . . on stage.

Michael is singing "Nothing can stop this burning desire," and nothing can stop my total and utter freezing. I can no longer remember any of the steps I carefully practiced for weeks. I look down and around, my black jazz shoes tied so tight that my chubby feet and toes push the leather out the sides. I'm completely frozen.

I look to the wings, tears in my eyes, and Peggy is there, wrinkles in her smile, cheering me on, "It's okay, Auntie Em; just pick it up again."

I look back to the audience, and somehow, someway, I come back into the steps. The muscle memory returns. I come back in stronger than ever on the instrumental part. When MJ says "ooh" in a strong beat, I mouth "Ooh" right along with him. The audience cheers for me, and I think, *Whew, I saved it.* But my blood is still cold. Tears swell out and make rouge streaks down my cheeks. I finish out the dance and travel offstage with a repeat of the step I entered on. As I grapevine-turn into the wings, I see that Dad is gone, and I realize I don't know how long it's been since he left.

I look to my right, where Mom, Grandma, and Grandpa always sit. The same seats they have been in for years. There they are, like always, giving me a standing ovation. Grandpa puts two fingers in his mouth and loud whistles for me. "Way to go, Em!" he yells.

I know I should focus on their love and support. I know I should be grateful I made it through the dance. I know I should be happy. But all I can do is collapse and sob. *My dad will never love me now, I think. It's all over.*

The NeverEnding Story II: The Next Chapter Recap

That night, after the recital, I'm inconsolable. Mom brings me a huge yellow Tupperware bowl of Pop Secret, a slice of grocery-store cherry cheesecake, some Fruit by the Foot, and a Blue Raspberry Squeezeit. Instead of reveling in yummy snacks, I pull my Kmart white-and-pink-flower comforter over my head and alternate between sniffling and heavy-moan crying, leaving my pillow tear splotched.

"I'm sorry," breath, cough, " . . . Momma", hiccup, snot. "I'm just . . . so . . . sad."

"I know, baby. It's okay. You can cry as much as you need to. Just make sure to have a snack at some point, I will leave your tray right here on your dresser. Want me to put on a movie for you?"

"Yes please, Momma." She ejects *Hello Dolly* from my VHS player. "You want to watch this again?" Instead, I tell her to put in my most recent Hollywood Video rental, *The NeverEnding Story II: The Next Chapter*, a movie I have seen many times, and it always seems to calm me. In this comfort sequel, I will lose myself in the make-believe land of Fantasia.

"I'm just gonna clean the kitchen, but holler if you need me, sweetie, and I'll come right back."

"Thanks Momma," gasp, snot. "I love you."

"Love you too, baby. More than all the oceans and all the skies."

Tears cloud my eyes during the opening credits, but I quickly become enthralled in the story. Suddenly I'm in a kitchen with Jonathan Brandis, that cutie from *Ladybugs* and *Seaquest*, and it's like seeing an old friend again. Inexplicably he is Bastian, (replacing Barret Oliver from the first film), and the actor playing his dad, (John Wesley Shipp from *Dawson's Creek* fame), is also a replacement from the first film, but meant to be the same character too.

It's not a remake, but it's loosely based on part two of the novel *The NeverEnding Story* by Michael Ende, German writer of children's fantasy books. *The NeverEnding Story II: The Next Chapter* is the continuing story of Bastian going back to the land of Fantasia to escape his reality. The reality of his father not being able to handle his mother's death. The reality of his father going out with women instead of paying attention to him. The reality that they are both grieving and his relationship with his father is not what he wants it to be. Bastian cries himself to sleep holding a picture of himself with his dad and mom, and he rubs his finger over her face.

I'm Bastian, crying in bed, longing for something that can't be. I haven't lost my mother, but my father is mostly absent, like Bastian's. As the movie plays, I look around my bedroom. In this rented house on Allegheny Street, I only have a few things, some books, a few ceramic clowns, a small *Singin' in the Rain* poster, a bigger New Kids on the Block poster above my bed, and pictures of my mom and grandma in thrift-store frames.

I think about the rest of the house and realize I don't even have a picture of my dad to hold on to at this moment. I keep replaying the moment when I saw him in the audience of my dance recital, and then, when I forget my dance, I look out and see nothing but darkness. The memory loop replays in my mind again and again. I feel empty.

Empty. "The Emptiness." Bastian, who is left alone to his imagination, soon discovers the *NeverEnding Story* book, and dives right in and back into the land of Fantasia. It's there that something called the "Emptiness" is threatening to take over the land. Like the "Nothingness" in the first film, the "Emptiness," is a threat to the land from the evil sorceress Xayide, who wants control of Fantasia. Atreyu (warrior and peacekeeper) and Bastian, try to capture her. But Bastian, easily influenced, falls under her spell where she tries to take away his memories.

Every time he makes a wish on the Auryn (the amulet on the cover of the *NeverEnding Story* book), he loses a memory. If I had my own Auryn, maybe I could forget about the recital and not feel so horrible inside. With only two memories left of his mother and father, Bastian needs help, and more help than even Atreyu can provide.

Bastian's father begins to worry about his son, and decides to delve into the book to try and save him. Meanwhile, in a fight with Bastian who is enraptured by Xayide, Atreyu is knocked off a cliff and killed. Bastian uses his last memory of his mother to bring Atreyu back to life and simultaneously wishes for Xayide to have a heart. When she realizes the errors of her ways, she returns Bastian's memories to him, both the ones he loves and the ones that are painful but necessary. Finally, peace is restored in the kingdom of Fantasia. The Emptiness is no more.

But Bastian's work is not done. In order to make it out of Fantasia, he has to give the Auryn to the Childlike Empress (remember her from the first film? And yes, she is also played by a different actor in this comfort sequel, a woman named Alexandra Johnes). She points the way home over a waterfall and cliff, saying that if he has found courage, he can return home. She is challenging Bastian's fear of heights, which was demonstrated in the beginning of the film when he is too scared to jump off the high diving board in swim class.

The Childlike Empress tells him to make a wish from his heart. He wishes to go home and tell his dad that he loves him. I grab the Pop Secret at this point, no longer able to contain my nerves and my tears, and also because my appetite is back. *You got this Bastian*, I think. Just then, his father's voice comes through the wind and trees. Bastian can hear him say, "You've found courage." Bastian's father has been watching him, reading the story along with him. He wills him to face

Can Bastian bring Atreyu back to life? Falkor and I can only hope.
(Photo courtesy of Warner Bros.)

his biggest fears, to keep going and to come back home.

Shoveling extra-buttery popcorn bits into my mouth, I watch as Bastian, so bravely, jumps over the waterfall. His dad gasps, holding his breath to see if Bastian makes it. I can feel the fuzzy blueberry on my tongue with each swig of Squeezeit, washing the kernels down the back of my throat.

Everything grows quiet. We are back at Bastian's home, and his dad is hoping, waiting, wondering. Finally, Bastian knocks on the front door, and his father answers. His father embraces him, tells him he loves him very much, and Bastian says he loves him too. Because his dad was there with him in the story, cheering him on and loving him, he could find his courage and his way back home.

As the credits roll, I undo my Fruit by the Foot. I unroll it all the way out, letting my tongue lap each section back into my mouth. I chew the synthetic strawberry flavor; it mixes in nicely with the artificial-blueberry drink remnants in my mouth.

Mom knocks and comes in to check on me.

"You okay, baby? Oh, I see you've had some snacks; that's good." Her knockoff Estée Lauder perfume and freshly sprayed Aqua Net suspend in the air.

"I'm better now," I tell her, through a mouthful of gummy treats and tears stuck in the corners of my eyelids.

"I love you, sweetie," she says, "more than all the oceans and all the skies," and she squeezes me into a hug.

"I love you too, Momma."

The "Emptiness"

My NeverEnding story is thinking that my dad will come save me in Fantasia. He never will. The times I've needed or wanted his help, he wasn't there.

My dad missed every one of my K through twelfth-grade assemblies, back-to-school nights, and parent-teacher conferences. He missed my plays, musicals, and dance recitals. My wedding. I even hear he almost missed my birth.

But when I was little, we had so much fun. On the every-other weekends I stayed with him, as mandated by the terms of the custody agreement, we ate at Long John Silver's and combed through antique and thrift stores looking for treasures. We sang along to songs from old musicals: *Singin' in the Rain*, *The Music Man*, and *Oklahoma*. When I was eight, he married Linda, and these rituals stopped. I rarely saw him. Mostly, they would stay in the bedroom with the door shut.

Once, I stayed up all night with an ear infection, afraid to wake them up and get in trouble. The next morning, I was punished for not waking them up and was reprimanded all the way to the doctor. When I spilled my Coke at the flea market, Linda grabbed my arm and yelled at me for being clumsy. Another time, Linda shoved me into a hallway closet, where I had to stay for hours, for a reason I have since blocked out. Over and over, I was punished, belittled, criticized, ridiculed, blamed, and shamed by her. Dad did nothing to stop it.

The Emptiness has been there my whole life. A hole where a father should be. As a kid, I thought it was because I wasn't good enough, not worthy enough, not lovable enough. I thought if I could only show him more of who I was, get his attention, say and do things I knew he liked, make things perfect, then I would finally have him. Maybe then he would show up to my activities, stand up to Linda, care about me, love me.

As a psychotherapist now, I understand where his neglect and inability to be a father come from. My dad never had a dad either. His father (my grandfather), the Con Man, was a Louisiana swindler. The Con Man stole my dad's identity to get credit cards and racked up debt my dad would have to pay off later in life. The Con Man was wild, always on the go, never to be pinned down. Years would go by, and my dad would hear nothing from him. The next day, there was the Con Man on his doorstep, when he was hungry and the money had run out.

My dad was also dealt an absent, alcoholic mother (my Gramma E.T.). When she left the house on a bender for awhile, he had to care for his younger sister and the house. They were poor Okies, trying to survive on scraps. He must have been so alone and scared. Between Gramma E.T.'s addiction and neglect and the Con Man's betrayal and unpredictability, his childhood was traumatic. So what happens when both of your parents are absent, abusive, and unstable?

When parents don't address their own trauma, the cycle continues. His neglectful and abusive caregivers, mixed with the trauma of poverty, meant that he never had a model of healthy parenting. I don't know anything about Gramma E.T.'s parents or the Con Man's parents, but we can only imagine that they likely experienced some of the same in their own upbringing.

My father never addressed his childhood trauma, which was then compounded by witnessing traumatic events as an adult and living with an abusive woman for thirty years. Of course the cycle was bound to repeat. The NeverEnding story of his unprocessed trauma perpetuated his unavailability and emotional neglect of me.

Knowing his family history does not excuse his behavior. But it does help explain where some of it comes from. After years of my own personal therapy and as a psychotherapist now, I know that he has limitations. I have learned that my suffering comes when I expect things from him that he is not able to give.

It wasn't until I studied and was trained in Dialectical Behavior Therapy (DBT) that things began to change for me. DBT, developed by psychotherapist Marsha Linehan, taught me the skill of radical acceptance. Rooted in Buddhism, radical acceptance taught me to accept things as they are, in the moment. It's an ongoing spiritual practice of letting go and being with what is.

Radical acceptance means I understand that I can't do anything to change my dad. Radical acceptance means that even though I don't condone his behavior and actions, I accept them, and I'm not in denial of the truth. When I radically accept him for who he is, I know his limitations are about him, not me.

While Bastian gets to have his father again, I will have mine only in small moments over the years. As I write this, Dad and I maybe talk once a year and send Christmas and birthday cards sometimes. I called him a few months ago to ask a question about canasta, a card game we played growing up. No answer. I called him again. No answer. I tried a few months later. No answer. He finally picked up when my partner called, and we all chatted for a bit.

The only way to see him is to go back to Tulsa to visit, which I rarely do. As I write this, I know that I do want to see him, even for a quick hamburger and a visit to a few antique stores. I know he deeply loves me in the ways he knows how to love. And I love him too. But counting on him for anything else only brings more suffering. I don't always get it right, but when I practice radical acceptance, I suffer less.

"P.Y.T." Take Two

The morning after the dance recital, I get up groggy, my eyes red and scratchy. Mom offers me a breakfast of Eggo waffles covered in butter and syrup and a side of scrambled eggs with extra American Cheese melted on top. I push the food around with my fork on my Lady Lovely Locks melamine plate, scraping her knee-length blonde hair with the prongs. I kick my feet back and forth underneath the kitchen table to the rhythm of the *The NeverEnding Story* theme song carouseling in my head.

I'm still so heartbroken, not even cheesy eggs and waffles can fill the Emptiness. I think about Bastian making wishes on the Auryn, and without thinking, I move my fork around my plate, recreating the pendant design. I use the color swirls of syrup and egg juice to make two snakes weave in and out of each other and finally meet in an infinity loop. It's more abstract than visually clear, but that's not the point.

"I'm here if you want to talk, sweetie," my mom's soft and gentle voice comes over the running faucet and clanging of dishes.

I respond with a slight "okay," then stack the Eggos on top of each other in the center of my plate, crushing the cheesy eggs underneath. That makes me thirsty, and I take a sip of Minute Maid orange juice, the new, pulp-free kind.

I'm indifferent to the phone ringing, and when mom tells me it's Peggy calling, I jolt awake from what feels like a murky dream.

"Peggy?" I whisper, and Mom nods smiling.

The fact that my dance teacher has taken the time to call me is exciting but makes my stomach drop. Am I in trouble for forgetting my dance on stage? I know she loves me, but I'm always afraid the people I love the most will leave.

"Auntie Em! Hiya, sweetheart." Her voice is cigarette ashtray raspy but as loving as can be. A balm to my nervous system, spun into tight rope knots.

"Listen, tonight is the second night of the recital, and I want you to do your solo dance again. I know you had a hard time last night, but I know you know the dance, so let's just do it over. Bring your costume, okay?" And before I can even process what Peggy has said, she tells me, "Keep your chin up! I'll see you tonight, sugar pie."

Night two of the recital is usually my group jazz number and that's all. But tonight will be different: I get the chance to do my solo dance over again. To make "P.Y.T." right. I'm ecstatic. Then I realize what this could mean.

Anticipating my anxiety, Mom asks, "Do you want to invite your dad again, sweetie?"

I freeze. My tongue is cemented in my mouth. I'm right back on stage, the music playing, the steps not coming to me. I don't think I can go through this again. Yes, of course I want him to come. But I could never call and invite him. And also I can't risk messing up my dance again.

"I could call him for you if that's what you want." She knows me so well.

"Yes, Momma, can you call him?" And she does.

I leave the room. I pace in the hallway, overhearing only every third or fourth word of their very brief call. I hear the receiver click, and she comes around the corner, eyes drawn, lips crunched, mood empathic. She says that he won't be able to come. He has to help Gramma E.T. during that time. And then her words are muffled, because all I can hear is he can't be there. Once again.

I figured as much. At least he knows it's happening. At least he knows I'm going to get it right this time. At least we tried.

I actually feel relieved. Knowing he won't be there frees me up to be excited about doing the dance again. Now it doesn't have to be perfect. I grab an Eggo from the top of my abstract Auryn and shove the whole thing in my mouth. I do a double pique turn that folds into a wobbly developpé and then small leap into the living room, humming *The NeverEnding Story* theme song under my breath.

"I'm gonna start practicing, Momma!" I say, my mouth full of sticky waffle.

And I do. All afternoon. I watch *The NeverEnding Story II* one more time while Mom applies my clown-level caked makeup and we head to the performing arts center.

My "P.Y.T." solo dance is later in the night. For now, I'm dressed in a teal bedazzled leotard with biker shorts for our group jazz number, "Whoop! (There It Is)." During the extremely long repeating coda, the girls in my group and I go out into the audience and get people to dance with us. I run down the steps and go right to my friend Lindsey, who has come to watch, and she's a little shy to be in the spotlight this way. But she ends up singing along and clapping, and we do the butterfly together. The whole thing goes off without a hitch.

When it's time, I throw on my homemade "P.Y.T." outfit once again, and Peggy brings me out onstage.

"This next dance isn't in the program, but Auntie Em here did this solo last night, and she forgot some of her dance. Right, Em?"

"Yep!" I say into the mic.

"So we are gonna do it again tonight for you. Are you ready?"

"Yes, I'm ready!" The audience cheers for me, and I can hear Grandpa's loud whistle.

Before the music starts, I look out and see Mom, Grandma, and

Grandpa in the seats where they always sit. Grandpa's bushy eyebrows smile when he gives me a big thumbs-up. Next to him, Grandma grabs a tissue from inside her longline bra and uses it to wave her love my way. Blowing air-kisses with her acrylic fingernails, Mom is careful to not smudge her mauve CoverGirl lipstick. I can see the white chrysanthemum-and-fuchsia daisy bouquets sitting in each of their laps, which they will give me after the show.

I take a deep breath. The music starts. This time, I'm not nervous. Everyone here loves me and doesn't care if I mess up. I'm filled with joy and newfound confidence. I'm filled with the love of the people who love me no matter what. Unconditionally. Sometimes in life you get a second dance that makes you realize what's important.

"The Emptiness cannot be destroyed; it had to be filled with love"
The Emptiness in me will never be filled by my dad. He will never yell "swim" or "fight" to me, hyping me up to overcome hard things in life as an adult. To do that, he would have to dramatically change who he is as a person, and when I think that might happen, I'm not practicing radical acceptance. I'm not loving him for who he is.

I spent so many years trying to disavow the Emptiness in me, reject it, prove to myself I didn't need my father, try to move on, only to come back again and again looking for his love. I would ask year after year for him to come to my dance recitals. When he finally did, I was so overwhelmed with his presence that I forgot my dance.

***

At the end of *The NeverEnding Story II*, the Childlike Empress arrives on a gorgeous pearly boat. Fantasia is restored to its former glory, before the Emptiness. The Empress reflects on these changes and says, "The Emptiness cannot be destroyed; it had to be filled with love." She means the love of a father, finding his son again after trauma, the love of Bastian and Atreyu's bromance, and the love of a community of misfits in Fantasia that comes together in solidarity against evil.

My own chosen queer family of Fantasia misfits give me the love and support I need. I work to practice self-love to counter the internal negative beliefs I have about myself as a result of neglect and emotional abuse. I remind myself, sometimes on a daily basis, that I am lovable and worthy and that not everyone in my life will leave me. When I radically accept things as they are, I experience less pain. When I start to feel insecure in my adult relationships because of my relationship with my dad, I have insight and I ask for what I need.

Over the years, I understand my dad's limitations are the result of his own traumas. I have empathy and have made spiritual peace with him. I still don't condone his behavior, but I do forgive him. And love him.

While my father will never show up the way I want him to, my mother always has. My grandparents always did when they were alive, and still do from the ancestral world. Peggy did too, by letting me have a second chance and for being there year after year like Falkor was there for Bastian. My chosen family continues to support and love me. The void, the longing, the Emptiness are filled by these loves.

The Emptiness from my dad has gotten smaller. It still sweeps up smaller branches and debris. Yet it leaves behind large stretches of land, mountains, and sky that are open and clear. Accepting that my dad will never come rescue me is what helps the Emptiness shrink and sometimes almost disappear. This makes room for space to be filled with love that feels limitless, freeing and NeverEnding.

The Evening Star

It's 1998, and I'm an almost-sixteen-year-old emo grunge teen visiting Gramma E.T.'s house. Gramma E.T. is the mother of my dad and my Aunt Sandy. Gramma says nothing of my trying-too-hard outfit. Pus oozes out of one side of my infected eyebrow piercing, and occasional blood drops on my left eyelid. It's fucking gross. No judgment from Gramma E.T. Gramma is all about the weird.

I sport black nail polish; my hair is dyed pink and blonde. Tight, acid-wash Levi's, ripped at the knees, are pulled over the tops of my black low-cut Doc Martens. I wear a baggy white Kurt Cobain memorial T-shirt with "1967-1994" on the bottom, red flannel tied around my waist. I didn't even like Nirvana all that much, but my look was dramatic, and I was trying so hard to fit in while standing out. Plus, this girl I had a crush on loved Kurt so . . . you know.

I'm here for my weekly hang at Gramma's house. Smoke from her Salem cigarette curls upward to the ceiling, hovering. It stops time and bleeds into the mustard-colored, tobacco-infused wall paint. I watch as she takes another puff, inviting the smoke into whatever is left of her lungs. A coal miner-level cough erupts from somewhere deep inside her, and it turns into a fit.

"Are you okay, Gramma?"

"Oh yes, fine." Her voice is gravel. She clears her throat by taking a sip from her QuikTrip thermos, filled with cheap vodka and Pepsi. Yum. It works, and her Salem smoke attack settles.

"Let me know if you need some water," I offer. She looks at me, cracks a tipsy smile, showing some missing teeth, a few cavities, and darkened gums. She fires out a "NAH," and we both laugh. The permanent puffiness around her eyes always makes her look like she just woke up from a nap, but that's just the alcohol imprint she wears underneath her JCPenney's bifocals. Despite her crow's-feet weariness, her face is warm, her smile gentle.

She sports a paisley floral caftan from the Mervyn's sale bin, now threadbare and sprinkled with moth holes. She is short (5 feet 2), like me, and her pudgy body, which always looks a bit swollen, pushes out the fabric so that her bosom and belly merge into a single teddy bear rotund. Curly brown and gray hairs encircle the tiny pink Styrofoam curlers all over her head, a way to do perm upkeep without paying for a new perm each month. Scrappy respect.

Gramma's house is always a breath of sweet tobacco-filled air. I can just be myself, grunge facade outside, theater kid underneath. Gramma and I kick it about whatever is going on with my theater friends, or she tells me stories about working at Shell Oil with "all those secretary bitches." We eat Hershey's miniatures and talk shit about people.

To others, she's Eloise; to me, she's Gramma E.T. E.T. are actually her initials, but also, the movie *E.T.* came out the year I was born, so that probably factored into her moniker. Sometimes her olive, wrinkly skin reminds me of *E.T.*, and I imagine she is trying to phone home in some way, like he was. Was *E.T.* a he? I just realized I don't know *E.T.*'s pronouns!

We sit in her living room, one window facing the street, a dead maple tree in her front yard blocking the view of latchkey kids running up and down the block. Midcentury modern furniture that hasn't been updated since it was purchased secondhand in the late fifties adorns the room. It's dusty. A set of *World Book Encyclopedias* from the seventies are the only books here. Gramma loves to read, like me, but we get our books from the local library; *Fried Green Tomatoes*, *Angela's Ashes*, and *Ethan Frome*.

It's a tiny, post-WWII home with lots of structural problems: mold, dirt, stained carpet, overgrown backyard, rodents and creatures setting up shop in its cracks and nooks. It's serving *Grey Gardens* realness and fits right into this poor, East Tulsa neighborhood. It has the style and vibe of Patrick Swayze and C. Thomas Howell's pad in *The Outsiders*. In fact, the house they used for filming is not too far away from Gramma's (it is now an *Outsiders* museum).

Today she puts out her smoke in the overflowing, amber-chipped glass ashtray and then reaches for another. She keeps her pack in a gray, faux-leather cigarette holder with kiss-lock closure. When I was little, I would open and close the pouch over and over again because I liked the little clicking sound it made. When she opens it this time, her cough returns and she takes another Okie cocktail swig to quell it.

We are going to see *The Evening Star*, the sequel to *Terms of Endearment*, in the movie theater later this afternoon. Gramma has the newspaper clipping stuck to the fridge with a Kool magnet. *The Evening Star* is circled in blue pen along with the show time, 4:45 p.m. at the dollar movie theater, Mall 31 Cinema. I loved the first film so much, I can't wait.

It's morning, edging toward noon, so we have time. Sunlight streaks through the window, highlighting the dust swirls and levitating smoke. In prep for our afternoon, we decide to rewatch the original. Gramma has a VHS copy somewhere in her house. "Honey, put on a record while I go look for it, will ya? I know it's here somewhere. I need some inspiration while I dig through all this shit." She leaves the room to find the Shirley MacLaine-Debra Winger classic, Mervyn's caftan billowing behind her.

"Sure, Gramma!" I head over to the record player and search through the land of Lawrence Welk and Beethoven symphonies. Ugh, yawn fest. Then I find the *That's Entertainment* double vinyl set. Sold. No question: we can rock out to Judy Garland, June Allyson, and Lena Horne.

I skip right to "The Trolley Song" and sing along with Judy: "Clang clang clang went the trolley . . . " I can hear Gramma singing along from the "junk room" (a bedroom where once my Aunt Sandy slept as a child, now designated hoarders' area of the house).

Ruffling through boxes, she throws things around, clanging and crashing along with the sounds of the trolley. A loud thump happens just in time with "Plop plop plop went the wheels," and Gramma's expletives mix in with the song build.

As Judy rounds into her grand finale, Gramma reappears in the hallway, holding a tape triumphantly as she belts out " . . . to the end of the line!" "Found it!" Victorious. Gramma takes a breath, coughs, sips from her QuikTrip thermos.

"Terms of Endearment" is handwritten in black ink on the side of a Fuji white, red, and green VHS box, recorded from a Saturday afternoon showing on TV. Likely this means it will have commercials and be G rated. Bummer, but that's okay; I have seen it a dozen times, and this is only meant to be a refresher.

"Pop it in. I'll grab the egg rolls and tea." She hands me the tape and disappears into the kitchen. I turn off Fred Astaire, now singing about how he will go his way by himself, and eject the movie already in the player, *Sunshine Christmas*. Damn, I love that one. Before the days of twenty-four-hour Hallmark, Gramma and I unapologetically watched Christmas movies all year.

I sit on the floor, inches from the TV, like I always do. I pull out the green tin dinner tray with foldout legs I've used since I was little. I unlace my Doc Martens and untie the flannel around my waist to get comfy.

Gramma arrives and then warns, "Pipin' hot!" She sets down a small Corelle bowl with three Pagoda brand egg rolls from the toaster oven. I know just by looking at them they are all still frozen in the middle. That's just how we egg roll.

"And here, my darling," she adds in a British accent, "is your high noon tea!" She places a delicately ornate and in-pristine-condition Royal Albert rose teacup and saucer set on my tray. A cube of sugar sits on the side with a teaspoon, also an antique. The Earl Grey is steaming hot and smells delicious. In a terrible Cockney attempt, I return, "Thank you, kind madam." We both smile, and Gramma sits down on the couch behind me.

I press play. The infamous *Terms of Endearment* theme starts. Credits fall over Shirley MacLaine (Aurora), an overbearing mother who is worried her baby (who will grow up to be Debra Winger/ Emma) will die from crib death in the night. She is so worried her daughter will die in her sleep that she actually tries to climb into the crib with her and ends up waking her up. The baby starts crying hysterically. Aurora leaves, satisfied. She can rest now, knowing that her baby is alive, although the opposite of sleeping soundly.

And it starts. The beginning of a complicated mother/daughter relationship that is all about what Aurora wants and needs. She is a mother who loves her daughter but who punishes her and administers consequences when she doesn't do what is expected. Aurora has clear specifications of what is best and right. Conditional love.

I watch Emma attempt to go her own way and have the life she wants outside of Aurora's demands. She marries asshat Jeff Daniels (Flap) and is unhappy. She has an affair with John Lithgow to actually experience love in her lifetime. She raises three kids pretty much on her own, Flap cheats on her; they are poor and run out of money. She dies of cancer.

Aurora judges all of Emma's decisions. She is self-centered and stubborn, refusing to talk to her as punishment. Aurora is all woe is me; she thinks Emma is ungrateful and trying to make her suffer. Aurora sees herself as the victim. At the same time, she loves Emma the strongest and the hardest. She fights to the nail for her at the hospital to have the best care before she dies. Aurora loves her deeply but has a funny way of showing it.

As I watch, I run my fingers along the cigarette burns in the once-beige living room carpet, my finger a ball in a maze puzzle game. I dig into one deep burn mark; pieces of charred carpet flick off underneath my black fingernail. Something clicks. *Terms of Endearment* is Gramma E.T. and my Aunt Sandy.

As close as Gramma and I are, as much fun as we have, she wasn't like that with her own daughter. With Aunt Sandy, Gramma was mean and punishing. It was all about Gramma, giving Aunt Sandy the cold shoulder when she didn't do something to her liking. She kicked Sandy out when she got pregnant at age sixteen. Sandy gave her baby girl up for adoption, had severe postpartum and no support from her mother.

Gramma didn't go to Aunt Sandy's wedding. She forgot birthday parties, left events early. She preferred to stay in her room drinking instead of being a part of her daughter's life. When Aunt Sandy and my dad were little, Gramma would disappear on benders and leave them to fend for themselves. They grew up too fast. Aunt Sandy died of a brain tumor. She was forty-six. She left behind four kids, all boys, my sweet cousins. Gramma sat at the back row of the funeral and left early.

As Jack Nicholson tells Shirley MacLaine she needs a drink to kill the "bug up her ass," Gramma cough-cackles. I look over at her, see the sadness behind her eyes even as she laughs. I pick up a half frozen egg roll; rust powder sprinkles off in my hand from the toaster oven. It rouges my fingers reddish brown. I raise my pinky as I take an Earl Grey slurp and set the teacup carefully back in its saucer.

"For She's a Jolly Good Butthole": Evening Star Recap

When it's time to head to the theater, we load Gramma's purse with movie snacks: a Twix, some nuts, peanut brittle, and a Diet Dr Pepper we will share. The door to her 1987 tan Buick is heavier than me, and the handle is broken, so after some careful maneuvering, I hop in the driver's seat. I like to practice with my driver's permit any chance I get (plus Gramma's a little too buzzed to be driving at this point), so it works out.

It's amazing her ride makes it a couple of miles to the dollar movies, but somehow it's the Energizer Bunny. We roll up, windows down, soft rock tunes up, cigarette smoke blowing out the windows.

As we settle into our theater seats (which are on their last legs), we look around and see we are the only ones here. Yes, *The Evening Star* did not do well at the box office, despite what we will soon see as Shirley MacLaine's Oscar-worthy revival of Aurora. Not to mention Juliette Lewis as Melanie, her granddaughter, commanding the screen and ripping my heart out in all the best ways.

I have so many questions coming in. What happens to Aurora? Does she stay with yummy next-door neighbor/famous astronaut

Garrett Breedlove (Jack Nicholson)? Does she find the great love of her life? Does she take care of her grandkids? Is she still overbearing and self-involved? What outrageous Southern-rich-white-lady outfits will she wear?

The opening credits offer a new heart-wrenching theme, piano and violin swelling and waning. A scrapbook opens, with carefully placed pictures of Aurora, Emma, and the kids reminding us of these character relationships from the first film. A child's hand uses blue and white crayons to draw a spaceship over the pages.

The white then becomes a perfect choice to make a star in the sky. *The Evening Star*. It's a little on the nose, but I expect this with this sequel. I want dramatic and predictable sappy camp; that's what we paid one-dollar tickets for. I came to cry, dammit.

Aurora's house comes into view, the same from the first film. We are in 1988 (about five years after the first film was set). We meet the grandkids, who are in their early-to-mid twenties now, which is a bit confusing and perhaps timeline inconsistent with the first film, but whatever.

Big surprise: all of the grandkids, raised by Aurora, has their own set of fucked-up issues. Tommy is in prison for possession of drugs and won't talk to her when she comes to visit him, homemade brownies in hand. Teddy is a struggling mechanic with a lackluster wife and a child who calls everyone a "butthole" and sings "for she's a jolly good butthole" to Aurora. The butthole segment is all kinds of adorable.

It becomes clear quickly that this comfort sequel is truly all about Aurora's granddaughter Melanie. As sassy, independent, and headstrong as her mother, she is the true reflection of Emma, trying to make a life separate from Aurora. In doing so, Melanie ends up with a dud of a boyfriend, played by Scott Wolf of *Party of Five* fame.

In an echo of Flap cheating on Emma, Melanie catches dud boyfriend with another girl and loses it. Melanie yells, screams, and ends up going to Patsy (Emma's best friend, played by Miranda Richardson) for help. In the end she attempts to die by taking sleeping pills, the pain of being cheated on too much for her.

Don't worry; she's fine. After a hospital stay, recovery and some hot makeup sex, Melanie forgives dud boyfriend and flies off to LA

Aurora and her grandkids
(Photo courtesy of Paramount Pictures)

to support him in his underwear modeling career. After he cheats on her AGAIN, she decides to take her life into her own hands and tries acting. She kills it, landing a TV show and her own dressing room. Badass.

Melanie yells to Aurora "You're suffocating me!" when she attempts to take over and tells her not to go to LA. Aurora's grandparenting is just like with Emma——she wants the best for her, but is overbearing, controlling, and too self-involved to step outside to see what Melanie actually wants. With lots of bumps, boundaries, and distance, they end up finding a way to be in each other's lives. They learn to accept each other without trying to change the other person. Aurora is who she is. So is Melanie. They are cut from the same fabric after all.

Gramma and I love this film. It has that kind of quick-witted-Southern-women-on-fire screenplay by Robert Harling (who also wrote the screenplays for *Terms of Endearment* and *The First Wives Club*) that I know will age well. We lose it at the one-liners from Aurora like "Now you go home and rethink your clothing." What really gets us almost to the point of pissing ourselves is the relationship between Aurora and Patsy.

Aurora and Patsy's rivalry is tea sweetened with too much sugar, where one drink makes you cough and the liquid comes out your nose. They're stab-you-in-the-back frenemies who are relatable, and you can still feel the love bubbling underneath. One scene ends in a showdown on an airplane after Patsy sleeps with the man Aurora is dating. Aurora grabs Patsy, pulls her into the galley, and throws what looks like red wine on her silk top, and Patsy goes after her with a coffee pot. It's so great.

In addition to all the hysterical dialogue and strong female characters, *Evening Star* is full of illness and loss. Rosie (Marion Ross), Aurora's lifelong best friend and maid, dies. Aurora is a mess. As Gramma and I watch Rosie transition, tears spill down our cheeks, and we take sips of Diet Dr Pepper to break up the heart pangs. It really gets me, the love between them. Tender, devoted, complicated, the love of chosen family.

Jack Nicholson returns (thank goddess) at the perfect moment, just when we need a laughter break from the sobbing. Like old times, he and Aurora flirt. They poke at each other; they catch up. In a nod to the first film, they take Rosie's ashes to the beach and, with the convertible top down, release her into the ocean air. "Goodbye, Rosie!" Aurora yells. The tears return. This time, quiet laughter breaks through.

Aurora decides (with the help of her very inappropriate therapist— more about him later—to chronicle her life. She makes scrapbooks documenting the years, her grandkids, her great-grandkids, parties, holidays, transitions. Her family is coming together as much as they can, more than ever before.

Tommy, now out of prison, is stable and married with a son named Henry. We soon discover that Henry is actually the child we met at the beginning of the film drawing in crayon: a spaceship, a house. Henry is Aurora's new project. She teaches him to play piano and love music the way she does. She spends all her time with him. He is the love of her life. The love she has always been looking for. In return, she gives him the unconditional love she couldn't give to Emma or Melanie. Their relationship is easy and brings me to tears again.

It's Christmas as the film comes to an end, wrapping up the story of the Greenway generations. Aurora suffers a stroke and is in the process of dying. The family surrounds her hospice bed. She's at home; her chronicles lie on the floor around her. A Christmas tree stands behind her, snow outside her window. Everyone is talking and laughing, flipping through old pictures. Her eyes are closed, and she says "Emma." We all know this is the end.

As she passes, Henry holds up a picture of Aurora and Emma as a baby. Mother and daughter together, the iconic image from the first film. Gramma E.T. and I are waterworks. Gramma reaches for her QT thermos; air passes through the straw, making a slurping sound, loud enough to indicate she is out of Pepsi and vodka. She takes Kleenex from inside her bra and hands me some before blowing her own nose. We are gonna need a lot more tissue than this. Napkins will have to do.

Conditional Love, Complicated Mothers

On the way back home, we stop at Freddy's, the neighborhood greasy burger hole-in-the-wall that makes the best damn Tater Tots in town. Gramma fishes out sticky quarters and dimes from between the car seats to pay for our snack. We order two extralarge Tots and a Coke to share.

Freddy's has the best ice cubes in town; it's like Sonic Drive-In ice, little hard pellets that make a soft crunch between my teeth. As I ice chomp, Gramma and I recount the moments in the film that we loved: the Aurora/Patsy showdown, the just-at-the-right-time phone call Aurora has with Melanie when they are both down-and-out. How Aurora carries Rosie back home to die instead of leaving her next door. The "for she's a jolly good butthole" song. All of that.

We both agree that what we love the most are Aurora's chronicles, the scrapbooks she makes and has around her until the very end. "You know I have some photo albums at the house?" Gramma offers, and she looks out the window of Freddy's. There's some yelling going on in the parking lot. Go figure, for this part of town. A young kid is screaming for more ice cream; a couple are yelling about tires. I swallow an ice pellet whole, holding back a slight choke in the back of my throat.

"You mean pics from like when dad was little?" "
Yep, they are in the junk room somewhere."

Her eyes stay on the screaming ice cream kid, but her mind wanders somewhere else. "I wanna see!" She nods to say yes, turns back to face me, and goes into a coughing fit. Even the Coke has a hard time quelling it.

"I'll take a look and see what I can find." Her voice is dry and stale. "Come on, sweetie!" She coughs some more. We grab the remaining Tots, grease blots seeping from the brown paper bag, and head to the car. She lights up a Salem as we head back home.

***

Aurora decided to chronicle her life at the encouragement of her therapist, Jerry (played by the late, great Bill Paxton). He is sexy, young, and let's say unconventional as a licensed counselor that Aurora meets with on a weekly basis. She loves him because he's cute and also because at their meetings she can talk about herself uninterrupted. With Jerry, she has someone to listen to her with full attention.

Aurora's narcissism is fed by these counseling sessions. Jerry mirrors back to her only what she wants to hear. He tells her she is right. He tells her she just needs time for herself. He tells her she is always just thinking about others and putting them first. She eats it up.

And on top of this, Jerry has mommy issues and ends up having a personal and then sexual relationship with Aurora. I know. WTF?! Just to be clear, NO MENTAL HEALTH PROVIDER SHOULD EVER DO THIS!

To add inappropriate and unprofessional insult to injury, he then gets drunk and has sex with Patsy (whom he previously met at a dinner party at Aurora's house), the enemy lines growing deeper in the Patsy/Aurora feud of the century. "Physician, heal thyself!" Aurora yells at him, storming off from a lunch she orchestrated to get back at both of them after finding out about their affair.

He is appealing to Aurora because he worships her, because he is sexy and young. He represents the qualities she seeks to have in the world and is a reminder that she's still got it! This is no excuse. I was always confused by this boundary crossing, and as a therapist now, I'm horrified and disgusted. It is an extreme violation of power, illegal for therapists to do, and totally inappropriate. It's hard to reconcile the

Aurora chronicles her life through scrapbooking.
(Photo courtesy of Paramount Pictures)

movie I love with this part of the story.

After the Jerry escapade, Aurora returns to be present for Rosie, for Melanie, for Tommy fresh out of prison, and for the people who matter most to her. Sex distraction over with, she continues chronicling her life. The gift of scrapbooking is about the only therapeutically appropriate tool Jerry offers, and she takes it and runs.

I explain narcissism like Aurora's as follows: you might grow up with all your physical needs met—a place to live, food on the table, clothes on your back—but if you don't have a caregiver whose attuned to you, narcissistic injury can occur. We don't see Aurora's upbringing with her mother but can imagine this may have happened to her.

An emotionally attuned caregiver might say, "I see you scraped your knee. It's okay to feel sad or scared, and I promise it will feel better soon." Or "If you need to cry, I understand it hurts." These are all messages of love that mirror the child's pain. A caregiver who is not attuned might say, "Stop crying; it's just a cut!" Or punish them. Or worse, never even acknowledge the child was hurt at all.

The lack of mirroring back the child's emotional states in an attuned way, can create narcissism. And not the Donald Trump-type-narcissistic personality we think of on an exaggerated scale. I'm referring to narcissistic injury that occurs on a more subtle level.

Someone like Aurora, who has trouble thinking outside of herself, represents this injury. A roll your eyes kind of self-centeredness. The world revolves around her. Where everyone else is wrong and she is right. Where she attempts to get closer to people by controlling them.

This is complicated mothering that makes Aurora look to her daughter and then to her granddaughter to have that emotional-mirroring need met. Aurora is looking to fill in the hole of not being seen. First Emma and then Melanie are the genetic mirrors that Aurora wants to look into and see herself reflected back.

This can't and shouldn't happen. Children aren't meant to meet that need. Children need to grow and develop their own sense of self. Children can't be lifelong extensions and appendages of their mothers. They need to individuate. To fly off, and in doing so, come closer.

But for Aurora, there are consequences to going outside of this narcissistic pull. Conditions to the love. Aurora not talking to Emma, cutting her off financially. Yelling, emotional withholding. Punishment. Emma did her best to be more attuned to her kids, but as a struggling mother of three with a cheating husband and complicated mother, it was hard.

Unlike Aurora, who has plenty of resources, Gramma E.T. was always poor, and she did not have much to stand on in the way of threatening to cut financial ties with Aunt Sandy. But taking away love is just as bad if not worse.

Kicking Sandy out, not going to her wedding, never reconciling with her. This is Gramma's version. Gramma's addiction is, in and of itself, a narcissistic endeavor. When you're drunk on Pepsi and vodka, how can you show up for your family? When you disappear for weekend benders, how do you mother? When you kick your daughter out, how do you repair that relationship? When you barely talk to your daughter when she's alive, how do you forgive yourself when she dies?

***

I shove a now-cold Tater Tot in my mouth; the once-crispy golden brown edges are soft and limp. A smoke stream from Gramma E.T.'s Salem slips into my nostril, and I dry cough through my tot chewing. My eyebrow ring itches, and I use the back of my flannel sleeve to gently scratch around the edges of the ring, where it's puffed out from infection.

Gramma's Jergens-soft lotion hands open the ruby-red cloth scrapbook she managed to find in the junk room. The pages, held together by a polka-dot string, are filled with pictures I've never seen before. There are a few photographs of Aunt Sandy and my dad together ages six and eight, playing outside with wooden toys, scabby knees, both laughing at something. I wish I knew what it was. It is rare to see them this way, happy and carefree.

Black-and-white glossy pics of my dad, age thirteen, working the pipeline with my great-grandfather one summer. My dad's hair is matted from the heat. He is smiling, with one leg propped up on a boulder. His looks a bit like the kid Michael from *Mary Poppins*, and I can imagine his sapphire-blue eyes like mine, underneath the black and gray of the photo.

I see a color photo of Aunt Sandy I've never seen before. It's 1955, and Aunt Sandy is about four years old, standing outside in the front yard of Gramma's house. It's the dead of winter, and a complete white sheet of snow covers the outside. The maple tree in front is dark brown, leafless, lifeless. The sun is shining high and bright, bouncing off of Sandy's skin, making her eyes squint.

Her face is my dad's, only softened. White blond curls make loops next to her cheeks. Her smile is missing a few teeth, bleached eyebrows blend into her face. Mismatched buttons climb up her long crimson wool peacoat. A black faux fur collar wraps around her neck with matching earmuffs covering her curls.

What I can't see from the picture is that it's one of the coldest days in Oklahoma history, the most snow they have had in years. What I can't see is Gramma E.T. behind the camera, telling her to smile, her tobacco breath coming out in misty puffs in the winter air.

What I don't know from looking at this picture is that she was about to take Aunt Sandy for hot chocolate at the Louisianne Diner in downtown Tulsa. What I don't know is that my dad was off staying somewhere with friends, and it was just the two of them, mother and daughter. What I can't see is the love in her eyes as she takes that picture with a Kodak portable box camera and afterward slides it back into its leather carrying case.

"Oh my gosh, I can't believe how cute she is in that outfit. I used to have one just like it too," I tell her. I think back to a picture of me as a baby, swaddled in the red London coat, my nose pink from crying all day at Sears Portrait Studio.

A soft E.T. wrinkled finger touches the page, makes a swirl around Sandy's face, traces the outline of the jacket. "That was one of the best days we ever had together." Gramma drops her voice as if she's about to cry. She doesn't. Instead she takes a drag from her smoke and turns the album page.

Chronicles

The Evening Star gave audiences what they were looking for: the continued story of Aurora and her family after the death of her daughter. It showed us the intergenerational aftermath of trauma and loss. A story of family, addiction, narcissism, rebellion, and complicated love. It showed us how a stubborn and self-involved mother can transform into an eccentric yet humble granny.

I did a rewatch of *The Evening Star* while writing this book. This time around, like the first time, the film fucked me up. It took me through all the emotions I felt watching it with Gramma all of those years ago. I laughed my ass off at Shirley MacLaine's comedic timing and her love/hate for Patsy. I split a gut during the butthole song; it's seriously so cute.

I hyperventilated-cried when Aurora picks up Rosie to take her home to die. When she becomes Rosie's caregiver, I was right there with her. As I write this chapter, my step-grandmother and stepfather (on my mom's side) are in hospice, and my mother is in the process of being diagnosed with Alzheimer's. I'm the only family caregiver for all of them. I feel Aurora in my cells, pill counting, food fixing, hospice-worker coordinating. It all takes a heavy emotional toll.

When Aurora dies at home during Christmas, I think about losing Gramma E.T. and how she wasn't at home with her family by her side during a holiday, instead at a nursing home, without speech, mostly alone.

I think about the last time I saw her, about six months before she died, a skeleton of her former, swollen self. I'm in my twenties and fly in from California to see her. "Hi, sweetie," she manages to say, and I feel she knows me. "Hi, Gramma! I missed you," and I really did miss her. I missed how we once were: the shit talking, the snack eating, the movie watching.

She looks at me, confusion behind her eyes, a quietness about her. Her coughing is relentless, her lungs basically disintegrated by this point. "I brought you a little something." I hand her a box and help her slide open the top. Pulling back tissue paper, I reveal a soft caftan in pastels, the likes of which she used to wear, and a pink organic cotton robe. She seems to like them.

"There's one more thing, Gramma." Underneath the clothes, I unveil a store-bought scrapbook, the letters spelling "Gramma E.T." stickered on the cover in purple, our favorite color. I sit next to her and show her page after page of pictures of her grandkids, their spouses, cute pets.

I tell her stories of who is doing this or that. I don't know if she follows me or not, but it doesn't matter. I land on a funny picture of me and her in matching hair rollers, singing into the air, mouths open, our eyes locked on each other in a knowing way. I just keep talking to her, loving her in stories and memories.

The last page of the chronicle is that picture of Sandy on a snowy day. She is framed in gold with black card stock covering the rest of the page. In white-colored pencil, I put snowflakes all around her, a blanket of protection covering her. On the top right-hand side of the page, ever so small, I drew an evening star.

***

There are times in life we get to do things over, right a wrong, repair a damage. In her way, Gramma did that with me. I was her sequel. The Melanie or Henry to her Aurora. Her relationship with Sandy was fraught, distant, abusive, neglectful. Ours was hilarious, close, kind, kindred. A couple of eccentric weirdos finding each other in a junk room of VHS tapes.

Gramma's love for me doesn't take away from the abuse and experiences of my dad and Aunt Sandy. But her story, like Aurora's, reminds us there can be more time to do things differently. More chances to get it right. Or at least more chances to fuck up a little bit less.

Aurora's chronicles are a scrapbook of each year. A way to remember and release. A person gone, a life transition, a memory. I realize I'm doing the same with this book.

Comfort Sequels started as a fun exploration of pop culture and psychology and ended up its own chronicle. Each chapter, a personal story. A part of my life that as I flip the pages I can see reflected back in film characters and story arcs.

We are all versions of sequels, attempting do-overs, wanting different results the second time, hoping to right wrongs, repair wounds, even achieve reparenting. Doing the same shit in a new way for a better outcome. We live in our own sequel cycles.

Comfort Sequels is all about the more of what we love. Stories get to continue on and on. We get to know more, to laugh more, to cry more. We get to see the same characters return, or meet new ones and see what they will do.

Special Thanks

I wrote this book in an RV, in various houses and apartments, and over most of the United States. *Comfort Sequels* wanted to be written and withstood climate change, surgery, shingles, family health issues, the passing of my grandma and my dog, job and housing transitions, and everything in between. Without my queer family, it never would have happened. Thank you.

Bowie: for asking me why I was writing this book in the first place and making me talk it out, which then became the book intro. For reading and rereading chapters every week over a period of years. My biggest writing buddy critic. For your honest and thoughtful feedback. I love you, my Bows. Bowies in space 4 Eva.

Scott: for being my BFF, my Linda Eder, Barbra, Sondheim, *Twin Peaks*, and Wasia Project co-enthusiast. And for making me snort laugh when I need it the most. Your friendship is dreamy. Your art inspires me every day. I can't understand that there was a time when we didn't know each other. Thanks for believing in me and for finally watching *Heartstopper*, dammit.

David Bushman: for your thorough and thoughtful editing and feedback. When we first met, you gave my book its title, and I'm so grateful.

Morgs: for bringing to life my words in the form of my book cover. Thank you for your patience, and artistry.

Interview Thanks: Stu Pankin, Chris McDonald, Maxwell Caulfield, Christine Ebersole, Steve Whitmire, Leif Green, and Peter Mosen.
The Magic of Bryan Johnson: for saying yes to what became a two-hour interview about Ghostbusters, our childhoods, and your artistic wizardry, which never ceases to amaze me.

Kerry Muir: Your art is outstanding; your steadfast support and excitement for this book has kept me going. You helped me lean into memoir so that the book could become what it needed to be, and you are my most constant cheerleader, whom I needed so much along the way. You inspire me. Thank you.

Also to my fellow Writing Salon folks, including Jake, Shirley, Kuang, Dorothy, Edna, Rupa, Stephanie, Mindela, and Karen. Y'all rock.

Amy Shearn: Why you gotta be so awesome though? And the amazing writers at the Yale Summer Writers Workshop for your feedback and support, thank you!

My Krist: for our life together of transformative salads, Lizzo karaoke, walks on the beach, and random trips to Sonic. Thank you for all your support every day. I love you, my Krist.

Cha: I adore you. I love our creative processes and playing Animal Crossing and Tetris side by side. I'm so grateful for your love and care every day. Thank you for all you do. AND thanks for being such an amazing cook. AND for never making me lamb, asparagus, or scallops.

Antonio: Thank you for talking me through all my interview anxieties and sharing your wisdom. You're the best! Thanks for being my sweet friend.

Mars! Monops! Murder on the Dance Floor! Thank you for always fixing my black bars on two and seven. And for being such an incredible and supportive friend. Oh, and your Virgoness is MUCH appreciated on every level, every day. Jeevan!

Ness: for your never-ending love and support, for allowing space for me to heal and create. Your Tarot readings, delicious foods, and witchy goodness are all I ever need! Love you!

Danny Pitt Stoller: for your incredible Batman knowledge. My *Batman Returns* analysis is possible because of your nerdy, wonderful brilliance.

Joe he's Joe!: for providing me with the *Batman Returns* comic book that gave me new insights into the character portrayal and just in general thank you for being a supportive and loving brother.

Bela: my *Heartstopper* soul friend. We have the best origin story ever. Thanks for your transitional object musings, for bringing me out of my shell, for our hilarious texts, belly dancing, and sweating without judgment in barre class. So glad we are queer family.

Travis and Christy: Your unwavering love and support helped me through this book and elevates me through life. Trav, thanks for chatting trauma and mutations at an AMC in Pensacola with buttered-popcorn fingers. I love you both so much.

Josh: I'm grateful for your ongoing support; your take on cinematic noir, caper, and heists; and your willingness to text all hours of the night on these nerdy topics.

Helpers, brainstormers, friends and artists: Kim, Jen, Colin, Cassidy, Jessica, Matt, Bullet, Charlene, Leslie, Jeremy, DDS, Sam, Kian, and my tap gurls: Lauren, Michelle, Lindsay, Claire, Lynn.

My mom: Thanks for all the snacks, the unconditional love, the unwavering support over my years of OCD ritualistic sequel reenactments. I love you more than all the oceans and all the skies.

To my ancestors: Geneva and Albert, Cindy, Gilda, Grandpa, Gramma E.T., I hope you're eating half-frozen egg rolls and watching Christmas movies right now. Grandma Gilleen, you are with me always, and every time I need a Kleenex I think of you having a stash in your bra and wonder how you did that.

To Lil, Goldie, and Sis: I love and miss you every day.

Finally, to Animal: thank you for all you do in your house husbandry and doggy-daddery to support me. You hold me through everything and are such a talented creative partner, sound engineer, and travel agent, and after a long day you will happily watch multiple episode of *Cobra Kai* and cry right along with me. As a fan of Bitch and Animal in high school, my nerdy teen self would never have imagined I would get to meet you, much less make a life together with you. After all these years, you still make my heart sing.

Land Acknowledgment:

I grew up in Tulsa, Oklahoma, where most of this book is set. The legacy of racism runs deep in Tulsa, as it does throughout the entire United States. Tulsa is the site of the 1921 race massacre, resulting in the genocide of Black Wall Street. This is a history I barely learned about in school. As a white person, I have white privilege that has allowed me to not know or be directly affected by this event.

If I hadn't participated in historical and cultural events put on by the Greenwood Cultural Center as a dancer and performer, I may not have ever been educated about the massacre. It wasn't until 2020 that the race massacre officially became part of Oklahoma school curriculum. It only took about a hundred years.

Oklahoma's history of Indigenous genocide has meant that I grew up on stolen land from tribes who were forcibly removed, including the Ni-u-kon-ska (Osage), Kitikiti'sh (Wichita), Kadohadacho (Caddo), Mvskoke (Muscogee Creek), and Tsálǎg (Cherokee) tribal nations. I give land acknowledgment to those original inhabitants and others who have been wrongfully displaced.

Tulsa Resources:
The Black Wall Street Times : theblackwallsttimes.com
This Land Press: thislandpress.com
Circle Cinema: circlecinema.org
Matriarch: matriachok.com
Indian Health Care Resource Center of Tulsa: ihcrc.org

About the Author

Emily (Em) Marinelli (They/Them) is a genderqueer, queer femme Virgo, psychotherapist, professor and writer. Originally from Oklahoma, they now split time between California and Vermont. Their essays have appeared in *The Blue Rose* magazine, *Film Obsessive*, and *TV Obsessive* and they host the *Twin Peaks Tattoo Podcast*. They are most likely cuddling with their rescue pup Radish and watching *Grease 2* at this very moment. Follow them online @emsmarinelli

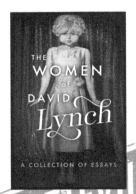
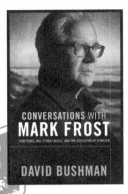